PERSONNEL MANAGEM
Made Simple

The Made Simple Series
has been created
especially for self-education
but can equally well
be used as
an aid to group study.
However complex the subject,
the reader is taken
step by step,
clearly and methodically,
through the course. Each volume
has been prepared by experts,
taking account of
modern educational requirements,
to ensure the most
effective way of
acquiring knowledge.

In the same series

Personnel Management
Made Simple

Shaun Tyson, BA, PhD, FIPM
Alfred York, BA, MSc, FBIM, FITD

MADE SIMPLE
B O O K S

Made Simple Books
An imprint of Heinemann Professional Publishing Ltd
Halley Court, Jordan Hill, Oxford OX2 8EJ

OXFORD LONDON MELBOURNE AUCKLAND
SINGAPORE IBADAN NAIROBI GABORONE KINGSTON

First published 1982
Second edition 1989
Reprinted 1990

British Library Cataloguing in Publication Data
Tyson, Shaun
    Personnel management made simple
    1. Personnel management. Manuals
    I. Title.   II. York, Alfred
    658.3

ISBN 0 434 98616 X

Typeset by R. H. Services, Welwyn and
printed by Richard Clay Ltd, Bungay

Contents

PART 4 THE EFFECTIVE EMPLOYMENT
AND DEVELOPMENT OF HUMAN RESOURCES

Contents

Contents

PART 6 INDUSTRIAL RELATIONS

PART 7 THE FUTURE OF PERSONNEL MANAGEMENT

Preface

The term 'personnel management' may be defined in specific or general terms. In its specific sense it refers to the professional function performed by personnel managers; in its general sense it refers to the management of people at work—a responsibility that most managers have to fulfil. In this book we are concerned with both meanings of this term.

The aim of all work-organisations may be described as the achievement of prescribed tasks by the use of available resources as effectively as possible. Of these resources people are the most important, the most valuable, the most complicated and the least predictable. Since people are the main resource, the effective management of people must be fundamental to the success of an enterprise. To reinforce this view, personnel management is now frequently renamed 'human resource management'. In practice, the effective management of people depends on contributions from two sources—line managers and personnel staff. Line managers are directly responsible for setting objectives, allocating work, monitoring and evaluating performance and achievement, and developing the human resources allotted to them by the employing organisation. Personnel staff have a special responsibility for managing the employment-relationship for the whole organisation, i.e. for ensuring that suitable staff are recruited, that their abilities are developed and used as effectively as possible in the interests of the organisation and the employees themselves, and that they are treated as fairly and as benevolently as possible.

There is no really significant difference between what is required of line managers and personnel staff in the management of people at work. Both are responsible for making the best use of available human resources in order to achieve the objectives of the employing organisation; both are responsible for the development, care, welfare, rewarding and protection of employees as individuals. They differ in the emphasis of their functions, but they need to work in the closest possible collaboration and harmony. This goal can only be achieved within the framework of a system.

The aim of this book is to describe the main elements of such a system and the inter-relationship of its various components. In pursuit of this aim it is our intention to lay particular emphasis on what long experience throughout this century has shown to be sound principles for the practice of personnel management, rather than to give what might be an arid account of all the possible variations in the details of current practice. In this way, we hope that the book may be useful not only as a foundation for students preparing for various examinations in personnel management, but also as a practical guide for practising managers.

SHAUN TYSON
ALFRED YORK

Note: We have followed the convention of using the masculine gender to avoid the repetition that our comments apply to men and women. No discrimination is intended.

Acknowledgements

We would like to thank Iona Tremlett, BA, LLM, Barrister at Law, for her comments on an earlier draft of the chapter on Employment Law and Doreen York for compiling the index.

SHAUN TYSON
ALFRED YORK

PART 1

People at Work

This part of the book is intended to provide a general background for all the subsequent chapters on specific aspects of personnel management. Since work and its management are human activities, set in motion, carried out, continuously supervised, monitored and assessed by people who are constantly inter- acting with each other, human factors are crucially important. Nevertheless, managers do not always act as though they fully understand and acknowledge that success in management has to be based on an awareness and at least a broad knowledge of human behaviour, including, of course, their own.

Throughout this century there have been continuous studies of the behaviour of people, and in particular of the special kinds of problems that modern industrial life creates. These studies are described collectively as the behavioural sciences and include contributions from specialists trained in a variety of disciplines, particularly in the different branches of psychology and sociology. In times of increasing academic specialisation we need to remind ourselves that the situations themselves have no such specialised distinctions. The value of the various special- isms lies in the difference of emphasis and perspective that they give in looking at the same situations, and hence in providing a broader understanding of their nature.

The behavioural sciences have sometimes been the subject of criticism for an apparently disappointing level of achievement in terms of the very considerable amount of time and money spent on research in this field. But criticism on these grounds is a misunderstanding of their purpose, which is certainly not to dispense prescriptions and solutions for the problems of managing people at work, but rather to provide a framework for analysis and to indicate possible courses of action and possible consequences. The opportunity costs of decisions, to use the language of economics, have to be evaluated by individual managers for themselves. In fact, there is tangible evidence that the research data accumulated during this century has had a considerable influence upon present day managerial thinking and behaviour: e.g. the significant growth in courses and literature concerned with management education; the general direction of much recent legislation; the establishment of governmental agencies concerned with employment and training.

In this preliminary phase of the book we are setting out to make a systematic survey of the important areas covered by research into the behaviour of people at work, which is, of necessity, no more than an outline. Apart from providing a necessary background for the main subjects of the book it will also, hopefully, indicate areas where further study may usefully be made.

1

Individuals

INDIVIDUAL DIFFERENCES

Human beings share certain common features, such as physical and mental characteristics. These attributes which link all the members of the species produce common patterns of behaviour. Thus, all humans have physiological and basic needs mainly concerned with survival, i.e. food, shelter, security, reproduction, affection, group-membership, etc., and unlike animals, they also reveal a higher range of needs, concerned with making sense of what might otherwise be a meaningless world. These needs show themselves in the form of exploratory, creative and self-fulfilling activities of many and varied forms. In consequence, a common feature of all human behaviour is that it is goal-directed, as the members of the species are driven to satisfy these needs. At the same time every single individual is the product of a unique combination of genetic and environmental factors. Apart from the exceptional circumstance of identical twins, every human is physically distinctive from all other humans at birth. Thereafter, everyone is subjected to a unique pattern of environmental influences, produced by the accumulative and distinctive features of a particular family, sex, region, race, education, religion, epoch, etc. This is a constantly changing process with the result that all of us are being continuously shaped and modified by new experiences and new relationships. The differing factors of heredity and environment produce an individual uniqueness which has important consequences.

As we grow physically and develop mentally, and join in, so to speak, the general human process of satisfying needs and making sense of the world, we are subjected to the socialising influences of other people with whom we have most contact, i.e. in the family, at school, at church, etc., and in the larger society or societies to which we belong, e.g. racial, national or religious. As a result of these influences we acquire attitudes, values and expectations which shape our behaviour to other people and strongly affect judgements and decisions about goals to pursue. When our beliefs have no rational basis, they may also be described as prejudices.

The condition of common, human similarity and individual

dissimilarity has a significance for the problems of interpersonal relationships and hence for personnel management. Information received by individuals from the external environment is processed in terms of their personal backgrounds and the results are used as a basis for judgements, decisions and actions. In the course of everyday relationships there is a general tendency either to assume that other people see and interpret the world as we do or to expect that they should do so.

The importance of awareness of the effects of individual differences on interpersonal relationships is not so much that assumptions and expectations about the behaviour of others will be eliminated or modified—although the possibilities of this will, no doubt, be increased. It is rather that we should have a framework for making as objective an analysis as possible of our own and other people's behaviour, which will lead to a greater insight into the nature of the basic problems, and hence may improve the quality of our interpersonal relationships, because we understand that reality is not absolute, but determined by individual perception and interpretation. In practical terms, this means that we may be less likely to become confused, frustrated or angry when the behaviour of others does not appear to match our own assumptions or expectations of what it should be. We are also correspondingly less likely to be impelled to explain apparently odd or unreasonable behaviour by other people by ascribing our own reasons and motives, e.g. stupidity, spite, jealousy, obstinacy, lack of interest, etc. This kind of insight and understanding is most important as a basis for studying specific areas such as communication, motivation, group and organisational behaviour and leadership.

COMMUNICATION

The problems that human individuality pose for interpersonal relationships lead logically to a study of communication. This may be seen as an extension of the study of the nature of individuals and their relationships with each other, the problems that human individuality creates, and the extent to which these barriers can be reduced. Since communication is a flow of information which humans use to pass messages and intentions to each other, it follows that no collaborative human action can take place without it.

Since pleas for improved communication are constantly voiced, it would be useful to pause for a moment to attempt to get some understanding of its essential nature, or at least not to assume that everyone means the same thing when talking about communication. Although the process is subtle and not easy to simplify, it is useful to think of communication as it is applied to wireless telegraphy, where a message is encoded by one person, transmitted over a certain wavelength, received and decoded by another. For the message to be received and understood as the transmitter intended, a number of conditions have to be fulfilled, i.e.

1. Both sender and receiver have to know the code.
2. They have to use the same wavelength.
3. There has to be the minimum of interference.

This simple analogy emphasises its essential nature—namely, that it is a two-way process, and that to be effective the intended meaning of the sender has to be received in as near an uncontaminated state as possible by the receiver. This basic prerequisite is not always understood in practice. Sometimes when managers speak about improved communication, they really mean turning the volume up, or sending more or different kinds of messages without any thought for the receiver.

It is common to think firstly of human communication as taking three forms: i.e. face-to-face, written messages from a distance, spoken messages from a distance. In all of these situations there is an emphasis on the use of words and their meanings. Of course, language is the basic form of human communication and here the slant of the message will be affected by the choice of words and their juxtaposition, and the tone of voice when the language is spoken. However, communication may involve all of the senses. As most of us are aware, there has been a marked growth of interest in non-verbal behaviour. The significance of non-verbal messages can be readily illustrated if we think of a telephone conversation and the difference between a situation where only the voice can be heard and another where both people are face-to-face. We usually have to be much more careful when speaking on the telephone where there is no opportunity to show by a twinkle in the eye or a smile that a remark is not meant to be taken too seriously.

The encoded communication signal is a combination of elements, comprising words used in particular ways, accompanied by expressions in the eyes, facial expressions, gestures and body postures, all of which contribute to the total meaning and the complexity of the message. It is most important, therefore, to realise that when we send messages to other people, the code, so to speak, is very much determined by the influences of the individual's heredity and environment. Our attitudes, value systems and expectations all contribute not only to the way a message is sent, but also to the way in which it is received. Receivers will decode information in the light of their individual perceptions of the world. Short of being able by some miraculous means to change identities with another person, there is no way that we can accurately check how other people receive our meanings. Nevertheless, we have to make the best of an imperfect world and since communication is vital to effective management, we need to seek every possible way to ensure that it is as sound as we can make it.

Despite the continued attention that the subject receives, the basic problems seem to remain as intractable as ever. Any newspaper any day will provide a catalogue of a wide range of human problems which all stem from a central problem in communication. Since the problem is inherent in the human condition, there can be no easy solutions. The best hopes for making any progress seem to lie firstly in acquiring a better understanding of the nature of communication, its inherent problems and their causes, and, secondly, in making use of this insight to create the most favourable conditions for the highest possible level of communication that can be achieved. We can now consider what these conditions are:

1. There has to be a genuine desire to communicate. In other words, the sender of a message must be truly concerned to help the receiver as much as possible to understand the intended meaning. A seemingly overt message sometimes hides a covert intention. Sometimes the sender even seems to be making more effort to obscure than to reveal a meaning. Bureaucratic correspondence regularly provides examples of this.

2. A climate of trust and openness is a very important factor in establishing effective communication. This style of management is much more likely to create a sense of security and of absence of threat, and hence to encourage the upward communication which managers need as a basis for sound decisions.

3. There has to be awareness of the problems inherent in the individual's uniqueness of perception. We need to deal with others not on the basis of our assumptions that their meanings are or should be the same as our own, but as far as possible in terms of their experience and possible expectations. For example, when communicating with young children, most of us recognise that we are dealing with people who have a very limited experience of the world and have a distinctive kind of perceptual framework. We naturally adapt our vocabulary and the way we present ideas to accommodate this limited experience and particular perception. The insight and sensitivity commonly shown in this situation is no different in principle from what is required in dealing with other adults. It seems that it can be achieved, but we frequently do not recognise that it is necessary.

4. The more experience is shared, the better the chances of communication are likely to be. Obviously the patterns of general experience are often shaped by forces outside our control. Neverthe-

less, the point is very relevant to working life where the more varied the managers' experience can be, the easier it is likely to be for them to communicate with the different kinds of employee with whom they come into contact. A real-life example of this principle is seen in the insistence by the police forces in the UK that everyone should begin on the bottom rung of the ladder as a police constable. In this way, the Commissioner of Police himself knows from personal experience what it is like to pound the beat and to deal with the drunk and disorderly. He will, therefore, speak the same language as his subordinates, and is unlikely to have problems of credibility.

5. We need to check regularly the understanding of our messages and intentions. In particular, we need to know specifically what others have understood, rather than whether they have understood. This is why a climate of openness and trust is especially important so that subordinates will not feel threatened or inhibited from saying what they actually think and feel, rather than what they imagine the manager might like to hear, nor be afraid to admit that they have not understood the managers' messages.

6. Finally, sound communication also means listening. This is a skill that does not come naturally. It requires much concentration and practice. Too often we become occupied with our own thoughts and seek opportunities to interject. The bore is an extreme case of deficiency in this skill. Real listening is an important skill that all managers need to acquire if they are to be successful. It is especially important for personnel managers who necessarily spend much of their time listening to the views, proposals, problems and complaints from line managers and their subordinate staff.

MOTIVATION

Motivation may be defined as an inner force that impels human beings to behave in a variety of ways and is, therefore, a very important part of the study of human individuality. Because of the extreme complexity of human individuals and their differences, motivation is very difficult to understand both in oneself and in others. Nevertheless, there are certain features of motivation which may be regarded as generally applicable, i.e.

1. The motivational force is aroused as a result of needs which have to be satisfied. Thus, a state of tension or disequilibrium occurs that stimulates action to obtain satisfaction.

2. The satisfaction of a need may stimulate a desire to satisfy further needs (e.g. 'The more they have, the more they want').

3. Failure to satisfy needs may lead to a reduction or a redirection of the motivational force towards other goals seen as more obtainable.

4. The motivational force has three basic elements—direction, intensity and duration, i.e. it is directed towards goals; its force may vary considerably depending on the strength of individual desires; it may last for long or short periods or be intermittently recurring.

5. There are two main sources of human needs:

(i) **inherited**, i.e. all humans share primary physiological needs that must be satisfied for survival.

(ii) **environmental**, i.e. through the main socialising influences in their lives people acquire attitudes, values and expectation, which lead to learned needs such as status, fame, wealth, power.

Some authorities would claim that needs for affiliation with others, creativity and achievement are also inherent in human beings.

Because of its central importance to the study of people at work, motivation has been a subject for continued research for the greater part of this century. Many theories have already been proposed and continue to appear. In very broad terms these theories are of two kinds. They may be based on assumptions by practising managers, resulting from experience and direct observation, or they may be the result of methodical research, usually by industrial psychologists and similar specialists.

MANAGERIAL THEORIES

Traditionally, assumptions made by managers about motivation have largely reflected a 'carrot and stick' approach. Ample evidence of the prevalence of this approach may be seen in the systems of rewards and punishments, applied in both direct and subtle ways, that are characteristic of very many work organisations. Sometimes described as a Rational–Economic Theory, it is exemplified in the ideas of F. W. Taylor and his followers in the so-called 'Scientific Management School', which introduced methods of time and motion study into work organisations at the beginning of this century. This theory is based on assumptions that workers are motivated mainly by material incentives. Such assumptions inevitably have a fundamental effect upon the organisational environment, managerial styles, working arrangements and methods. In Taylor's system, for example, time and motion studies were used to maximise efficiency and productivity. Workers were regarded as a factor of production. Little heed was paid to the potential influence or importance of human factors upon work-performance.

RESEARCH STUDIES

Because of their variety it is not easy to classify theories of motivation without over-simplification. However, for the convenience of a general survey, two very broad categories may be distinguished. In one group of studies the emphasis is directed mainly towards the importance of needs as an influence on motivation. Because most of these studies are concerned with higher human needs for creativity and self-fulfilment, they represent a form of reaction to managerial assumptions about the dominance of economic motives. The main authors in this category are A. Maslow, E. Mayo and colleagues, F. Herzberg, D. McLelland and D. McGregor.

Maslow's Hierarchy of Needs

Based on the premise that man is a wanting being whose behaviour is goal-directed, Maslow postulates a catalogue of needs at different levels ranging from the basic physiological and biological needs to the higher, cultural, intellectual and spiritual needs, i.e.

1. **Physiological:** these are essential to survival, e.g. food, drink, sleep, reproduction, etc.
2. **Security or safety:** these refer to needs to be free from danger and to live in a stable, non-hostile environment.
3. **Affiliation:** as social beings, people need the company of other humans.
4. **Esteem:** these include self-respect and value in the opinion of others.
5. **Self-actualisation:** these are needs at the highest level, which are satisfied by opportunities to develop talents to the full and to achieve personal goals.

Two important concepts are fundamental to Maslow's theory: higher needs do not become operative until lower needs have been met (e.g. the hungry professor in prison is likely to be more interested in food than philosophy); a need that has been satisfied is no longer a motivating force. Research into the applicability of this system to real situations has indicated that it is an over-simplification. Nevertheless, the classification of needs into categories has provided a very useful basis for subsequent research.

Mayo's Theory of Social Needs

Between 1927 and 1939, on-site experiments were carried out by Mayo, Roethligsberger and Dickson at the Hawthorne Plant of the Western Electric Co., Chicago, which have assumed a classical status in the study of human relations. The initial objective was to study the effect of illumination on productivity, but the experiments revealed some unexpected data on human relations which had very significant consequences for subsequent research in the behavioural sciences. Very briefly the main conclusions of the experiments were these:

1. Industrial life has taken much of the meaning out of work so that

workers are driven to fulfil their human needs in other directions, especially in human relationships.

2. Workers are not solely concerned with economic needs and material comfort.

3. Human factors play a very significant part in motivation, and in this respect the research work emphasised the importance of social needs and the influence of the work group.

4. Workers are likely to be more responsive to the influence of colleagues than to attempts of management to control them by material incentives.

5. If management styles produce a threatened, frustrated, alienated work-force, worker-groups will tend to form with their own norms and strategies designed to counter the goals of management.

The main lessons for managers which emerge from the Hawthorne data are that the personal and social needs of employees are very important and that concentration by management exclusively on productivity, material and environmental issues will prove to be a self-defeating aim.

Herzberg's Two-factor Theory

The two-factor theory is a development of Maslow's system. F. Herzberg classified two categories of needs corresponding to the lower and higher levels of human goals. He calls one group 'hygiene factors' and the other group 'motivators'. The 'hygiene factors' are the environmental factors in the working situation which need constant attention in order to prevent dissatisfaction. They include pay and other rewards, working conditions, security, supervisory styles, etc. They are essentially negative factors in that neglect leads to dissatisfaction, but they cannot actively promote satisfaction or motivate workers. Motivation and satisfaction, says Herzberg, can only come from internal sources and the opportunities afforded by the job for self-fulfilment. According to this theory, a worker who finds his work meaningless may react apathetically, even though all the environmental factors are well looked after. Thus, managers have a special responsibility for creating a motivating climate and to make every effort to enrich work. Herzberg's ideas have provoked much controversy, because they imply a general applicability and do not seem to take enough account of individual differences. His insistence that motivation comes from within each individual and that managers cannot truly motivate, but can stimulate or stifle motivation, is, nevertheless, an important contribution to the study.

McLelland's Power–Affiliation–Achievement Model

McLelland's research has identified three basic categories of motivating needs, i.e. power, affiliation and achievement, into which people could be grouped, according to which need appears to be the main motivator in their lives. Those most interested in power seek positions of control and influence; those for whom affiliation is most important seek pleasant relationships and enjoy helping others; achievement seekers want success, fear failure, are task-oriented and self-reliant. These three needs are not mutually exclusive. Many people are well motivated by all three, but invariably one area is predominant. McLelland's research has also indicated that motivational patterns can be modified by specially designed training programmes. The achievement drive, in particular, can apparently be increased by this means. The implications of the theory in practice are that managers can identify employees who are self-motivated, those who rely more on internal incentives and those who could increase their achievement drive through training.

McGregor's Theory X and Theory Y

D. McGregor proposed that management makes two kinds of assumptions about people, which he calls Theory X and Theory Y. Theory X is seen as a set of traditional beliefs that man is inherently lazy and unambitious and will avoid responsibility. The main incentives to work are provided by the carrot or the stick and constant supervision is necessary. Theory X attitudes, in McGregor's view, are the main reasons why workers adopt defensive postures and group together to beat the system whenever they can. Management expects them to behave in this way and they fulfil the prophecy. Theory Y, on the other hand, takes a benevolent view of human nature. It assumes that work is a natural human activity, which is capable of providing enjoyment and self-fulfilment. According to Theory Y, the chief task of the manager is to create a favourable climate for growth, for the development of self-reliance, self-confidence and self-actualisation through trust and by reducing supervision to a minimum.

The second category of studies is more concerned with the dynamics of the motivational process. In this group there is much more emphasis on the importance of individual differences, of individual expectancy as a function of motivation, and of the contingencies of different situations.

Lewin's Field Theory

Believing that behaviour is the result of an individual's reaction with his or her environment (i.e. B, Behaviour is a function of P, Person and E, Environment), Lewin reached the following conclusions about motivation: it depends upon the individual's subjective perceptions of his relationships with his environment; behaviour is determined by the interaction of variables, i.e. tension in the individual, the valency of a goal and the psychological distance of a goal (or in other words, the existence of a need, the perception of the possibility of fulfilment and the reality of this possibility); human beings operate in a field of forces influencing behaviour like the forces in a magnetic field, so that people have different motivational drives at different times; in the context of work some forces inhibit (e.g. fatigue, restrictive group-norms, ineffective management) whilst others motivate (e.g. job satisfaction, effective supervision, rewards).

Vroom's Valency–Expectancy Theory

Vroom proposes that motivation is a product of the worth or value that individuals place on the possible results of their actions and the expectation that their goals will be achieved. The theory is expressed by the formula: Force (F) = Valency (V) × Expectancy (E). The importance of this approach is the emphasis that it places on the individuality and variability of motivational forces, as distinct from the generalisations implied in the theories of Maslow and Herzberg.

Porter and Lawler's Model

This model is in the same genre as the theories of Lewin and Vroom in its concern with the influence of perception and expectancy on motivation. However, it is a more comprehensive account than the other theories. The model is based on the following propositions:

1. The motivational force of an individual depends on how he or she perceives the value of the goal, the energy required to achieve the goal, and the probability that the goal will be achieved.
2. This perception is, in turn, influenced by the individual's past experience of similar situations, because this will enable a better self-assessment of the required effort, the ability to perform as required, and the probability of achieving the goal.
3. Performance—achievement is mainly determined by the effort expended, the individual's understanding of the task requirements and self-assessment of ability.
4. Performance is seen by the individual as leading to both intrinsic and extrinsic rewards, which produce satisfaction, if the individual perceives the reward as fair.

This model is probably the most comprehensive and adequate description of the motivational process in its potential, practical application. It underlines the need for a system of management by objectives, performance appraisal and very careful attention to the organisation's system of intrinsic and extrinsic rewards.

Schein's Theory of Complex Man

Schein's thesis is an appropriate conclusion for a survey of motivational theories. His view is that whilst all theories contain some

INDIVIDUALS
Uniqueness of each individual derives from inherited and environmental factors. Individuals develop unique systems of attitudes, assumptions, values, expectations, etc. These fundamentally influence personal motivation and interpersonal relationships.

COMMUNICATION	MOTIVATION
Its essence is a two-way process of transmission—reception. Each message is a complex of signals, e.g. spoken messages comprise words, tone, expressions, gestures, postures, etc. Encoding and decoding are filtered through each individual's personal system of assumptions, expectations, values, needs, etc. This process is the fundamental cause of communication barriers. The problem may be mitigated by: 1. A genuine desire to communicate. 2. Trust and openness. 3. Awareness of the nature and problems of the process. 4. Sharing experience. 5. Checking understanding. 6. Listening.	In essence it is an inner force driving humans to satisfy needs –inherited and environmentally acquired. The force has three elements: direction; intensity; duration. There are three main groups of theories: Managerial assumptions (e.g. Taylor's Rational–Economic Theory) Human needs (e.g. Maslow, Mayo, Herzberg, McLelland, and McGregor); Expectancy/contingency (e.g. Lewin, Vroom, Porter and Lawler). Schein's 'Complex Man' summarises the complexity of motivation. A general analysis model: 1. Forces within individuals. 2. Nature of the job. 3. Work-environment.

Fig. 1. Summary of studies of individuals, communication, motivation.

truths about human behaviour, no single theory is adequate by itself. His position may be summarised as follows:

1. Man is driven by nature to fulfil a variety of needs—some basic and some on a higher plane.

2. Needs once satisfied may re-occur (e.g. basic needs); other needs (e.g. higher needs) are constantly changing and being replaced by new needs.

3. Needs vary, therefore, not only from one person to the next, but also within the same person according to differences of time and circumstances.

4. Effective managers are aware of this complexity and will be as flexible in their approach to their subordinate staff as possible. Above

all, they will learn to avoid generalised assumptions about the motivation of others based on projections of their own views and expectations.

Because of the complexity of motivation, managers cannot expect to be able precisely to gauge the various motivational forces that influence their individual subordinates. They can, however, use the available data to broaden their understanding and to provide a framework for analysing the general influences that may inter-relate to produce a variety of individual motivational patterns, i.e.

1. **Forces within individuals themselves:** attitudes, beliefs, values, assumptions, expectations and needs.

2. **The nature of the job:** extrinsic and intrinsic rewards; component tasks; responsibilities; work arrangements; feedback on performance.

3. **The environment of work:** superior managers and their styles; other colleagues and relationships with them; organisational climate and practices.

QUESTIONS

1. Briefly describe the essential nature of human communication.

2. What are its inherent problems and the conditions that are necessary for communication to be effective?

3. Give a brief definition of motivation.

4. What are the distinctive features of the theories of the following authorities: Maslow, Herzberg, McGregor, McLelland, Porter and Lawler?

5. Describe a simple framework for a systematic analysis by managers of motivational factors.

2

Groups and Leadership

GROUPS

The behaviour of groups has important consequences for management. Research into this subject has produced some very interesting data from which has emerged the main conclusion that a variety of behaviour takes place in working groups that is often not apparent on the surface. Various studies that have been made throughout the past fifty years have indicated the existence of phenomena of group behaviour, and in particular of informal patterns, which are not described or taken into account in formal, official prescriptions about work, issued by management. These revelations are especially significant because of the implication that, if managers are unaware of these phenomena and their causes, they will make unwarranted assumptions based on their own perspectives, and establish goals, structures, plans and work arrangements that are inappropriate to the groups that they lead. In fact, some of these phenomena may be a reaction to inappropriate, insensitive behaviour on the part of management, so that a vicious circle of negative behaviour may be set in motion which is virtually self-perpetuating.

The main concern of managers about their work-groups is that they should work cohesively in order to achieve required results. Their interest in group behaviour is centred, therefore, on basic questions such as what factors make groups work cohesively and what factors cause disruption. In order to find likely answers to these questions we need to examine a series of related questions, i.e. what are the characteristics of work-groups, why and with what expectations do people join them, how in general do they operate, and what kinds of problems may arise within the group, between groups and managers, and between different groups. These questions will provide a useful framework for a systematic analysis of the subject.

Work-groups differ from other groups in the following important ways:

1. Except for prisons, mental institutions and military national service, members join voluntarily.
2. There has to be a common purpose or goal which is achieved by the collaboration of the group members.

3. The individuals in a group have to perceive that they are members of a particular group, to know what they have to do and what contribution is expected from each member.

4. The members of the group have to reach a degree of cohesive collaboration in order to perform effectively and fulfil their purpose.

5. To maintain collaboration and to keep the group moving towards its goal a co-ordinating leadership function is needed.

Reasons For and Expectations from Group Membership

The reasons why individuals join groups and the expectations that each person has will naturally cover a very wide range. The main, identifiable reasons closely match the categories of Maslow's Hierarchy, i.e. material or economic; social; self-esteem or status; self-development of fulfilment. Evidently, the satisfaction of material needs is only one of a number of possibilities.

When people join work-groups a contract is formally drawn up which makes precise statements about what employers require and what they will give in return. These terms and conditions are invariably expressed in material language. They do not say for example that the firm will undertake to satisfy the employees' needs for self-esteem or self-fulfilment. Nevertheless, behind the formal language of the official contract there is always implied what C. Argyris has described as a 'psychological contract'. This means that employers assume that employees' decisions to join organisations indicate a willingness to accept the principle of subordination and to recognise the authority of the organisation as legitimate. The employees' perception, on the other hand, is that since the relationship is voluntary, they have some freedom for the exercise of influential behaviour, which could, if necessary, lead to changes in the work-situation.

Interaction Within and Between Groups

Before the particular manifestations of group behaviour revealed by specialised studies are examined, it would be useful to consider the subject in general terms. B. Tuckman, for example, has proposed a four-stage model as a general description of the chronology of a group's progress towards cohesive collaboration, i.e.

Stage 1 **Forming.** The initial stage, when members are tentative about the task, about each other and the group leadership. Extremes of view are usually restrained. Members test each other and draw up rules of conduct. In a leaderless group, leaders may be chosen or begin to emerge. These may be changed in later stages.

Stage 2 **Storming.** The members are getting to know each other better and are prepared to put forward their views more vigorously. This leads to conflict between individuals, leaders or sub-groups, which may have been formed.

Stage 3 **Norming.** The conflicts begin to be controlled as the members realise the need to co-operate in order to perform the task. The group produces norms of behaviour, i.e. an accepted code of attitudes and conduct which all the members accept.

Stage 4 **Performing.** The group has now developed the required degree of cohesion to work as a team and to concentrate on the problems it has to overcome to attain its goal.

This is only a very generalised model and it would apply literally only to groups whose members all meet for the first time to complete a specific task. A committee or a working-party is a good practical example of such a group. Nevertheless, the basic principles have a wider application and give a useful insight into the behaviour of groups with a continuous existence and an on-going task.

Another useful, general model of group behaviour is the result of specific studies carried out by R. F. Bales and colleagues of Harvard University. This data is based on the observation of small discussion groups, and like Tuckman's model, these conclusions would be directly applicable only to work-groups of a similar nature, such as committees. However, some general principles may be derived to describe the behaviour of people in working groups whose relationship extends over much longer periods. Briefly to summarise Bales' data, he found that behaviour fell into two main categories, i.e.

1. Task-oriented.
2. Socio-emotionally oriented.

His observations showed that apart from efforts which were directed towards the task, there was another type of behaviour which concerned the human aspects of the group and its individual members. Bales further distinguished two sub-categories of the so-called socio-emotional behaviour, i.e.

1. Emotionally positive.
2. Emotionally negative.

Emotionally positive behaviour is directed towards enhancing the cohesiveness of the team and expresses itself in tension-releasing humour, action to support other members of the team, etc. Emotionally negative behaviour is egocentric, and expresses itself in the form of antagonism, signs of tension, appeals for help, withdrawal of co-operation etc. This study also indicated that some people tend to give a lead either in the task-oriented or socio-emotional roles, e.g. one person would be primarily concerned with the task and another would be more interested in maintaining group cohesiveness. Occasionally, the two functions might be combined in the same person.

These two general models are not only helpful for providing a broad understanding of group behaviour, but particularly for emphasising two basic orientations, namely task fulfilment and group cohesiveness. On this basis we can now look in rather more detail at particular phenomena of group behaviour and associated problems with which managers have to contend. Certain factors have been identified as fundamental in their influence on the behaviour of groups, namely:

1. **The task:** its nature and the arrangements imposed by management in terms of methods and work conditions.

2. **The group:** its size, composition, relationships and norms.

3. **The leadership function:** styles and their appropriateness to the task and the group.

4. **The environment:** relationships with other groups and the main organisation.

The influences of these factors are described below and illustrated with examples from work situations and data from various research studies.

The Task The nature of the work and the way it is arranged can have a very important influence on either stimulating or impeding group cohesiveness. For example, where the tasks of the group involve prestige and esteem such as, for example, the public-display or special-service units of the armed forces, there is seldom much difficulty in obtaining recruits to the group, retaining members, or developing a high level of group cohesiveness. Similar cohesiveness is found in groups who share dangerous or hard conditions, e.g. miners or seamen. On the other hand, where the technology of the task reduces social interaction to a minimum, as for example in the production lines of the motor industry, then the problem of creating a spirit of group unity may become virtually impossible.

Some well known and valuable studies have been conducted on the effects of the task upon the group. A team from the Tavistock Institute of Human Relations studied the effects on groups of coal miners of a technological change from traditional short-wall to long-wall methods of mining. Traditional methods had been based on small, highly autonomous, cohesive teams. When new mechanical equipment was introduced, which revolutionised the working arrangements, the traditional small groups were replaced with much larger groups under a supervisor, divided into three shifts, each performing different stages of the total task. Although the new arrangements were very sound in technical terms, the human consequences were very serious: the former cohesiveness of the small group was destroyed; workers developed feelings of social disorientation and low productivity became an accepted norm.

Data which underlined the findings of the Tavistock Institute were produced in a classic study of a gypsum factory in the USA by A. W. Gouldner. Here, management introduced a series of new working arrangements into a factory which had a long tradition of highly autonomous working groups and well established group norms. The new-broom methods were intended to produce greater efficiency, but, in fact, they created much tension, counter measures and a series of bitter disputes.

Both of the examples quoted above illustrate the possibly serious consequences of management's lack of awareness of the general nature of group behaviour and of the particular influence of the task and working arrangements.

The Group Relationships within the group are affected by factors such as size, composition, individual personalities and their roles, group norms, etc. Managers need to understand these factors and their influence as a basis for analysing possible sources of unity or disunity inside a group. All the evidence suggests that highly cohesive groups are generally more productive than groups that are less cohesive. At the same time, it would be wrong to assume that group cohesiveness necessarily correlates with high levels of productivity. A group may become cohesive as a reaction to and a defence against the tactics of management of which it disapproves, or because of perceived threats from other groups.

The size of a group may influence possible patterns of behaviour, and it has an obvious relevance to questions of communication. No hard and fast rules can be laid down because of the varying requirements of varying situations. However, if the group is too large, it may divide into sub-groups that may collaborate for reasons other than productive work. In large groups, leaders have problems of control. It is difficult for them to know their subordinates well, and communication barriers are more likely to occur.

The composition of the group will also influence patterns of interaction. Managers cannot normally be expected to plan or manipulate composition of their groups to take care of all possible subtle influential factors of personality, experience, social class, age, etc. In theory, the greater the homogeneity a group has, the more cohesive it is likely to be. Except for circumstances where there are too many dominant personalities, a blend of personality traits could be as much an advantage as a disadvantage.

A brief reference has already been made to group norms. They occupy such a prominent role in the general behaviour of all groups, that more needs to be said about them. Norms are to a group what the individual perspective is to each separate human being. Thus, a group will develop an identity of its own in terms of common patterns of behaviour and attitudes, as in clubs, gangs, societies, etc., which attract people of a like mind. Work groups develop norms about work, e.g. standards, quantity of output and attitudes to managements. They may also develop other norms which act, as it were, as the unwritten 'rules of the club', e.g. members of this work group will dislike certain other groups, will read certain kinds of newspapers, will hold certain kinds of political views and so on. Newcomers to the group are expected to comply initially whilst they pass through what is termed the socialising process of learning the expected behaviour. Eventually they will find that they have unconsciously made the group's behaviour and attitudes their own, i.e. they have internalised the norms of the group, or else they will reject them and remain outside the group.

Closely linked with the phenomena of norms is the pressure exerted by the group on members to conform. Non-conformists may well be rejected by the group. In extreme cases, this means being totally ignored. A number of authors, especially in the USA, e.g. S. Millgram, S. Asch and J. Janis, have made special studies of conformity which have produced some rather disturbing conclusions about the degree to which people may succumb to social pressures to toe-the-line and to suppress their real beliefs. Applied to working situations, this data indicates that group decisions, as for example those made by committees, are often not nearly as sound as is popularly supposed. Strong pressures within a group to reach consensus may well result in the suppression of wiser counsels.

Leadership This has a crucially important bearing on group behaviour. As an influential factor we are especially concerned with different styles of leadership and their possible effects upon groups. Because of its special importance, leadership will be discussed later in detail. For the present, it is enough to say that the effective performance of a group is obviously much determined by the skill of the leader in co-ordinating the efforts of the individual members, but also by the degree to which the style of leadership is appropriate to the task and the nature of the group. An important factor that studies of group behaviour has revealed is the possible presence and influence of informal leaders. In the work situation most leaders are appointed by the organisation, but there are very often other unofficial and influential group leaders, who emerge from the informal behaviour of groups.

The Environment Work groups operate mainly in the environment of the organisation to which they belong. The significance of the group's environment lies chiefly in its relationship with the organisation as a whole and with the other groups that comprise the organisation. At best there might be what could be termed as friendly rivalry or healthy competition between different groups, but in the work situation, where there is often competition for limited or scarce resources, intergroup feelings may well extend even to hostility. Paradoxically, such negative feelings can arise from the very force of cohesiveness which gives an individual group its strength, and depends on tasks and norms, not shared by other groups. Some valuable experiments to study intergroup relationships were carried out by M. Sherif in the USA with groups of boys at a camp. Situations were deliberately contrived to stimulate intergroup hostility, in which one group could only win at the expense of another. The results were markedly increased intragroup solidarity and intergroup hostility. Tensions were reduced or removed by giving common goals to all groups and deliberately increasing social contacts in non-competitive situations.

Finally, it has to be emphasised that although we have been considering the task, the group itself, its leadership and environment as separate factors of possible influence, in practice the influences of these factors inter-relate and overlap in a variety of subtle and complicated forms.

Conclusions

To achieve cohesiveness within individual groups, collaboration between different groups and hence total effectiveness certain basic requirements, it seems, need to be met:

1. An equilibrium has to be maintained within a group between the energies directed towards the achievement of tasks and maintaining the team as a cohesive unit.

2. Conditions have to be established which make membership of the group worthwhile and meaningful to the individuals in the group.

3. The effectiveness of the organisation as a whole rather than the effectiveness of individual groups needs to be emphasised. Measures need to be taken to develop collaboration between groups and to establish sound communication links.

4. Exchanges of members of groups should be encouraged to reduce insularity and to promote mutual understanding of problems.

5. Situations that produce winners and losers should be avoided.

6. Leaders of groups need to meet regularly to discuss common problems and to concentrate on total effectiveness rather than the interests of individual groups.

7. Group leaders need to be aware of the significance of the

informal behaviour of groups, of group norms and of the possible existence of leaders other than those officially appointed.

LEADERSHIP

Leadership is obviously a subject of extreme importance in management. As modern research has clearly shown, leadership is a part of the study of group behaviour. Leaders cannot operate in isolation, and groups with tasks to perform cannot perform these tasks without leaders. Leaders are members of groups, influencing them and being influenced by them. They are especially concerned with the cohesive development of the group as a prerequisite for the ultimate achievement of the group's goals. If management is defined as a process of making the most effective use of available human and material resources for the achievement of specified goals, then leadership may be described as the component of management that is most concerned with the use of human resources.

Until recently, nearly all the emphasis of leadership study had been concentrated on leaders themselves, usually by examining the careers of well-known leaders of history in an attempt to analyse the secrets of their apparent success. Thus, a belief predominated for centuries that leadership was dependent on the circumstances of one's birth. Some became leaders because they had the good fortune to be born into noble, naturally ruling classes; others because they were endowed with certain innate qualities. The idea that leadership is a facet of group behaviour has only emerged in recent times from studies of the human problems of industrial society. It has led to some profoundly important conclusions, i.e.

1. Leadership has no meaning outside the context of tasks to be performed and groups to perform these tasks.
2. Studies of leaders as isolated individuals provide little useful insight into the nature of leadership.
3. This can only come by analysing what leaders and groups do in a variety of specific situations.

Studies on leadership published in earlier times invariably included lists of what their authors regarded as the essential traits of a good leader. Whilst these lists naturally coincide in a number of important respects, at the same time they inevitably vary in their total contents, their priorities and their emphases. These variations clearly illustrate the fundamental limitations of attempts to study leadership on a basis of personal qualities. Such an approach has been shown to provide no means for answering some of the fundamental questions that need to be asked, e.g. if there is no consensus on what makes effective leaders,

by what criteria are they to be identi.
Even if a consensus on essential qualities
valid test could be devised to identify thos
requirements, are we then to believe that su
with equal effectiveness as leaders in any circ
wide variety of possible work situations immediate
cannot be so.

The functional approach to leadership as an ele. ... up
behaviour has dispelled much of the mystique th. ...nally
surrounded the subject. Above all, it has provided a fran. work for
meaningful analysis and for the systematic selection, training and
assessment of leaders. The emphasis has shifted from the study of
leaders to leadership as a function of co-ordinating the efforts of a
group to achieve specified tasks. At the same time, it is apparent that
there is considerable variation in the nature of tasks and in the
composition of groups. From this, certain conclusions may logically be
deduced, i.e. people can be trained to gain insight into the nature of
group behaviour and to develop the interpersonal skills required to
accomplish a productive co-ordination of human efforts; the very wide
variety of situations means that certain styles of leadership will be
more appropriate to some situations than to others. Therefore, leaders
should be trained to be as flexible and adaptable as possible or if, in
fact, people cannot significantly vary their leadership styles, then
particular types of leaders should be matched with particular
situations.

After the Hawthorne experiments had aroused the initial interest in
group behaviour, serious research into leadership soon followed and
has continued ever since. The change of emphasis from the personality
of leaders to leadership as a function in a collaborating group has had a
profound effect during the post-war years, firstly on the selection and
training of military leaders, and subsequently of managers in general.
However, the innovation of the functional approach caused some
problems of misunderstanding, because traditionalists interpreted this
approach to mean that personal qualities are not important—a view
which misrepresents this theory. The personal qualities for effective
leadership are not in question. The message of the functional approach
is simply that an analysis of personal qualities gives little help in
understanding what leadership means in action.

The quantity and variety of research is so extensive that a
comprehensive summary cannot be attempted in this brief survey.
Nevertheless, the findings and conclusions of some of the most
important works merit a brief description because of what they have to
say about effectiveness in the management of people. Many of the
studies of leadership have been carried out by direct observation of
people at work. Others have taken the form of 'armchair philosophy',

...sonal experience or the re-orientation of previous works.
... the research has been carried out by university teams and
...ne by particular individuals.

University of Iowa

This was the first serious attempt to study leadership in groups in action. It was based on the activities of boys who were members of a model-making club, and were quite unaware that they were being observed for experimental purposes. They were divided into three groups and subjected in turn to three quite different styles of leadership:

1. Autocratic, whereby they were given no scope for initiative and were tightly disciplined.
2. Democratic, whereby the leadership was positive and firm, but allowed participation and freedom of expression.
3. Laissez-faire, whereby the boys were allowed to do as they pleased.

The results clearly indicated the superiority of the democratic style for all three groups in terms of general contentment, group cohesiveness and productivity. The other styles produced apathy, disunity and low productivity. It would be dangerous to seek correlations between the behaviour of juveniles in leisure activities and adults at work, but the data of the experiments at least emphasised for the first time the importance of leadership styles.

Harvard Department of Social Relations

The work of R. F. Bales and his colleagues has already been mentioned in connection with group behaviour. Since there is a very close link between the study of groups and leadership, it is not surprising that this research has important messages for managers in their leadership roles, which are:

1. They need to be aware of the equilibrium problem, i.e. to balance the demands of the task against those of personal and interpersonal feelings.
2. They need to recognise the main kinds of contributions to a group's work, i.e. task-oriented behaviour and socio-emotional behaviour, and especially to distinguish between the positive (group maintenance-directed) and negative (individually oriented) aspects of this behaviour.
3. The leader's constant task is to move the group in a co-ordinated way towards the achievement of its goals, but at the same time to keep relationships harmonious and personal outcomes at a high level (i.e. to motivate people who want to retain membership).

4. The two facets are interdependent. In practice there could sometimes be high quality work, but a rapid turnover of staff, which reduces total efficiency.

Ohio State University

A team from this university carried out an extensive on-site study with employees of the International Harvester Co. to study the effects of leadership which covered a very wide range of different types of behaviour that leaders use in their dealings with subordinates. A statistical analysis of results revealed two broad categories of behaviour, one directed towards fulfilling tasks and goals, the other concerned with group reactions and individual feelings. Applying these categories to different levels of managers, the team found that some managers showed clear preferences for one of the two styles, whilst others exhibited both in fairly equal measure. It was also found that, in general, extremes in task-oriented styles correlated with high grievance-rates and that the subordinates of leaders who strongly favoured people-oriented styles had lower grievance-rates.

University of Michigan

These experiments took place at the offices of the Prudential Insurance Co. and looked at the correlation between work performance and leadership styles. Taking sections engaged in similar work, the team identified those with high productivity and those with low productivity. Next, they established that there were no significant differences in the supervisors of the sections in terms of age, sex, experience, etc. A study of the supervisory styles produced most interesting results. The supervisors of high-performance groups revealed similar behaviour. In particular, they exhibited concern for their employees, allowed them to share in decisions affecting work and generally established an atmosphere of trust. The supervisors of low-performance groups exhibited opposite types of behaviour and in general were much more concerned with productivity than their subordinates.

Likert's Four-systems Model

Rensis Likert, also of the University of Michigan, has made a prolonged study of management and in particular the effect of leadership styles upon people at work and in consequence upon group cohesiveness, effective performance and productivity. His research has led him to propose four main identifiable styles which he calls Systems 1–4, described as follows:

System 1 **Exploitive-authoritative.** Managers are very autocratic, do not trust subordinates, motivate mainly by fear and punishment, attempt to communicate only in a downwards direction and make all decisions unilaterally.

System 2 **Benevolent-authoritative.** Managers have a less harsh attitude, but still keep a tight control, especially in decision-making. They motivate with rewards and sometimes punishment and allow a limited measure of upward communication.

System 3 **Consultative.** Managers are much more employee-oriented than those of Systems 1 and 2. They motivate with rewards, participation and occasional punishment. They allow fairly unrestricted two-way communication. They tend to keep decision-making on major issues mainly to themselves.

System 4 **Participative-group.** Managers show complete trust and confidence in subordinates, who share in communication and decision-making at all levels. They operate with themselves and their subordinates as a group.

Likert's research into actual work-situations indicated a clear correlation between the four systems and the managers' success as leaders and the groups' achievement of goals and productivity. System 4, needless to say, was found to be superior to the others, a conclusion which closely matched the research data at the Prudential Insurance Company.

F. E. Fiedler's Contingency Model

Fiedler has made a unique contribution to the study of leadership. He has proposed that there are three critical dimensions for classifying leadership situations, i.e.

1. The leader/group relationship.
2. The ease or difficulty of the task (e.g. structured or unstructured).
3. The leader's vested authority.

He further proposes that in these three dimensions the situation may be favourable or unfavourable for the leader (e.g. he may not have enough authority to deal with a particular kind of group). Matching favourability and unfavourability with the three basic dimensions, he then produces eight possible combinations, ranging from dimensions 1, 2, 3 all favourable to dimensions 1, 2, 3 all unfavourable. This is the model for determining the nature of the situation.

Next, he produces a model for categorising leadership styles. An individual leader's style is determined by scoring a questionnaire designed to reveal the individual's attitudes towards persons that they themselves choose as the work colleague with whom they have had most difficulty in working (designated by Fiedler as 'the Least Preferred Co-worker'). Each tested subject is then given an LPC rating in which high scores indicate leaders who are people-oriented and low scores those who are task-oriented. The essence of Fiedler's Contingency Theory is that in practice we need to identify the nature of the situation and then select leaders most likely to be suited to a particular situation. Thus, for some situations, a people-oriented leader (i.e. high LPC) will be more effective, whilst other situations call for the task-oriented style (i.e. low LPC). This theory differs from other theories on leadership in that Fiedler inclines to the view that individuals tend to have preferred styles and that these need to be adapted to situations. Most other authors urge the need for developing flexibility in leaders to meet the needs of varying situations.

Tannenbaum and Schmidt

These authors are concerned with problems of leadership style and with questions such as whether managers can be democratic towards subordinates and yet maintain the necessary authority and control. For purposes of analysis they have produced a 'continuum of leadership behaviour' ranging from authoritarian styles at one extreme to democratic styles at the other, which they call 'boss-centred' and 'subordinate-centred' leadership. Unlike other models which advocate a preferred style, this model attempts to provide a framework for analysis and individual choice. The authors propose three key factors on which choice of leadership pattern depends, i.e.

1. Forces in the manager (e.g. attitudes, beliefs, values, etc.).
2. Forces in the subordinates (e.g. their attitudes, beliefs, values and expectations of the leader).
3. Forces in the situation (e.g. pressures and constraints produced by the tasks, organisational climate and other extraneous factors).

The summary of their conclusions is:

1. In deciding which point along the continuum represents the appropriate style, leaders need to begin with an analysis of these three factors, but in particular they need to clarify their own objectives.
2. Leaders need to develop skills in reading situations in these terms and then being able to behave appropriately in the light of their perceptions.
3. No one style of leadership is always right and another always wrong. Successful leaders are neither assertive nor permissive, but are consistently accurate in their assessment and application of the continuum.

The Blake-Mouton Managerial Grid

This is a well-publicised system for identifying leadership styles as a basis of training. Following the data of other authors, Blake and Mouton identify two critical basic dimensions, i.e. concern for the task and concern for the people. To find the precise location of a leader's style they have produced a grid with 'concern for people' along one axis and 'concern for the task' along the other. Each dimension ranges from 1 (low) to 9 (high) so that an 81-square grid is produced. The extremes are found in each corner, i.e.

1. Highest concern for people, lowest for task = 1.9.
2. Lowest concern for people and task = 1.1.
3. Highest concern for task, lowest for people = 9.1.
4. Highest concern for people and task = 9.9.

A moderate concern for both is in the middle of the grid and scores 5.5. The ideal which leaders should aim to achieve is 9.9.

J. Adair's Functional Leadership Model

This model was developed whilst the author was lecturing at the Royal Military Academy Sandhurst. It is based on the research data of studies of leadership, groups, etc. and the author's own experience at Sandhurst. The model is three-dimensional and proposes that, in all leadership situations, there are three crucial areas to which the leader must attend, namely:

1. The task.
2. The maintenance of team-cohesiveness.
3. The needs of the individuals.

All three areas require constant attention, but effective leadership depends upon the leader's skill in giving appropriate emphasis to particular areas at particular times. The special importance of this model is its usefulness for training purposes, i.e. activities can be meaningfully analysed and assessed in these terms. It has had a marked influence on military training and is now widely used in many other organisations.

Conclusions

The broad conclusions which emerge from research on leadership are these:

1. Democratic-participative styles are generally likely to be more effective in creating group cohesiveness and productivity than strongly task-oriented styles.
2. At the same time, varying situations require different leadership

NATURE OF GROUP BEHAVIOUR

Tuckman's model proposes four stages:

1. Forming.   2. Storming.
3. Norming.   4. Performing.

Bales' data indicates two areas:

Task-oriented; socio-emotional
(positive and negative).

Fundamental influential factors
are:

Task — nature and work-arrangements.
Group — size, composition,
relationships and norms.
Leadership — styles and appropriateness.
Environment — relationships with other
groups and the organisation.

CONCLUSIONS

1.   Balance between task-requirements
and team-maintenance is essential.
2.   Membership of group must be
worthwhile.
3.   Total organisational harmony
is paramount. Positive steps
are needed to reduce inter–group
rivalry.

NATURE OF LEADERSHIP

Modern studies emphasise superiority
of a functional analysis of leadership
in action rather than leaders' personal
qualities. Main contributions are:

Univ. of Iowa : study of leadership
styles at boys club (autocratic;
democratic; laissez-faire).
Harvard (Bales): theory of task-oriented
and socio-emotional axes.
Ohio State Univ.: data on effects of
task-oriented and people-oriented styles
at International Harvester Co.
Univ. of Michigan: similar data from
studies at Prudential Assurance Co.
Likert's four-systems: Exploitive-authoritative;
Benevolent-authoritative; Consultative;
Participative-group.
Fiedler: Contingency Theory, i.e.
matching leaders' LPC ratings with a
three-dimension model (leader/group
relationship; nature of task; leaders'
vested authority).
Tannenbaum and Schmidt: Continuum of
leadership behaviour ('boss-centred'–
'subordinate-centred').
Blake and Mouton: 9 X 9 Managerial
Grid (concern for task/concern for
people)
Adair: Functional Leadership Theory
(Needs of: Task, Team, Individuals)

CONCLUSIONS

In general, democratic-participative
styles are more effective.
However, much depends on
situational variables. Styles
have to be adapted to suit these.
Effective leadership requires
awareness of task, group,
individual and self.

Fig. 2. Summary of studies of group behaviour and leadership.

styles, which have to be adapted or selected to suit these different circumstances.

3. Effective leadership depends upon awareness of the nature of the task, the group and its individual members, the environment, and particularly upon the self-awareness of the leaders themselves.

QUESTIONS

1. What are the main features of Tuckman's and Bales' methods for analysing group behaviour?

2. What are the main factors that influence group behaviour?

3. What are group norms and why are they important in the study of group behaviour?

4. Summarise the main conclusions that have emerged from studies of group behaviour.

5. What are the significant differences between the former and present-day approaches to the study of leadership?

6. Briefly summarise the main features and conclusions of the studies of leadership carried out by the universities of Iowa, Michigan and Ohio.

7. What are the distinctive features of Fiedler's theory?

8. Summarise the main conclusions that have emerged from research into leadership during the past forty years.

3

Organisations

THEIR NATURE

Individuals and groups operate within the framework of larger groups, called organisations. Although much of what has already been said about the behaviour of individuals and groups will be applicable to organisations, they merit a special study because of the internal complexity of their structure, the inter-relationships of their component groups and their relationships with the external environment. The importance of managers of organisational studies is this: firstly, when we reach the organisational level of study, we are considering the total effectiveness of the system; secondly, having considered how an organisation does and should control its component elements, we are still left with the very difficult question—how is the organisation itself to be controlled? Is it capable of controlling itself? Northcote Parkinson, for example, has acquired a special fame for his comments about the uncontrolled ways in which organisations behave and expand.

The basic problem of size and complexity in organisations is something which everyone experiences sooner or later. It is seen in everyday working life in the difficulties that employees find in describing the organisation or in relating to it. It is much easier to identify oneself with the smaller group. It is as though individual employees are dealing with a mystical, unseen, indefinable force that controls their working lives, but with whom, like God, they can never come face to face. Like the other aspects of the study of people at work there has been considerable research into organisations and a vast quantity of literature has now accumulated. These works could be classified in various ways, but there is a common thread running through the diversity of particular themes, which is the implicit assumption that organisations as a phenomenon of modern industrial life need to be studied and analysed to provide a basis for designing structures that are as effective as possible both in terms of productivity and human contentment.

From the very wide variety of research data it is possible to distinguish four broad categories of approach, which reflect different emphases in studying the subject, namely:

1. **Structural approach:** this group includes authors who form the so-called classical or traditional school. They are mainly concerned with formal organisations, and related questions such as structural design, the definition of responsibilities and the legitimacy of authority.

2. **Human relations approach:** those who follow this approach stress the importance of individuals, their needs and reactions to organisational life, and the existence of an informal system which needs to be taken into account when organisations are designed.

3. **Systems approach:** authors included in this category are interested mainly in the significance of the interaction and inter-relationships between the component elements of organisations and between organisations and their environments.

4. **Contingency approach:** this is the most recent development in organisational studies. It has links with the structural and systems approaches, but emphasises the need for on-site, comparative studies to find out what organisations are really like, to analyse the interactions of all the internal and external variables, and on this basis to design organisations to take account of the contingencies of differing situations.

This categorisation is a simplification of a very complex field of study, but is adequate as a basic framework for a broad analysis of the subject. All four groups have combined to produce the sum total of our current insight into organisational life, the problems that it creates and possible remedies. For the purpose of this review, it would be useful briefly to examine some of the important contributions in each group as samples of the main trends of thought about problems that typically occur, their causes and possible remedies.

STUDIES OF ORGANISATIONAL STRUCTURE

The first major study of organisations was made by Max Weber. This work was doubly important because it laid a foundation for subsequent studies and raised the very important question of authority types:

1. **Charismatic:** here, authority stems from the personality of the leaders of the organisation and is typified in religious, political and industrial organisations by people like Gandhi, Churchill, Ford, etc.

2. **Traditional:** here, the basis is precedent and custom. The commonest example is a monarchy. In industry, examples are found in family firms, where the leadership is passed from father to son, even though initially at least the son may derive no authority from experience.

3. **Rational–legal:** this is described as a normal basis for democratic society and formal work organisations. The main requirement is a

hierarchy of levels of authority, which is based on the assumed ability of managers to perform better than their subordinates either through superior professional or superior administrative experience, knowledge and skills, or a combination of both. This authority is then incorporated into a set of rules and codes governing the arrangements for work and the conduct of employees.

Weber described the rational–legal organisation as a bureaucracy, which he considered to be the predominant and most effective form of organisation. Its particular virtue in Weber's view—and hence its name—is that once the roles of office at various levels have been defined, the organisation continues to function independently of individuals. A simple analogy would be a long-running play, where different actors join and leave the cast over the years, but the play continues. Weber was not so concerned with what later authors have described as the dysfunctions of bureaucracy, e.g. the potential for the misuse of authority by the substitution of power by certain individuals who seek to pursue personal ends by means of coercion or manipulation; conflicts which arise from personal interpretations of the meanings of organisational rules, etc. Furthermore, whilst the basic model of the typical bureaucracy is useful for general analysis, it also does not take account of the importance of role interpretation. Employees interpret their work roles in the light of their own attitudes, values, beliefs, needs and expectations. Weber has adequately described the formal pattern of organisational behaviour, but beneath the surface there is an informal pattern which is just as important, as the Human Relations School has shown. People interact socially at work and take part in activities not prescribed in the formal system. Nevertheless, the introduction of the idea of authority and legitimacy has made a most important contribution to the study of organisations, especially in terms of the psychological contract, discussed earlier.

Another significant contribution to the theme of organisational authority has been made by A. Etzioni. This author is interested in the idea of matching types of individuals' attitudes and expectations with types of organisations. He identifies three main types of organisation, according to their authority base and three types of individual involvement, i.e.

1. Organisation-types.
(*i*) **Coercive:** used in prisons, mental hospitals and sometimes in military units.
(*ii*) **Utilitarian:** used mainly in industry, related to Weber's rational–legal type and relying mainly on economic rewards.
(*iii*) **Normative:** used mainly in organisations where voluntary service predominates, e.g. religious, welfare, political and professional associations.

2. Individual types of involvement:
   (*i*) **Alienative:** members are forced to join and have no psychological involvement.
   (*ii*) **Calculative:** members join mainly to satisfy economic and similar needs.
   (*iii*) **Moral:** members place a high personal value on the objectives of the organisation.

There is a general correlation between the organisational type and the type of involvement. This model may also be useful when related to the idea of the psychological contract between employer and employee and possible problems of misperception. For example, if an organisation, that is expected to be essentially utilitarian, tries to introduce patterns of authority that are coercive in nature, then an alienative response is likely to be produced. Similarly, if this type of organisation expects a moral involvement, such as a heart and soul commitment from employees to the firm and its products, it could be making a psychological miscalculation in asking for more from its employees than it is really prepared to give in return.

THE HUMAN RELATIONS APPROACH

This approach to organisational life is concerned with the effects that the dispositions of management, as expressed in the form of organisational structures, rules of conduct, hierarchical systems of authority, working arrangements etc., may have upon the individual employees. The principal contributors to the school of thought which emphasises the importance of the individual are Mayo, Maslow, McGregor, Herzberg and Argyris. The essence of these theories has already been examined in discussions of motivation and group behaviour and does not need repetition. Their value has been to draw attention to the existence and significance of the informal system of behaviour and relationships which are not considered in the traditional approach to organisational structure.

THE SYSTEMS APPROACH

Chronologically, the theories which belong to this group are more recent in origin. The emphasis of the approach is concentrated upon the interactions between the different elements of an organisation—the people, the structure, the technology and the environment, which could be seen as a response to the greatly increased pressures upon organisations and their employees in recent years as a result of the very rapid changes in political, technological, economic and social environments.

The studies of coal-mining made by the social scientists of the Tavistock Institute and the conclusions that they reached about the impact of the task upon group behaviour have already been mentioned. Strongly advocating the view that an organisation is a complex of interacting variables, this group has produced two important ideas, namely:

1. The concept of **the socio-technical system:** this implies that an organisation is a combination of two systems: the technology (the tasks, the equipment and working arrangements) and the social system (the interpersonal relationships of employees). The two systems are in constant interaction and each influences the other.

2. **The open-system model:** The essence of this idea is that organisations import resources and information from the environment, which are processed within the organisation and then exported to the environment in the form of products or services.

The significance of these ideas lies in their emphasis on the organisation's dependence on its environment and on the need to design organisations which take full account of the socio-technical system.

A well-known example of the systems approach to organisational studies is R. Likert's theory of overlapping groups and linking pins, the main theses of which are:

1. The significant environment for a group is composed of other groups.

2. Groups are linked to their environment by people holding key positions and being members of more than one group (e.g. the Head of Department who is also a member of the Organisational Management Committee).

The total system comprises three levels: society as a whole, organisations of similar function, and sub-groups within a larger system, which are connected by people in key positions, acting as linking pins. Likert's model emphasises the importance and the possibly far-reaching consequences of relationships and dependencies.

A theory which is very similar to Likert's in concept, but adds a further important idea has been developed by R. Kahn and colleagues. On the basis of Weber's view that organisations should be regarded as a hierarchy of offices and the behaviour of office holders as roles, Kahn proposes that all those with whom office holders have contacts can be described as their role sets. In this way an organisation can be regarded as a complex of overlapping role sets. The model is useful for analysing organisational problems of relationships and integration. For example, there may be role conflict because members of the role set have different views about the ways role holders should behave; role ambiguity may arise if office holders are not given adequate information to perform their roles; office holders may experience role stress when members of their role set have different expectations of their behaviour, as often happens to supervisors, for example, when dealing with the expectations of management on the one hand and those of their subordinates on the other.

The systems approach to organisational study has made a particularly valuable contribution in emphasising the possible extents of influence, i.e. what Rosemary Stewart has called 'the concept of boundaries'. For example, in studying an organisation, we need to think beyond the internal confines of the organisation's immediate environment and consider the clientele that it exists to serve and its general social environment. This idea is closely related to the model developed by P. Blau and W. Scott who propose that an organisation's survival and growth depends on its ability to clarify its purpose and to be aware of its beneficiaries. On this basis they propose four categories of organisations.

1. **Mutual–benefit associations**—serving their own members (e.g. unions, political, professional and religious groups).

2. **Businesses**—serving their owners, shareholders and the general public.

3. **Services**—serving particular clients (e.g. hospitals, schools, etc.).

4. **Commonweal organisations**—serving the public at large (e.g. police, fire, welfare services, governmental departments, etc.).

CONTINGENCY STUDIES

In recent times, there have been some developments in organisational research which are different in approach from, but related to, the structural and systems approaches. The authors of these studies have this in common; they are especially concerned with current problems faced by organisations, such as the suitability of structures for different organisational purposes, their capacity to adapt to their environment in times of considerable instability, and the organisational designs likely to be most effective for various situations. Unlike traditional structural theories, this research has usually been very practical and carried out at work-sites over long periods of time by means of direct observation and questioning. The authors are concerned with what organisations are really like and what they need to do to be effective, rather than what they seem superficially to be.

In the 1950s, Joan Woodward carried out detailed research of a wide variety of firms in Essex with reference to certain characteristics, e.g. the number of levels of authority, the span of control, definitions of responsibilities, communication patterns and divisions of labour, and the effects that environmental variables such as technology have upon them. Three types of productive technological environments were distinguished, i.e.

1. Unit and small batch, including self-contained units making products for customer specifications.
2. Large batch and mass, where the technology is characterised by mass-production.
3. Process, in which the technology is directed towards an intermittent or continuous flow production of chemicals, etc.

When the types of internal organisational variable mentioned above were examined, relative to the three categories of factories, it was found that there was a direct relationship between these and the technological processes employed. The main conclusions drawn from these studies were:

1. Variables in the environment, and especially technology, should be a fundamental factor in organisational design.
2 It is inadvisable to think of organisation design in terms of universally applicable principles.

A sociologist T. Burns collaborated with a psychologist G. Stalker in a similarly important on-site study of manufacturing firms in Scotland. They were particularly interested in problems of introducing modern electronic technology into traditional organisations. As a result of these studies, the authors have produced a well-known model based on the difficulties that different firms experienced in adapting to change. They propose a continuum of organisational structures, with what they describe as 'mechanistic' and 'organic' types of organisation at the extremes. The 'mechanistic' organisation is typical of Weber's bureaucracy in structure and works satisfactorily in stable conditions. In unstable conditions, such as those of rapid technological change, the 'organic' type of organisation has much more flexibility. Its significant differences compared with the traditional organisation are these:

1. Functions and duties are not enshrined in organisational charts.
2. Interactions and communication are not restricted by a hierarchical structure of authority, but depend on the specialist requirements of the situation.
3. There is continuous readjustment to meet changing circumstances.

A major study, typical of the contingency approach, has been produced by P. Lawrence and J. Lorsch, based on the work of Woodward, Burns and Stalker. These authors studied ten firms from three different industries in terms of different rates of technological change and the influence of different elements in the environment.

They analysed the internal structures of these firms according to two dimensions:

1. The 'differentiation' of different functional departments (i.e. differences in objectives, time-allocation, interpersonal relationships, etc.).

2. 'Integration' (i.e. the degree of inter-departmental co-ordination, collaboration and relationships).

Then they analysed the relationships between differences in external environments and differences in internal environments. They found that the internal variables have a complex relationship with each other and with the external variables. In contingency terms, their findings may be summarised as follows:

(*i*)   In an unstable and varied environment, the organisation needs to be relatively unstructured.

(*ii*)   In a stable and uniform environment a more rigid structure is appropriate.

(*iii*)   If the external environment is very varied and the internal structure is highly differentiated, positive measures need to be taken to ensure integration.

There is a clear similarity in the data from all of these contingency studies, i.e. organisational effectiveness is much influenced by the degree of harmony between the internal and external environments of organisations and this is a fundamental factor to be taken into account in their design.

CONCLUSION

Research data has produced the following general conclusions about organisational behaviour and management's responsibilities.

1. Managers need to be aware of the general nature of organisations and especially of the complexity of the interactions between the organisations' component elements, and between an organisation and elements in the external environment.

2. Managers need to be aware of the existence and significance of informal systems and their relationships with formal systems in the organisation.

3. No universal principles should be assumed in the design of organisations, which should be tailor-made to take account of interactions between internal and external variables. The predominant technology is a fundamentally important factor affecting design.

4. The design should encourage the maximum possible integration of groups and prevent intra- and intergroup conlict as far as possible.

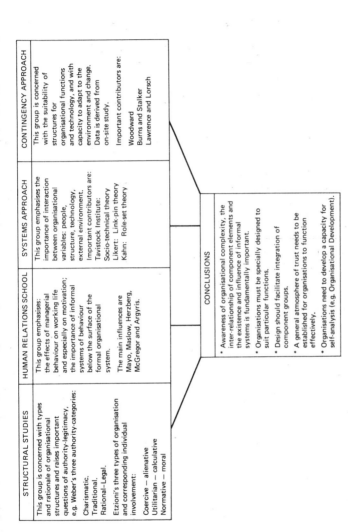

Fig. 3. Summary of studies of organisations.

5. A general atmosphere of trust and openness has to be established, whereby clearly defined objectives are communicated to all employees and the psychological contract (i.e. what the organisation can give and what it expects) should be clarified.

6. Finally, in order to survive and grow, organisations need to develop a capacity for self-analysis, whereby they may diagnose and solve their own problems. In this connection, the emergence and application in recent years of the idea of Organisation Development (OD) is particularly promising. The essential objectives of OD are:

(*i*) to help organisations to become much more aware of their own structures and of their internal and external relationship.

(*ii*) to become more adaptive to change.

(*iii*) to programme a process of continued self-analysis as an integral element of organisational life.

OD requires the employment of external or internal consultants on a long-term basis to fulfil a catalytic function in helping managers at all levels to achieve the objectives described above.

QUESTIONS

1. What different kinds of categories of organisational theory can be distinguished and what are the distinctive features of each?

2. Describe briefly the essential features of the theories of the following authors: Weber, Etzioni, Likert, Kahn, Burns and Stalker.

3. Summarise the main conclusions about organisation design and behaviour that have emerged from studies of organisations.

4. What is Organisation Development and its principal objectives?

FURTHER READING: PART 1

Argyle, M., *The Psychology of Interpersonal Behaviour*, Penguin, London, 1967.
Argyle, M., *The Social Psychology of Work*, Penguin, London, 1974.
Child, J., *Organizations*, Harper & Row, New York, 1977.
Gahagan, J., *Interpersonal and Group Behaviour*, Essential Psychology, Methuen, London, 1975.
Gibb, C., *Leadership*, Penguin, London, 1969.
Handy, C., *Understanding Organizations*, Penguin, London, 1976.
Kirby, R., and Radford, J., *Individual Differences*, Essential Psychology, Methuen, London, 1976.
Lassey, W., *Leadership and Social Change*, University Associates, USA, 1973.

Murrell, H., *Motivation at Work*, Essential Psychology, Methuen, London, 1976.

Porter, L. and Roberts, K., *Communication in Organizations*, Penguin, London, 1977.

Pugh, D., *Organization Theory*, Penguin, London, 1971.

Schein, E., *Organization Psychology*, Prentice-Hall, Englewood Cliffs, N.J., 1970

Stewart, R., *The Reality of Organisations*, Penguin, London, 1972.

Vroom, V., and Deci, E., *Management and Motivation*, Penguin, London, 1974.

PART 2

Personnel Management as a System

Managers are expected to organise and to be accountable for the work of other people. In this process, managers act as employers and as such they create and sustain the employment relationships of their organisations. The occupation of personnel management specialises in the technical skills of managing this employment relationship. As we defined specialist personnel management in the Introduction, it is the occupation which exercises a responsibility throughout the organisation for creating, maintaining and adjusting the policies which form the employer's part of the employment contract. In this section, we shall look at how specialist personnel management has emerged. After we have seen how different models of personnel management have developed, we shall explore the interdependence between the activities which make up the personnel function of management by looking at how these activities interlock as a 'system'.

4

The Nature and Development of Personnel Management

When we come to consider the essential nature of personnel management we immediately encounter the question of what are the goals of specialist personnel managers, and how do they assist in the achievement of the organisation's goals?

Since the early years of this century, writers such as Fayol and, more recently, Urwick and Brech have classified the activities of managers under the headings 'planning', 'co-ordinating', 'controlling' and 'motivating'. These headings demonstrate an awareness of the primary managerial task of pushing work forward, adapting to changes in the environment and overcoming obstacles. Although this classification is helpful as an analysis of management deploying economic resources, when we observe managers at work it is difficult to see their actions in this simple way. For example, all their work involves co-ordination and control. Management work is better described as part of the continuous social processes which apply in organisational life, as Mintzberg (1970) and Stewart (1968) have shown.

The actions of managers are usually very much concerned with achieving results through other people, and therefore the inter-personal skills they demonstrate—notably their capacity to communicate and to receive information, the climate of trust they establish, the degree of enthusiasm they generate, their sense of fairness and their own humanity—will be more significant than a grasp of techniques such as how to discount cash flow or to prepare a critical path analysis.

We can now venture a description of what lies at the heart of managerial work. The essential characteristics seem to be that managers exercise their authority in such a way that it is regarded as legitimate, they maintain the adherence of subordinates to the organisation's goals, and build teams which are capable of achieving these goals. Personnel management in its specialised sense is concerned to help in the widest possible way with these managerial tasks.

The personnel department is the unit with organisation-wide responsibilities for personnel policy, and should be considered as quite separate from the personnel function, which all managers carry out in the management of people. Definitions of personnel management vary. North American authors stress the responsibility that all managers have for their staff. The specialist personnel role is not seen to detract from the key tasks in managing people which all managers are required to perform. The personnel manager is an integrated member of the team, responsible for putting forward policies which will help managers achieve the profit objectives. For example:

'Personnel Management is the recruitment, selection, development, utilisation of, and accommodation to, human resources by organisations.' (French, 1978, p. 3)

Similarly, Beach (1975) describes personnel management as a frame of reference, and as a way the manager applies theory to his particular circumstances.

British definitions of personnel management grant it a professional status in its own right. For example, Barker's definition suggests that it is the department which copes with the central problem of all organisations, in finding methods of organising people to achieve the organisation's objectives. Definitions from this side of the Atlantic frequently accord the personnel manager a normative role. Thus Cuming (1975) represents the main concern as 'obtaining the best possible staff for an organisation, and having got them, looking after them so that they will want to stay and give of their best to their jobs'. Armstrong (1977) describes the model of personnel management meeting legal obligations and social responsibilities, and the Institute of Personnel Management suggests that personnel management aims to achieve both efficiency and justice: 'neither of which can be pursued successfully without the other'.

There are, therefore, a number of different traditions of personnel management. It can be perceived as a kind of social conscience, reminding the senior management of their social responsibilities. Personnel departments can spend much of their time operating on personal welfare problems. If manpower control is the main consideration, the role of personnel will be principally concerned with issues such as the reduction of absenteeism, labour budgeting, head count, etc. Other traditions in personnel management include organisation development, in which the personnel manager helps the company to adapt to change, and strives to have a beneficial influence on relationships through the application of the social sciences to personnel problems with job redesign and job satisfaction schemes and communication techniques. In some organisations, personnel departments perform a kind of low-level administration, dealing with routine requests from managers for recruitment, transfers, and termination, whereas in other organisations they are concerned with strategic planning, developing long-term manpower plans and industrial relations strategy.

How the work is conducted will depend on the particular organisation, and there is no common standard applicable throughout the public sector, industry and commerce. The way the company is organised and its size—whether, for example, it is broken down into divisions, profit centres, or part of a group—will also influence the way specialist personnel departments fit into the policy-making and decision-making arrangements of the organisation.

Different emphases are sometimes given to parts of the specialism, such as manpower planning, selection, industrial relations, training, and management development. In some cases, personnel directors sit on company boards, advising their fellow directors on the influence of decisions on personnel policy. There is, therefore, a multiplicity of types of relationships between personnel and line managers.

The personnel manager is often depicted as an adviser to senior line managers. The amount of executive power he possesses to carry out decisions without referring them to others will be dependent on what the Chief Executive has delegated but, unlike some other managers, the amount of power personnel staff possess to carry out policies is usually limited. If, for example, the personnel manager wanted to introduce a new pension scheme, or to change the remuneration policy, it is extremely unlikely that he would do so unilaterally. Yet, as we have suggested, personnel managers are sometimes given a general remit to improve relationships. The reason for this paradox can readily be found in the accountability that line managers have for the achievement of the organisation's objectives. To illustrate this point, we may consider the case of the sales manager who is given a sales target to achieve, but no say over the number, quality or deployment of his sales force. In such circumstances, he could hardly be accountable for the attainment of his target.

In their 'staff' role, personnel managers act as advisers to management on policy and strategy, whilst the conduct of the policy is often left in the hands of their line manager colleagues.

Recent developments within this strategic role have given rise to the phrase 'Human Resource Management', as an alternative to 'personnel management'. Human Resource Management is sometimes defined as a qualitatively different approach which seeks to use the personnel policy areas employee resourcing, employee development, employee relations and rewards within a broad strategic plan for the people part of the business, in order to improve or sustain an organisation's competitive advantage.

So far we have outlined the complexities of line manager/personnel manager relations, and we have mentioned some of the various traditions in personnel work that exist. The history and development of personnel work is a good starting point for understanding how different conceptions of personnel management have emerged.

THE EARLY HISTORY OF PERSONNEL MANAGEMENT, UP TO 1914

The 'industrial revolution' which spread throughout Britain during the middle of the nineteenth century was brought about by the application of the principle of the division of labour combined with the harnessing of steam and other power sources. Concentrations of working people in factories and the related growth of towns led to the helter-skelter existence which we associate with modern industrial life. The rapid increase in population, new markets, new technology and expansion by vertical integration were conditions which helped to create the need for a large-scale organisation of resources.

During the first half of the century, a ground-swell of criticism appeared against what seemed the unchecked greed and exploitation of man by his fellows. Movements for democracy, agitation for the repeal of anti-trade union legislation and for some minimal controls on employers found their expression through the Chartists, the Ten-Hour movement and the Anti-Corn Law League and in sporadic riots and petitions. In the works of Dickens and the later social investigations of Mayhew, Booth and Rowntree, the worst abuses of sweating (excessive hours), child mistreatment, and oppression by employers were revealed, and a working-class counter-culture was described.

Even amongst enlightened liberal opinion, public acknowledgement of the reasons for poverty had usually supported the beliefs underlying the 1834 Poor Law. There was no understanding of structural unemployment or the effects of a down-turn in the trade cycle. The general image of the pauper was a lazy profligate brought down by his own failings, notably excessive drinking. Such a vision was congruent with the middle-class ideology which was a celebration of capitalist economics. Management and the owners of business were drawn from the upper middle class, where a high value was placed on individualism, competition and the survival of the fittest. Artisans, foremen and shopkeepers would also have subscribed to such views. Little had changed for working people in the nineteenth century. Their conditions and life chances had always been poor. As John Clare, the Northamptonshire poet wrote:

'. . . the poor man's lot seems to have been so long remembered as to be entirely forgotten.'

Pressures for reform and for the protection of working people came towards the end of the nineteenth century, mostly from trade union leaders and members of the labour movement. The extension of the franchise added to these pressures in the last quarter of the century. Active campaigning by individuals such as Rowntree was also effective, and the large Quaker employers set out to provide an example of how good working conditions and profitability could be compatible. What has been called the movement towards 'industrial betterment' came on the fringes of a wider claim for improvement in living conditions. Out of this movement emerged the earliest attempts at welfare policies. One interpretation of the industrial betterment movement is that it was a response by employers to the demand for change in society.

Early welfare workers belonged to the property-owning classes and at first were concerned only with women. The protection of women was seen as a worthy objective, and even the most harsh employer would have found it difficult to oppose these aims openly. Extra-mural welfare workers visited sick employees, and helped to arrange accommodation for women and girls, often including an oversight of moral welfare as part of their work. Welfare workers were usually employed in the newer industries, where women were engaged on light machine work, packing, assembly and similar routine jobs, and it was in these factories that full-time welfare staff were first in service. The scope of the welfare officer was allowed to grow in those companies where she could demonstrate a successful integration of welfare and managerial objectives, so that she became concerned with the recruitment, training and transfer of hourly-paid women factory hands.

Up to 1900 there were still only a dozen or so full-time welfare secretaries, but their number had grown sufficiently by 1913 for them to seek a recognisable identity by forming the Welfare Workers' Association, this being the forerunner to the Institute of Personnel Management. They often found that managers and supervisors were suspicious of their work, and they were also attacked by the unions as a management device for controlling employees. The problems of being the 'man in the middle' were not unlike the difficulties faced by first line supervisors. Work people were not sure whether the aims of welfare were altruistic and felt that there was an element of hypocrisy in the welfare secretaries' actions. Managers saw the possibility of another standard besides economic efficiency being applied, and were antagonised by the thought of any restriction on their power.

The reasons for the development of a welfare movement can best be seen as a response to the wider trend of greater interest and concern for general living conditions. Although it has been argued that Quaker employers such as Cadbury may have been expiating their guilt feelings by becoming leaders of the welfare movement at a time when they had not yet reconciled the profit motive with Christian ethics, it is more accurate to see in their sponsorship of the welfare movement a belief in good organisation, good health, hygiene, and a broad mission of pastoral care for their workers. Individual welfare workers probably had mixed motives, but there is no doubt that most of them wanted to help improve conditions for working people.

What was the purpose of welfare work?

1. It was an assertion of a paternalistic relationship between employers and their workforce. This outlook was in the spirit of the old guild masters, which meant that employers might expect a reciprocal sense of service from their workers.

2. To grant some form of moral protection over women and children just as the Factory Acts sought to provide a form of physical protection.

3. To achieve higher output by control of sickness and absenteeism, and by the early resolution of grievances and problems.

4. To provide sanitary and acceptable working conditions. Much of the early welfare work was in food factories where cleanliness also benefited the consumer.

5. To make the organisation of women by trade unions unnecessary through removing the employees' grievances.

From these early days some of the conflict and confusion about personnel work has persisted. In fact, welfare work was always undertaken to meet the interests of management, since ultimately it was a cost met by management. To some degree, the areas of welfare covered by welfare officers, or 'secretaries' as they were sometimes known, were on behalf of society as a whole, at a time when there was no help from the State.

THE FIRST WORLD WAR

The First World War occasioned a 'step change' in the development of personnel management. There was a large increase in the number of welfare officers (to about 1300), largely in munitions and war factories, where men were also recruited to oversee boys' welfare. State regulation of employment was instituted through the Munitions of War Act, 1915, which, with its amendments, sought to control the supply of labour to war factories and made welfare services obligatory in these factories.

The extension of controls into such matters as timekeeping, attendance and 'diligence' gave the State an unprecedented impact on working life. However, there were initially a number of different approaches adopted towards personnel problems, and it was not until towards the end of the war that the controls became well organised and effective. Welfare work was performed on an impersonal, bureaucratic basis.

The Government gave direct encouragement to welfare development through the Health of Munitions Workers' Committee, which was the precursor to the National Institute of Industrial Psychology, and which continued the research into psychological problems of working—boredom, fatigue, monotony, etc.

Women were recruited in large numbers to fill the manpower gap caused by the demand for war materials and the expansion of the armed services. In 1915 one man was expected to do the work of two. The employment of women necessitated agreement with the trade unions on what was termed 'dilution'—that is, accepting unskilled women into craftsmen's work, the abandonment of formal apprenticeship schemes, and changed manning levels. Although compulsory arbitration was introduced, there were many bitter wrangles. Lloyd George, as Minister of Munitions, was obliged to go to the Clydeside shipyards to try to resolve a dispute over 'dilutees' and discharge certificates, for example.

After 1918 various forms of joint consultation were proposed. The only enduring form was the Whitley Joint Consultative Committee in the Civil Service, which is still in existence. However, for the first time the State had to open up a dialogue with the trade unions, and a recognisable policy on industrial relations was evidenced in this period.

GROWTH OF EMPLOYMENT MANAGEMENT

Employment management accented labour control, recruitment and discharge of labour and had separate origins from welfare. Labour managers came into being in the engineering industry and in large factories—for example, in process industries—and in some cases developed from more routine jobs such as 'timekeepers' or record-keeping assistants on the works office manager's staff. Often, wages clerks saw job applicants and came to deal with queries over absences, bonuses, piece rates, etc. The employers' federations had industrial relations responsibilities, and employed officials to help settle disputes. In engineering and shipbuilding there was national negotiation of rates, but districts plussed-up on these rates according to tradition and the supply of skilled labour. Records of grievances and disputes were kept by engineering employers because of the need to follow procedures within the employers' federation, and therefore specialists in the procedures evolved in some companies.

EARLY PERSONNEL DEPARTMENTS (1920–39)

In the 1920s and 1930s employment managers with various job titles such as 'Labour Officer', 'Men's Employment Officer', etc., were increasingly common. The number of employers' associations which had traditionally fulfilled the major industrial relations role fell from 2403 to 1550 between 1925 and 1936. This was partly due to employers wanting to follow an independent tack, and because with the growth in complexity of their businesses, they created their own personnel departments with industrial relations policies. In the large organisations, such as ICI, Courtaulds, Pilkingtons, London Transport and Marks and Spencer, the first specialist personnel departments were formed between the wars.

Specialist personnel management in organisations such as these was a response to the problem of control. Complex organisation structures resulted in differing standards and divergent policies unless a central controlling influence was exercised. Mergers, acquisitions, and expansions led to the establishment of personnel departments. These were usually in the newer industries, such as plastics, chemicals, mass-produced consumer goods, and in multiple retail, whereas there was no attempt to develop employment management as a specialism in industries such as shipbuilding, textiles or mining which were hit by the slump. This was because employment management addressed itself to the question of manpower control in matters like absenteeism and recruitment with the intention of improving output. In the older industries, the pressing problems were those of structural unemployment and no techniques such as retraining adult workers, redeployment or work-sharing were considered by managements. The size of the problem (for most of the 1920s and 1930s there was never less than 10 per cent of the working population unemployed), and the world-wide recession made it unlikely that solutions would be sought by the application of new techniques.

As trade began to pick up, and rearmament began in the late 1930s, the larger companies in the new industries showed an interest in management development and training. Management trainees were recruited, who followed a central training scheme, and in this way the latent purpose of spreading a common managerial philosophy throughout diverse organisation structures was ensured when the trainees moved between divisions. Since the First World War the National Institute of Industrial Psychology had begun to develop selection tests and to contribute to the solution of training problems.

In the larger modern companies, the welfare and employment management sections were merged in the later 1930s. Personnel management in all but these few enterprises was a low-level affair until after 1945. The employees covered were usually hourly-paid operatives and junior clerical staff. In retail distribution some moves towards including sales staff and buyers took place in the 1930s and the Staff Management Association was set up in 1934 specifically to cover the difficult personnel problems of managing staff scattered in small units. Industrial relations was not regarded as the mainstay of personnel work, and was frequently the main responsibility of senior line managers.

The effects of large-scale unemployment retarded advances in techniques. With a cheap supply of labour available, and uncertainty about future demand, there was no pressure for sophisticated manpower planning, and the threat of unemployment averted attention from questions of motivation. Similarly, after the General Strike in 1926, and the weakening effect of structural unemployment, power was passing from the hands of trade union leaders. However, from 1937 onwards, rearmament and the prospect of war caused a change. There were also social pressures emanating from the Depression, for security and a better life. This was the period of improvements in suburban housing, of a national movement for holidays with pay, and it was a time when big corporations saw the value in improving employee benefits such as pension schemes as a way of ensuring a stable, tractable workforce.

THE SECOND WORLD WAR

In the Second World War, personnel management was expanded in its manpower control aspects to virtually all factories, and the designation of welfare and personnel occupations as 'reserved' (i.e. those occupying them were exempt from conscription into the forces) shows the importance that was attached to the personnel role. The growth in numbers of personnel officers was again a feature of wartime, as had been the case with the First World War, there being around 5700 by 1943.

The three instruments of labour regulation were 'protected establishments' (engaged in war work), the registration of all employment, and 'essential work orders'. These gave an expanded Ministry of Labour and National Service considerable power to direct labour, to prevent the call up of those with special skills, and to influence conditions of employment.

Welfare and personnel work was inaugurated on a full-time basis at all establishments producing war materials, and the concept of a total war carried with it the belief that no effort should be spared to ensure high productivity. In addition to the administration of the rules, all aspects of the management of people came under scrutiny, and the Government saw specialist personnel management as an integral part of the drive for greater efficiency. For example, the Ministry of Aircraft Production stipulated that specialist personnel management was mandatory in aircraft factories.

The evacuation of large numbers of civilians, the extension of shift working, and the problems of training large numbers of women and young people, gave welfare and personnel departments the same central place in the organisation of production as had emerged during the First World War. Welfare was again part of the rule-governed environment created for large-scale production. The pervasive aspects of the role were resented by work people, but less so in the Second World War than in the First.

The acceptance of the vital importance of the struggle and the feeling of involvement by ordinary people in view of the blitz were perhaps the main reasons for this different response. Nevertheless, personnel and welfare officers were seen as part of the operations of management and the two World Wars helped to create the image of the personnel officer as a bureaucrat.

To achieve wartime production targets strikes were made illegal and compulsory arbitration was introduced. In 1940 three men were expected to cover the work of four, and once again the manpower gap necessitated the employment of women in unfamiliar jobs, such as crane drivers, and in war factories. Of necessity, restrictive practices had to be suspended by the unions, and the State entered into a dialogue with the unions to try to maintain harmony. The relationship was more intentionally fostered in the Second World War, when Ernest Bevin, as Minister of Labour (and an important pre-war trade union leader), and a coalition government were able to persuade the unions that the suspension of normal practices was not a surrender. The linking of productivity improvements with joint consultation made a lasting impression on management thought, and the principles of joint consultation have come to be regarded as important in the training of personnel managers. After 1945, successive governments have found various forms of consultation with the TUC necessary, continuing the tradition.

Three significant tendencies deriving from both World Wars can be summarised as follows:

1. The belief, sustained by research, that output and employment conditions are related, and the development of specific personnel techniques.

2. The integration of employment management and welfare work into the broad function, under the umbrella of personnel management, and the massive increase in the number of people in the occupation.

3. The Wars demonstrated that the regulation of employment by the State could produce the desired outcomes in the short term at least, but that this required large-scale controls, and could only succeed with the agreement of the work people who needed a commitment to victory, if they were to be convinced of the necessity to relinquish their freedoms.

1945 ONWARDS

Industrial Relations and Personnel Management

An understanding of the different facets of personnel management is not possible without an appreciation of what role personnel managers have played in employee relationships. The term 'industrial relations' is frequently used to describe only formal, institutional arrangements for relationships between the mass of the workforce and managers as representatives of those in whose interests the organisation is controlled.

However, the differences between the 'formal' and 'informal' relationships have never been so strictly drawn for an analysis on that basis to be sufficient. Power relationships are central to our understanding of industrial relations, and these have fluctuated.

A brief account of the development of trade unionism is given in Chapter 18, so in this section we shall confine ourselves to the development of industrial relations responsibilities in the personnel job. The broader views of 'industrial relations' as the whole spectrum of relationships and the negotiation processes between power groups in an organisation reveals at once the cardinal place that personnel management occupies.

Trade unions were suspicious and hostile towards the early welfare workers. They felt that welfare workers were extending the employers' control into the private lives of the work people. The welfare movement had sprung up in non-unionised companies. Shipbuilding, engineering, mining and transport, for example, were industries where trade union traditions were strong and regulation of labour was largely in the hands of both district and local trade union officials, and the employers' federations.

Although large companies began to establish their own personnel departments from the late 1920s onwards, it was difficult for personnel officers to gain credibility quickly. This is a problem which has dogged the occupation to the present day. Institutional arrangements in the engineering industry militated against importance being granted to personnel management. The 'procedure' for settling disputes tended to favour the involvement of senior executives at the later stage rather than local personnel officers. Union negotiators, although now reconciled to personnel work as part of management, typically preferred to negotiate with the more senior members of companies, recognising then as now the value of dealing with those who had the power to grant their case.

Post-1945 industrial relations have witnessed an enormous growth in the number and power of shop stewards, and the breakdown of national level bargaining through employers' federations. Local-level bargaining has given greater scope for personnel staff and the larger companies have preferred to develop their own industrial relations policies which are in tune with their investment plans, and their overall corporate strategy. There was a growth in productivity bargaining in the 1960s as employers and unions negotiated about shares in wealth that were to be found from improvements in technology, such as the Fawley agreements. The involvement of line managers in productivity bargaining was essential both because of their technical knowledge, and because they were the managers who had to make the bargain work.

The Donovan Report of 1968 on Trade Unions and Employers was a Royal Commission report which examined British industrial relations in the light of the large number of unofficial strikes which were taking place. Donovan was particularly critical of what the Commission's members saw as the failure of personnel managers either to cope with the changes that were taking place, to be skilled in negotiation, or to plan industrial relations strategy. The immediate, *ad hoc* responses that were typical of management's reaction to the disagreements which so often led to unofficial action were seen as a failure of management's part to give personnel management a high priority.

This was one of a series of criticisms against management, and the personnel occupation seems destined to have periodic crises of confidence, although there may be some justification for the view that personnel staff had not been sufficiently innovatory in their responses to the changing industrial relations scene. Donovan failed, however, to offer a solution or a range of techniques which would resolve the problems.

All kinds of organisations (Local Authorities, hospitals, service industries, for example, as well as manufacturing) were starting to employ full-time personnel staff by the mid-1960s and the spread of ideas and of specialisation within the field began to establish personnel management as an occupation within its own right. The staff-cum-advisory role, the 'consultant-problem solver' as we shall describe it later, is often the most acceptable one in an organisation's authority structure, so there may be greater involvement for line managers in day-to-day negotiation. The research, co-ordination and backup activities of personnel officers are often an essential part of the management's control and direction of relationships, however.

The most significant contribution of personnel management to industrial relations is through the creation of conditions under which certain industrial relations policies come to be accepted. Wage payment systems and conditions of service which create different status groupings are examples of how personnel systems come to create relationships.

Industrial relations strategies are rarely explicit. Examples of personnel managers operating latent strategies can be found in motor manufacturing, for example. The issues over which negotiation with the unions is now accepted have widened to include pension schemes, training, working procedures, safety, discipline and even individual appointments, in some industries. This is noticeable in the public sector where the growth in 'white collar' unionisation has brought staff associations into the arena of collective bargaining.

Union leaders have been heard to call for better personnel management since personnel managers bring order and have often been able to promote good relationships, for instance through organisation development schemes, which started to be prescribed as solutions to difficulties in relationships in the later 1960s. Attention to personnel management might be expected to ensure some minimum standards and to curb the rogue employer.

National Economic Policy, Legislation and Personnel Techniques

In post-war Britain we have suffered a boom-slump cycle in which both Labour and Conservative Governments have tried fiscal and monetary policies to control the economy. Following the Second World War came a period of low unemployment for 25 years. During this period the stability of sterling and the rate of price inflation dominated economic thinking.

State legislation on prices and incomes ranged from voluntary regulations by individual employers to statutory controls maintained by special Commissions and Boards. Whatever form has been used, the regulation of wages in accordance with national economic policies has entailed the control of wage policies by personnel managers and other senior staff on a company-wide basis. This encouraged the use of job evaluation schemes and incremental scales.

Entry to the EEC came at a time when multinational companies were expanding, which gave some personnel departments an international dimension. In these circumstances, compensation planning became more complex since different payment systems had to be reconciled within a single status hierarchy.

In addition to prices and incomes policies, the State was extremely active in formulating new employment legislation during the early 1960s. The Contracts of Employment Act, 1963, Industrial Training Act, 1964, and the Redundancy Payments Act, 1965, were the forerunners of comprehensive legislation on job security, equal opportunity and the position of trade unions. Various State agencies were also set up during this time to encourage good employment practice. One of the major consequences of all this activity has been the enhancement in formal authority of personnel departments and these changes have also been a factor in the spread of personnel into small organisations.

The burst of legislation coincided with the development of personnel techniques. Management training courses with both

Table 1. Traditions in personnel management

Traditions	Period	Description
Welfare	Up to 1920s	Personnel management as a personal service to employees, who are the 'clients' of the personnel or welfare officer. Major concerns were the provisions of canteens, sick visiting, the supervision of moral welfare in anticipation of a reciprocal sense of service from the employee.
Employment Management	Up to 1930s	Emphasised the control of numbers and budgets and placed stress on economic efficiency plus a high value on performance investigation by O and M type studies. Employees have not always shared these beliefs, thus leading to a 'theory X' view of work people by managers.
Bureaucratic	1914 to present	The 'personnel administrator' typical of many large organisations operates a comprehensive set of rules based on a belief in order and rationality, and on the intrinsic merit of the organisation's internal status system, to which employees are expected to subscribe.
Professional Personnel Manager	1945 to present	A belief in specialisation is sustained by the application of techniques applied for the benefit of the 'client', who is the line manager, and is supported by a general social acceptance of 'experts'.
Liberal/Radical	1930s to present	This personnel manager sees his role as that of improving communications and leadership. Approach is that of a radical liberal, a belief in individualism, and in the need to participate with employees, anticipating agreement and enthusiasm from those at work.

educational and vocational aspects expanded, and theories drawn from the social sciences became popular in the 1960s to explain motivation to work and organisational behaviour. Some would argue that American psychologists such as Herzberg and McGregor have been over-exposed. Communication techniques such as briefing groups were emphasised and greater attention was paid to the social and technical environment of work, largely due to the influence of the Tavistock Institute and the 'socio-technical systems' school. The Institute of Personnel Management drew heavily on sociology and psychology when restructuring its examination scheme, and the IPM was active in the move to 'professionalise' personnel management.

Manpower planning had become more sophisticated with the advent of computer models which could predict future requirements by manipulating the many variables of labour supply and demand. Similarly, record-keeping for large concerns was aided by microfilm and computer storage. Selection tests had been available since the early 1920s, but they began to be used more frequently, often by specialised agencies. Following the recession of the early 1980s, organisations have driven through new approaches to quality improvement and efficiency. Productivity improvements were achieved by new investments and by introducing more flexible working practices: flexibility of time, task and contract. Employers have retained a shrinking core of full-time permanent employees while expanding in the secondary labour market of part-time, subcontract, temporary, casual and short-term contract employees who are now in the majority.

The demographic changes are potentially the most significant influences on human resource management. The large reduction in the number of young people coming on to the labour market in Western Europe, and increasing longevity mean organisations must gear their employment policies towards the middle-aged and towards women. This has stimulated interest in equal opportunity policies.

The routine personnel administration is now often performed under the direction of a senior line manager (for example, at Divisional or local Company level) and a strategic, Human Resource Manager role is performed at or near Board level. In this latter position, human resource managers have been active in managing fundamental changes within their companies.

SUMMARY

This chapter has shown that there are various traditions in personnel management, and that each has its own historical pedigree. A brief summary of the traditions of personnel management we have touched on is given in Table 1.

No generalisation about personnel management is possible, therefore, at the level of description, and different models may be appropriate in different organisations. The capacity to switch between models as required is one of the most important capacities for those working in this field. In the next chapter we shall see how the interdependence between line and personnel managers is indicative of successful personnel work, by showing that the way the personnel function is discharged is as important as what is done for the achievement of the organisation's objectives.

QUESTIONS

1. Define personnel management, showing the distinction that should be made between the personnel department and the personnel function of management.

2. What are the main trends in the history of personnel management?

3. What impact does personnel management have on 'industrial relations'?

5

The Elements of a System and their Inter-relationship

This chapter sets out a systematic way of conducting the personnel function of management, and shows the respective spheres of line and personnel managers.

As we have seen, specialised personnel departments were frequently established by organisations responding to change, often as a consequence of acquisitions and mergers, or due to the increased size and complexity of their businesses.

Specialisation in personnel management has contributed to the success of famous companies, and through such companies has played a part in advancing the cause of civilisation. The improvement of working conditions, the creation of job satisfaction, the development and training of employees, the maintenance of harmonious relationships and the fairness of rewards, for example, exist in organisational life because managements have seen the importance of a professional approach to personnel management. However, there is evidence of failure in some organisations. The problems of low productivity, unofficial strikes, absenteeism, accidents and social abuses such as sexual and racial discrimination are still with us as we go through the closing decades of the twentieth century.

In the previous chapter we described how some of the different traditions of personnel management developed. The variability of organisation cultures and the changing environment in which people are managed would lead us to believe that there is no regular trend in the development of personnel management which applies to all organisations. No one model of personnel management can meet all requirements. The problems arise when there is unsufficient flexibility by personnel managers in their response to the changing demands of their role. The co-ordination of this kind of variable, responsive attitude towards personnel problems does require senior management to possess an outward-looking philosophy which questions the assumptions on which decisions are predicated. The approach advocated looks towards changing values in society, to the impact of market and technical changes on the workforce so that a comprehensive, sensitive and accurate response is made.

By operating a comprehensive, systematic coverage of the employment relationship in all the activities of personnel management, and by following the appropriate process, personnel managers can help to adapt their organisations to the changing environment and can contribute to the success of their organisation's goals. In the remainder of this chapter we wish to describe in detail the inter-relationship between all the activities that go to make up the personnel function and to look at the process of personnel management.

We shall therefore examine personnel management at two levels of analysis: the descriptive level at which we set out the activities which must be performed for personnel management to be successful, and the 'process' level of relationships between the members of the management team.

THE ACTIVITIES OF THE PERSONNEL FUNCTION

The labels we give to these activities are rough descriptions of a collection of related events and tasks which make up the work of managing the employment relationship.

In this section we shall try to examine the relationship between the activities, using the notion of a 'system': that is, a set of interdependent parts each providing an input to another. This helps to explain the activities of the personnel function as logically related, and adjustable to meet the changing needs of the organisation. It is another feature of a system that feedback is possible to adjust the system to change. The system of activities we will be describing is therefore a related set of activities which adjusts to circumstances and which provides a comprehensive coverage of the employment relationship.

At the heart of all personnel activities is the manpower plan. This is the centrepiece, where corporate manpower objectives are set out, in numbers of people within each area of production, sales, and administration, the skills required and the costs. The plan may cover any period, but most typically it will be for the period of one to five years, and will be a part of the company's budgetary programme. Corporate planning is often undertaken on a five-year rolling cycle, with each successive year being brought up to date as it comes closer to the current year, and it would be usual for the manpower plan to be part of this procedure. In the manpower plan the organisation's demand for labour is set out, and this results in an examination by the personnel manager of the internal labour supply. Where possible, posts are filled from within as the most efficient source of labour, but it would be unusual for the right mix of skills and experience to be available for every vacancy, and so recruitment into the organisation is necessary. The transfer of employees, their promotion and recruitment results in the establishment of training schemes.

Training is also an adjunct to appraisal. Appraisal is an activity designed either formally or informally to measure the performance of subordinates against the achievement of agreed objectives. Welfare policies are available to help individuals who have personal problems which inhibit their performance. Along with the activities of appraising and training, there is concurrent attention to manpower control, by the application of reporting and discipline procedures.

Throughout all these actions there may be a requirement to consult and/or negotiate with the appropriate trade unions, and this will almost certainly be the case in that part of the manpower plan where projected labour costs and output have to be translated into actual costs. The stage at which negotiations take place will obviously vary with the practice of the industry, but in view of the crucial importance of wage costs for determining prices, and thus sales revenue and net profit, the earlier the negotiation, the greater the certainty that costs will be as predicted.

The chart in Fig. 4 is a simplified version, and there may be more complex links that could be made—for example, Joint Consultative Committees are often concerned with training matters, and in areas such as apprenticeship schemes the recruitment is for projected demand for labour rather than for meeting an immediate (or next year) demand. Some of the links in the chart may also not be applicable in particular companies. There are many people who would dispute the notion that performance appraisal, although linked to the setting of individual standards which unquestionably should fit into the corporate objectives, should necessarily be linked with pay. These kinds of issues we will explore fully as we consider each of the items mentioned in the succeeding chapters.

The essential message here is that each 'personnel' activity is linked to the other and that therefore failures in any one part of this system may result in the breakdown of the whole. As a system, there are links between corporate and individual objectives, joint agreement on the approach to be taken between management and work people, a monitored and flexible manpower plan which allows for the development of individuals who are appraised and rewarded in accordance with their contribution to the organisation's objectives.

The activities we have outlined are not the exclusive province of the personnel manager but are activities which managers in all parts of the organisation share. The manpower plan must be integrated with the corporate plan, and we would anticipate that all senior managers would make an input to this planning activity, just as managers are originators of job descriptions, appraisers, initiators of salary increases for their staff, and of action within the discipline procedure. In other words, managers have the major role to play in the management of people, and the supporting role is performed by the personnel department.

Without the advice and support of specialist staff, however, managers would find their tasks difficult to achieve. It is worth remembering that when Great Britain faced its most difficult struggles, in the First and Second World Wars, the way to victory on the home front included the expansion of specialist welfare and personnel management. In the list of managerial contributions to the personnel function outlined in the paragraph above, we can note that the appraisal systems, the salary administration policies, the discipline procedures and the policies within which managers manage their subordinates, are created and monitored by specialists in personnel management to an increasing extent. The responsibilities of management are shared, and in addition to their central 'resourcing' role, of specialising in finding, deploying and developing employees, personnel managers must co-ordinate and administer the whole range of personnel policies.

The ways in which personnel managers interlink their work with line managers is often a source of difficulty, but conflict is not inevitable. The relationships between personnel and line managers are crucial to the success of both parties. This is more easily seen if we can understand personnel management not only as a series of activities but also as a process.

THE PROCESS OF PERSONNEL MANAGEMENT

When we described the nature of managerial work in the previous chapter, we emphasised management as a social 'process'. The process relies on interpersonal skills. It is the process by which views are formed, decisions are made and actions are conducted. We can subdivide the process of personnel management under five headings:

1. **Analysis:** In this role, the personnel manager acts on his own initiative, involving others as necessary, and diagnoses problems, individual and group difficulties such as disputes between trade unions, problems of high labour turnover, arguments between groups.

2. **Consultancy:** The consultancy role is performed when the personnel manager is called in by his colleagues to advise. This may lead on to participation in projects, as exemplified by the co-operation between personnel manager and line manager in organisation development programmes. Frequently in those cases, the personnel manager gives specialist advice, but the line manager takes the ultimate responsibility.

3. **Problem-Solving:** This is the personnel manager's search for

acceptable and practical solutions to problems. It is a pragmatic role, one could almost describe it as a political role. Negotiating in its different forms is typical of problem-solving, the objective being to resolve divergent interests.

4. **Resourcing:** The personnel manager's central role is finding, deploying and maintaining human resources. It is the role of the recruitment interviewer, the training instructor, the management coach, and the implementer of the manpower plan. The tasks which are determinants of this role are all concerned with making use of people, trading in jobs and their constituent skills.

5. **Executing:** The executive process in personnel means executing agreed policies in any sphere of managing the employment relationship, such as authorising pay cheques, forming contracts of employment, enforcing conditions of service, etc. It is in this role that the mass of routine work of the personnel department is executed.

These roles are interdependent with each other. Clearly it would be difficult to solve problems without some previous analysis or consultancy work, for instance, and so the combinations of these roles will depend on the tasks to achieve and on the preferred authority relationships in the organisation. The degree of autonomy practised by the personnel manager, and the extent to which he uses a consultancy role and works through other managers, could also be a function of the personalities concerned and the experience of each manager. Some of the roles described are more compatible than others, and some will result in conflict and ambiguity in personnel work. A list of combinations of the roles is given below, and it should be noted that combinations of three or more roles at the same time in relation to an event will make the process of personnel management even more complicated, and difficult to sustain.

THE MOST AUTONOMOUS ROLES FOR PERSONNEL

Analyst and Resourcer: An independent and expert role for the personnel manager, who is expected to be a self-starter and to ensure that the organisation's needs are met by using his resourcing expertise. This is probably best suited to a small organisation.

Analyst and Executive: This would imply that having decided what the problem was, the personnel manager had the executive authority to solve it without working through other people. Such a role might best be sustained if the personnel manager reported directly to the Chief Executive of his company.

Analyst and Problem-Solver: This is a very acceptable role in most companies with a well-established personnel department. In producing solutions after his analysis the personnel manager is relying heavily on his own experience and knowledge, which may, of course, be at fault.

PERSONNEL MANAGEMENT ROLES WHICH ENTAIL WORKING WITH AND FOR OTHER MANAGERS

Consultant and Problem-Solver: An arrangement where the personnel manager is called in to advise and then to implement practical solutions will work well where there is a high element of trust amongst management, when the personnel manager is one of a team of senior managers. If he is not careful the personnel manager may find himself undertaking tasks which line management ought to perform, but which they find distasteful: for example, the first stage of a discipline procedure.

Consultant and Resourcer: This tends to be a role best accomplished when the personnel manager is formally a level below those he serves. In this role, he takes the requirements of the line manager and tries to meet them. His opportunity for influence lies chiefly at the time the requirement is first discussed. Resourcing by using expertise and conducting a client relationship with the line manager needs great skill in handling to avoid either manipulation of the client's wishes with what the personnel manager is capable of doing (for example, persuading a manager that he needs an assistant just because a particularly well-qualified person is looking for such a post to the personnel manager's knowledge), or by disturbing the client relationship by failing in any aspect of the resourcing role.

COMBINATIONS OF ROLES WHICH PRODUCE PROBLEMS FOR PERSONNEL MANAGERS

Resourcer and Problem-Solver: In this combination of roles, the personnel manager is 'fire-fighting', responding to problems which are observed on the surface, in an *ad hoc* way, but never coming to grips with fundamental causes. He tends to be working at a low level in the organisation, and may be useful if he is part of a larger department. The danger is that the solutions he implements may make the situation worse, since he has not really discovered what the problem is. Aware of this, his problem-solving becomes increasingly ambiguous as he tries to avoid being wrong.

Executive and Problem-Solver: This is also a conflictful role. The personnel manager acts as an executive, giving instructions, authorising requests from others, but also expects to resolve problems for other managers in an acceptable way. Since he is bound by the precedents of his own actions, and will wish to maintain his executive authority, the personnel manager's solution to problems are dictated by self-interest rather than pragmatism. The conflict arises because this thought will not be lost on his manager colleagues.

Consultant and Executive: The combination of consultant and executive has a similar inherent conflict to the one described above. The difficulty here is that the 'contract' between the line manager and the personnel manager will tend to bind the personnel manager to the line manager, so that he exercises executive authority in favour of the person to whom he is a consultant. As he may have a number of similar

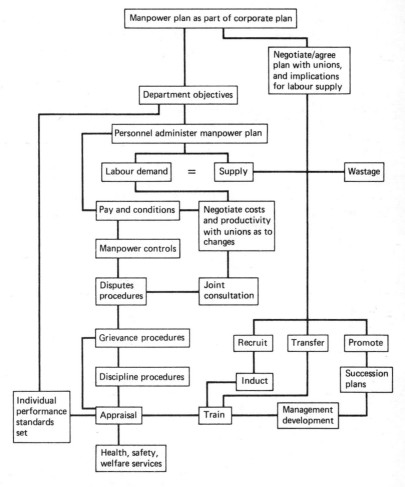

Fig. 4. Personnel activities.

'contracts' with other line managers, he will find it difficult to serve all of them honestly. Accusations of favouritism and the formation of cabals amongst management are the probable consequences.

The roles of analyst and consultant have not been described in combination above, as in the definition given they are mutually exclusive—i.e. the analyst is starting from the position of knowing which problem he wishes to research, whereas the 'consultant' is brought in by line management and forms some kind of 'contract' or agreement on which his intervention is to be based.

The intention here has not been to present a counsel of perfection. The 'process' of personnel management assumes that there may be problems and that a systematic approach to the solution of these has to take place concurrently with the activities of personnel management. To conduct the personnel process successfully, the personnel manager will require a range of interpersonal skills—notably skills in counselling, interviewing and negotiating. In this way, the process of managing people becomes linked to the activities of personnel management. Interpersonal skills are the 'cement' which joins together the process of personnel management with its activities. Thus, for example, in recruiting a senior manager, the personnel manager interviews candidates. His success as an interviewer will be reflected in the accuracy of the information he gleans and arising from which an appointment is made. Similarly, grievance and discipline procedures require the possession of counselling skills of a high order if they are to be workable, and if the processes of consulting and problem-solving, which both these procedures imply, are to be convincing to line managers.

SUMMARY

This chapter has set out how the process of personnel management can be conducted so that line and personnel managers can resolve problems in the management of people. The activities by which human resources are managed have been described, in a logical system, which permits flexibility. These activities can only be pursued successfully when the managers involved exercise interpersonal skills in a way which makes possible the social processes of managing people.

A GLOSSARY OF THE TERMS USED

Corporate plan: A plan devised by functional heads, showing *inter alia* the marketing changes anticipated, the net profit projected, and the investment decisions that are necessary. The manpower requirements derive from these considerations.

Manpower plan:	A plan showing the demand for labour over a period of time, which incorporates assumptions about productivity and labour costs. The supply of labour available within the company, and the shortfall that will need to be made good will be revealed.
The negotiation of pay and benefits:	This is now frequently undertaken on an annual cycle, and it would be sensible to phase the negotiations to fit the manpower planning sequence, as the assumptions about costs and output that are built into the plan may need adjustment. Negotiation throughout the year may be necessary as contentious issues arise out of joint consultation.
Pay and conditions:	The regulation of pay scales and associated benefits such as company cars are a personnel department responsibility.
Manpower controls:	Controls on attendance, overtime, commission or bonus payments, as well as monitoring of line management requests for labour to ensure that any alterations to the manpower plan are authorised.
Disputes procedures:	Procedures agreed between management and employee representatives concerning the methods adopted in resolving disputes. Should there be a disagreement over the authorisation of overtime, control of sickness absence, etc., this would be resolved through the disputes procedure, which may contain a clause allowing for arbitration.
Joint consultation:	Arrangements for management to discuss any proposals affecting the organisation with employee representatives on a regular basis. Differences which emerge would be subject to a negotiated agreement.
Grievance procedures	Procedures whereby individual employees may take up grievances which are of concern to them, such as complaints about their own managers. These procedures would involve other senior managers, and ultimately the personnel department.
Discipline procedures:	Formal procedures for improving performance/ behaviour which is judged inadequate for the job. These result in a series of warnings, verbal and written, to ensure compliance with the organisation's rules, and penalties for misconduct and poor performance, including dismissal.

Recruitment:	Undertaken as an activity by personnel to fill vacancies from external sources to comply with the manpower plan.
Transfer:	Where a vacancy can be filled by level transfer, this may be done as part of the development of the individual, or it could be a fortuitous circumstance. Transfers are sometimes arranged also to resolve interpersonal disharmony.
Induction:	Induction is a formal programme, designed and partly carried out by personnel to introduce new employees to the organisation, in all its social as well as work aspects.
Management development:	A term used to cover a series of arrangements by which organisations, help to ensure that individuals with potential for managerial work are given experience and training to fit them for the likely opportunities that will become available.
Succession plans:	These are the plans made between senior management for succession to managerial posts which best fulfil both the organisation's needs, and the needs of the management development programme.
Promotion:	Promotion, as part of the succession arrangements to fill vacancies as they occur, by which time the person promoted should have completed the necessary experience and have been trained through the management development programme.
Training:	Formal and informal instruction designed to improve the individual's performance at work, so that he can achieve his performance standards. Training needs may derive from appraisal reports or be assessed on all new entrants to the posts in question.
Appraisal:	Formal techniques for assessing individuals, with a view to advising them of their progress, improving their performance, identifying potential and helping with any personal difficulties.
Health/safety welfare services:	The services provided by the company to ensure acceptable standards are maintained in respect of the health and safety of their employees (such as regular medical checks), and that where the company can prevent personal difficulties from inhibiting performance, the welfare of the individual is taken into account.

Individual performance standards
These are the performance standards which derive from the objectives of the department where the employee works. They may be expressed as 'key tasks' or 'objectives' which have to be achieved in a given period of time. It is against these that the individual's performance is appraised. Where there is provision, merit or commission payments may be made to reward good performance.

QUESTIONS

1. Why is it helpful to think of the activities of personnel management as a 'system'?

2. Describe the roles performed in the process of personnel management.

3. What are the most problematic roles performed in the process of personnel management, and why?

4. What skills are needed in personnel management?

FURTHER READING: PART 2

Beach, D. S., *Personnel: The management of people at work*, Collier Macmillan, London, 1975.

Cuming, M. W., *The Theory and Practice of Personnel Management*, Heinemann, London, 1975.

Legge, K., *Power, Innovation and Problem Solving in Personnel Management*, McGraw-Hill, London, 1978.

Lupton, T., *Industrial Behaviour and Personnel Management*, IPM, London, 1969.

Marks, W., *Politics and Personnel Management. An outline history 1960–76*, IPM, London, 1978.

Mintzberg, H., *The Nature of Managerial Work*, Harper & Row, New York, 1973.

Niven, M. M., *Personnel Management 1913–63*, IPM, London, 1967.

Stewart, R., *Managers and their Jobs*, Macmillan, London, 1968.

Torrington, D. and Hall, L., *Personnel Management – a new approach*, Prentice Hall, London, 1987.

Tyson, S. and Fell, A., *Evaluating the Personnel Function*, Hutchinson, London, 1986.

Watson, T. J., *The Personnel Managers*, Routledge & Kegan Paul, London, 1977.

PART 3

Obtaining Suitable Human Resources

The task of finding people who either possess or have the potential to develop the knowledge, skills and attitudes that will enable a work organisation to carry out the tasks necessary for the achievement of its aim and objectives, is obviously of fundamental importance. However, the whole process from start to finish is very complicated and to be effectively accomplished it requires an understanding of the nature of the process, of the inter-relationship of its component stages and a systematic application in practice. As with all systems, apart from the importance of each individual element the neglect or omission of any stage will inevitably adversely affect the total system.

The main elements of this system and their inter-relationship are the subject of this part. They are:

1. The definition of the aim and objectives of the organisation as the basis for any assessment of the human resources needed to meet the organisation's commitments.

2. Manpower planning, which is the process whereby the quantity and quality of the required human resources are assessed and planned in the light of their availability.

3. Job analysis, which provides essential information about jobs as a basis for the recruitment and selection processes.

4. Recruitment, which is the positive action following the manpower plan to find the human resources in the number and quality that the organisation needs.

5. Selection, the final stage in the system when the organisation examines the suitability of applicants that the recruitment process has produced.

6

Manpower Planning

ITS NATURE AND PURPOSE

Manpower planning must have been applied in a general sense ever since people have collaborated in working groups to undertake tasks. The idea itself is, therefore, certainly not new. What is new is the emergence of the term as part of the vocabulary of management, the ever-increasing awareness of its crucial importance, and the development of a scientific approach to the use of human resources. The discipline as we know it developed from studies carried out shortly after the last war by the Tavistock Institute of Human Relationships in subjects connected with labour wastage and turnover, and from Operational Research, which was initially concerned with the application of scientific and mathematical principles to solving the operational problems of military and industrial organisations. Inevitably it was realised that the manpower component of these problems could not be ignored. Thus, in 1967 the Manpower Study Group emerged from the Operational Research Society to become the Manpower Society in 1970. At about the same time, in 1969, the Institute of Manpower Studies was formed as a research unit, based on the London School of Economics and the University of Sussex.

The importance of planning the material resources of an enterprise has never been in question, and much effort has been devoted to optimising financial and capital resources. Paradoxically, the human resource, which is ultimately the most important and least predictable asset, has not attracted the same level of attention. Despite significant developments and recent changes of attitudes towards manpower planning, it continues to arouse some scepticism, apparently because the sceptics feel either that a process which ought to be largely common sense has become unnecessarily complicated, or that the many variable factors in an uncertain future make the returns for the investment of effort of very doubtful worth. Such views, however, indicate a misunderstanding of the nature and purpose of manpower planning. Manpower planning has certainly become a specialised field in which statisticians, economists and others have a disciplinary interest. However, it is also very much the concern of every manager in an organisation and especially of the senior staff responsible for policy, commitments of resources and accountability for achievement.

All management is about decision-making in an environment of risk and uncertainty. Effective management aims to reduce the risk and uncertainty as far as this is possible in an imperfect world by the acquisition of the best available information and the use of a system. Manpower planning is an expression of this philosophy in the most important area of all, the use of human resources. Whatever scepticism may remain, there are strong indications that the impetus that manpower planning has now acquired will become increasingly evident in managerial practice. The changes and pressures brought about by economic, technological and social factors compel organisations of all kinds to study the costs and human aspects of labour much more seriously and carefully than ever before. The demographic shifts which characterise the period up to the turn of the century make planning essential in order to source the demand for labour and improve productivity.

The general purpose of manpower planning has been described, but there are specific purposes in crucial areas of management which manpower planning serves, namely:

1. Balancing the cost between the utilisation of plant and manpower: this involves comparing costs of these two resources in different combinations and selecting the optimum. This is especially important to making sound decisions when costing projects.

2. Determining recruitment needs: it is an essential prerequisite to the process of recruitment, i.e. to avoid problems of unexpected shortages, wastage, blockages in the promotion-flow, and needless redundancies.

3. Determining training needs: it is fundamentally important to planning training programmes, for which it is necessary to assess not only quantity but also quality in terms of the skills required by the organisation.

4. Management development: a succession of trained and experienced managers is essential to the effectiveness of the organisation and this depends on accurate information about present and future situations in all management posts.

5. Industrial relations: the corporate plan will of necessity make assumptions about productivity and the manpower implications of merger, acquisition, and divestment decisions will have an impact of the organisation's industrial relations strategies.

In practice, manpower planning is concerned with the demand and supply of labour and problems arising from the process of reconciling these factors. Whilst there is a consensus amongst the specialists about the general purpose and basic elements of manpower planning, they sometimes show slight variations in the shape of their proposed systems. Any system has to be based on analyses of demand and supply and the plans and decisions which follow these analyses.

A SYSTEM OF MANPOWER PLANNING

The main elements of a system of manpower planning are:

1. Defining or redefining organisational objectives.
2. Determining and implementing the basic requirements for sound manpower planning.
3. Assessing future requirements to meet objectives (demand).
4. Assessing current resources and availability of resources in the future (supply).
5. Producing and implementing the manpower plan in detail, i.e. balancing forecasts for demand and supply, related to short-term and/or long-term time-scales.
6. Monitoring the system and amending as indicated.

The first two of these stages are preparatory; the last three are directed towards the detailed production and implementation of the plan itself.

DEFINITION OR REDEFINITION OF ORGANISATIONAL OBJECTIVES

The effectiveness of the manpower plan will depend on how soundly the organisation has considered and planned its corporate strategy and integrated the objectives of its component departments. Once these fundamental details have been thoroughly examined and decided, the senior directing staff of the organisation can consider the implications in terms of human resources. Because of the constantly changing environment in which all work organisations operate, whether they market a product or provide a service, the corporate strategy and objectives will necessarily require continuous monitoring and revision from time to time. This will entail a corresponding, regular review of the manpower-planning system.

DETERMINING AND IMPLEMENTING BASIC REQUIREMENTS FOR MANPOWER PLANNING

Sound manpower planning needs to be based on the following principles and actions:

1. It has to be fully integrated into the other areas of the organisation's strategy and planning.

2. Senior management must give a lead in stressing its importance throughout the organisation.

3. In larger organisations a central manpower planning unit responsible to senior management needs to be established. The main objectives of this unit are to co-ordinate and reconcile the demands for human resources from different departments, to standardise and supervise departmental assessments of requirements and to produce a comprehensive organisational plan. In practice the personnel department would normally play a leading role in the task. In smaller organisations these responsibilities would probably be carried out by a senior member of staff, e.g. the senior personnel manager or even the managing director.

4. The time-span to be covered by the plan needs to be defined. Because of the abiding problem of making forecasts involving imponderable factors, a compromise is often adopted in which a general plan is produced to cover a period of several years, and a detailed plan for the first year. If the system is operated as a continuous, overlapping plan, the five-year period of general forecasting is maintained and each first year is used in turn for purposes of review and revision for the future. For example, 1980–5, 1981–6, 1982–7, 1983–8, 1984–9, 1985–90 is a series of 5-year rolling plans covering a total of ten years.

5. The scope and details of the plan have to be determined. For large organisations separate plans and forecasts may well be needed for various subsidiary units and functions. In smaller organisations, one comprehensive plan will probably suffice for all employees. Where particular skills or occupations may pose future problems in recruitment or training special provisions will be required in the planning.

6. Manpower planning must be based on the most comprehensive and accurate information that is possible and necessary. Such personnel information is essential in any case for the effective management of the organisation. Details of format and contents will naturally vary, but they will normally need to include details of age, sex, qualifications and experience and of trends likely to affect future forecasts, such as labour wastage, changes in jobs, salaries, etc. Apart from the routine collection of data for personnel records, special analyses may sometimes be necessary to provide particular information.

THE ASSESSMENT OF FUTURE REQUIREMENTS (DEMAND)

This task is concerned with estimating the quantity and quality of human resources needed to meet the objectives of the organisation. Several methods of forecasting are in regular use—some of them simple and non-technical, others sophisticated and involving specialist mathematical and statistical knowledge and skills, e.g. estimates based on managers' experience, opinions and calculations; statistical methods; work-study methods; forecasts based on measures of productivity. In practice, these methods are often used in combination, especially in larger organisations. The essential features of each type are briefly summarised below.

1. Estimates made by management: This is the simplest method of assessment and is, therefore, the commonest method in use, especially in small organisations. Assessments of this kind are provided from two main sources: the estimates submitted by individual line managers and the corporate estimates produced by senior management, advised by the personnel department. Since these forecasts rely entirely on personal judgements, they have an obvious potential weakness of subjectivity. However, this can be mitigated in the following ways: firstly, in submitting assessments managers should include explanations and reasons to support their claims; secondly, these assessments 'from the bottom up', so-called, should be compared with those prepared by senior management, perhaps by an *ad hoc* manpower committee with the purpose of discussing and reconciling discrepancies.

2. Statistical methods: A number of statistical methods are now used for forecasting, which vary in their degree of sophistication. This is a task for specially qualified staff and such methods are used, therefore, mainly by particular kinds of large organisations for whom manpower planning poses complicated problems. Some of the techniques which are most often used are: simple extrapolation, which attempts to predict growth or decline of a variable or set of variables for a period of time; regression analysis, based on assumptions about the stability of certain relationships; econometric models in which past statistical data are studied, on the assumption that relationships between a number of variables will continue in the future.

3. Work-study methods: Work study is a systematic analysis of work in terms of people, skills, materials and machines, and, in particular, the man-hours needed per output-unit to achieve maximum productivity. Work-study data may be used for forecasts of productivity, for detailed production schedules for specific periods of time within the plan, for estimating the total numbers needed to achieve production targets within a specific period. The production schedules may comprise the following details: product quantities; production methods; machinery needed and available; times for individual operations; quantity and quality of labour needed and available. Work-study techniques are particularly appropriate for estimating manpower requirements for work which is directed towards end products.

ASSESSMENT OF CURRENT RESOURCES AND AVAILABILITY OF RESOURCES IN THE FUTURE (SUPPLY)

Current Resources

As a basis for estimating the future supply of manpower a detailed and accurate account of the current situation is needed. Although accurate and comprehensive information is vitally important in manpower planning, there is a danger of producing records in excessive detail, which may make it difficult to see the wood for the trees, waste valuable resources and increase the possibility that information may not be kept up-to-date. In the end, each organisation has to decide for itself the quantity and quality of information it needs, but some broad bases can be established for analysing existing resources, namely: operational functions; occupations; status and skill-levels; other specific categories (e.g. qualifications, trainees, age-distribution, etc.).

Operational Functions An initial tally of all employees is made, based on divisions into functional units, (e.g. sales department, stores branch, repair workshop etc.). Specific categories produced by subsequent analyses may be related to these units, if desired.

Occupations Employees are categorised according to occupational groups. These categories may be particularly related to critical occupations and anticipated recruitment problems in terms of detail required. Although broad homogeneous groupings will normally suffice, for certain key occupations detailed and specific categorisations may well be needed. In order to facilitate and standardise the task of occupational analysis and definition, HMSO publishes, on behalf of the Department of Employment, *The Classification of Occupations and Directory of Occupational Titles* (CODOT) in three volumes. The broad groupings conventionally used for occupational analysis are: managers, supervisors, professional staff, technical staff, clerical staff, manual and other staff (skilled; semi-skilled; and unskilled).

Status and Skill-levels To a certain extent the categorisation of employees by occupations also implies a categorisation by status and level of skills. Nevertheless, it may also be necessary to make a further distinction between, for example, senior, middle and junior managers, senior and junior clerical staff, administrative and technical supervisors etc. This kind of analysis is especially relevant to the task of producing data for planning succession to senior levels.

Other Specific Categories In addition to the basic kinds of analysis described above, it is normally necessary to produce other particular kinds of information, especially for critical groups and occupations, such as the qualifications of employees, records of employees under training, age groups and distribution.

Apart from the purposes of manpower planning an organisation will need to have detailed records of its employees, showing their qualifications, experience, particular skills and aptitudes, which are relevant to its functions and objectives. On this basis it can assess the strengths and weaknesses in its general pools of skills and experience and in particular areas, and will be in a better position than it might otherwise have been to plan for recruitment and selection, transfer or promotion, training, retirements, etc.

Training is systematically integrated with and dependent upon other important areas of personnel management such as job analysis, recruitment and selection and performance appraisal. It is an extremely costly and time-consuming activity and must be taken into account when the supply of manpower is being analysed. For the period to be covered by the plan, the analysis will project the flow of numbers of employees passing through all forms of training programmes, both internal and external.

The age distribution of employees in an organisation has a strong influence on questions of promotion, retirement and especially wastage. It is most important that an organisation should always be aware of the current and future age structure of its employees. It is essential information, if employers are to take timely measures to anticipate and remedy the effects of any imbalance in experience, excessive losses of all kinds of employees or those in key occupations because of simultaneous retirements.

INTERNAL AND EXTERNAL FACTORS INFLUENCING CHANGE

As manpower planning is basically an exercise in projecting likely future situations based on past trends, it is important to obtain information about those which indicate any significant changes. These data are invaluable as a background against which the forecasts, produced by other methods already described, may be finally assessed. The changes which are likely to be significant and worth analysis are those that affect shifts in the relative numbers of employees in the various categories represented in the personnel record system. A well-known example in organisations with high-cost operational goals is the tendency for administrative and supporting staffs to grow disproportionately to the relatively small number of operational staff.

One of the commonest factors which complicates the task of

manpower planning is unforeseen wastage. In making forecasts over a future period it is a fairly straightforward task to allow for employees whose retirement dates are known. However, there will always be unplanned losses of employees for a variety of reasons. The most significant source of loss is through voluntary wastage, i.e. when employees leave of their own accord. This can be very high and difficult to predict, except, perhaps, where an organisation has acquired a reputation for a high labour turnover and achieves, paradoxically, some form of predictable consistency in this factor. In very large organisations it may also be necessary to include transfers or promotion of staff across divisions, departments or branches in these calculations.

Labour wastage has traditionally been calculated by the following formula:

$$\frac{\text{Number leaving in a year}}{\text{Average number of employees}} \times 100 = x\%$$

This index can be considerably distorted, however, by untypical features in the organisation's employment pattern. For example, the significant element of wastage may be limited to a particular category, which may give a false impression of movement in an otherwise stable labour-force. In recent times, more sophisticated methods have tended to be used. A commonly used guide to movement in the labour force is the Labour Stability Index which is deduced by the formula:

$$\frac{\text{Number of employees exceeding one year's service}}{\text{Number of employees employed one year ago}} \times 100 = x\%$$

Even more sophisticated results can be obtained by the use of the actuarial/statistical techniques known as cohort and census analysis. In the same way that life expectancy for age groups can be actuarially assessed, a so-called survival curve can be graphically plotted to enable predictions to be made about the relationships between employees' length of service or age and rates of wastages.

Apart from wastage as a factor complicating manpower planning, any internal variations in working conditions such as a reduction or increase in working hours or retirement ages will affect the situation.

Finally, there are external factors which also need to be taken into account when the availability of human resources is being considered. They may be categorised as macro- (national) or micro- (local) influences. At the macro-level the factors which are commonly significant are:

1. The intervention by the state in the field of employment as a user and protector of the labour-force in the form of employment legislation, regional development schemes, governmental and related agencies.

2. National trends affecting the working population such as, for example:

(*i*) The percentage of elderly, retired people.
(*ii*) The percentage of people pursuing courses of higher education.
(*iii*) Immigrants, their available skills and concentrations in certain locations.
(*iv*) Married women available for employment.

The important factors at micro-level are:

1. The nature of the local population in terms of numbers, growth or decrease, reserves of skills, availability of part-time labour etc.
2. The level of unemployment.
3. The competition from other employers.

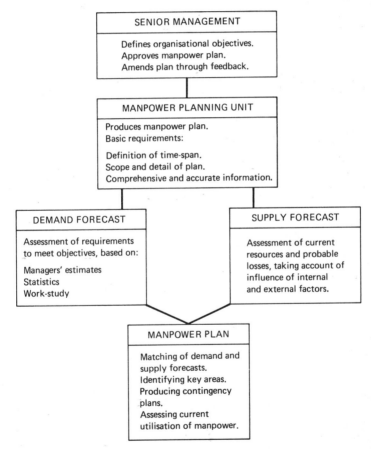

Fig. 5. Summary of the main elements of a system of manpower planning.

4. The degree of development of the area, accessibility and transport facilities.

5. Plans of central and local government and other organisations which may significantly affect the area.

The possible influences of these factors can never be easily assessed. Those responsible for manpower planning should be aware of their existence and possible effects and should take them into account when making manpower plans.

THE PLANNING STAGE

The last stage, in which the manpower plan is produced, is based on the information that the preceding stages have provided. This involves:

1. Matching the forecasts for supply and demand.
2. Identifying key areas essential to the achievement of objectives.
3. Making plans to minimise the effects of possible shortages or excesses of manpower.
4. Considering whether the best use is currently being made of the organisation's human resources.

Until the preliminary analyses have been made and the final plans formulated, no meaningful plans can subsequently be made for recruitment and training staff. Finally it is worth emphasising once again that manpower planning cannot guarantee any particular levels of success in ensuring that the right number of employees of the necessary quality will be provided to meet an organisation's requirements. It is essentially an exercise in foresight, in anticipating potential difficulties in human resources in time, and, above all, increasing flexibility in order to be able to cope with unforeseen crises. In practice, the plan has to be able to be constantly monitored and forecasts compared with reality, so that adjustments may be made in good time as the need arises. Additionally, there should be a regular review at various periods throughout the lifespan of the manpower plan. This review could be incorporated into an annual general review of corporate objectives, achievement, budget-planning, etc. in accordance with the system for a running, overlapping plan, already discussed.

QUESTIONS

1. What is manpower planning?

2. Name five specific purposes of management that manpower planning may serve.

3. What are the main elements in a system of manpower planning?

4. Name the methods of forecasting the manpower demand that are commonly used; give a brief description of each and their uses.

5. What are the main areas of information needed in forecasting the manpower supply?

6. What internal and external factors influencing change need to be taken into account in forecasting manpower supply?

7. What are the main steps in producing the manpower plan?

7

Job Analysis

ITS NATURE AND PURPOSE

Job analysis is a key function in personnel management. It is an essential foundation for all processes leading to the effective performance of work, the recruitment, selection, performance appraisal, training and development of staff. It is also a pre-requisite for job evaluation and for a system of health and safety at work. Since all of these areas are vitally important in the management of people at work, the effectiveness of an organisation will inevitably be adversely affected unless the importance and principles of job analysis are understood and skilfully applied in practice.

Job analysis has produced its own terminology to describe its component and related elements. In 1967, the Ministry of Labour produced a set of definitions in its *Glossary of Training Terms* with the intention of standardising usage and interpretation throughout industry. Nevertheless, a cursory study of the mass of management literature will immediately reveal that no uniformity of descriptions and meanings exists. The terms job description, job specification and person specification are in common use. The confusion arises because of the different items that various authors include under these main headings. The system that will be examined in this chapter is based on the three headings mentioned above and our definitions for each of them are briefly described below.

1. **Job description:** a statement of the component tasks, duties, objectives, standards and environmental circumstances of a job.

2. **Job specification:** a specification of the skills, knowledge and attitudes required effectively to perform a job. It is usually expressed in behavioural terms.

3. **Person specification:** an interpretation of the job specification in terms of the kind of person needed effectively to perform a job. Its main use is in personnel selection.

There are no standard formats for these three elements of job analysis. How they are used may vary considerably from one organisation to another. For our purposes, it will be best to give as comprehensive a description as possible, although, in practice, the job and person specifications may, for example, be combined, at least to some extent, and certain headings given here may be omitted for a variety of local reasons.

JOB DESCRIPTION

The items listed below will provide a comprehensive account of the job which can be flexibly adapted to suit varying requirements of particular organisations. For example, a brief abstract of this format may form the basis of an advertisement for recruitment purposes.

1. **Basic details** Exact title and grade (if applicable). Numbers engaged in the job. Location(s).
2. **Purpose** Objectives and relationship to the aim of the organisation.
3. **Tasks** Main tasks and key areas. Occasional tasks. Secondary duties. Hours of work.
4. **Standards** Standards for effective performance of tasks. Criteria indicating that tasks have been effectively performed.
5. **Responsibilities** Position of job in organisation structure. Managers/supervisors to whom job holder is accountable. Subordinate staff for whom job holder is responsible. Responsibilities for:
   (*a*) Finance.
   (*b*) Materials, equipment, etc.
   (*c*) Classified information.
6. **Physical and social environment** Particular features of work-environment (e.g. sedentary, static, indoor-outdoor, mobile, dirty, hazardous, etc.). Contacts with others (e.g. small/large groups, isolated, external contacts, etc.).
7. **Training/education** Training planned to bring new job holders to required levels of performance (e.g. induction programme, job-rotation, visits, external courses, etc.). In-job training and educational courses normally associated with the job.
8. **Advancement opportunities** Opportunities open to job holders for promotion and career development.
9. **Conditions of employment** Salary and other emoluments and benefits. Possible overtime requirements. Sickness and pension schemes. Welfare, social and other facilities. Leave entitlement. Special employment conditions applying to the job.

10. **Trade Union/ Associations** — Appropriate unions/staff associations. Closed shop conditions.
11. **Job-Circumstances** — Aspects of the job commonly accepted as pleasant/unpleasant, easy/demanding.

JOB SPECIFICATION

The job specification describes the knowledge, skills and attitudes required to perform the job effectively. The most systematic format consists of four columns. The first column is a list of the component tasks of the job, based on the job description, followed by the three headings mentioned above.

The knowledge column requires no particular elaboration. It contains all the various kinds of knowledge needed for each task, e.g. technical, professional, administrative, etc.

The skills column presents rather more difficulties because of the problems of identifying and defining skills. Briefly described, skills are forms of behaviour which are essential for the effective performance of tasks. They are developed by regular practice and depend on innate mental and physical attributes. Since these vary from person to person, the levels of skills attainable by individuals will likewise vary. Skills may be intellectual, manual and social (interpersonal).

The attitudes column creates similar problems of identification and definition and especially of measurement, because of the psychological complexity and general lack of knowledge of the subject. Often the items included in this column are virtually social skills. The need constantly to attach great importance to safety at work is an example of the kind of item that might be included under this heading.

PERSON SPECIFICATION

A person specification expresses the requirements of the Job Description in personal terms i.e. what kind of person would be needed to meet the requirements of the job description? It is a vitally important document as a basis for systematic personnel selection, because it determines the selection methods and is essential for the final judgement i.e. does the candidate meet the specified requirements? Formats for person specifications will vary with individual organisations, but in general they need to cover the following headings:

1. General requirements (e.g. age range, health, appearance etc.).
2. Any specific academic or professional qualifications.
3. Any work experience required.

Table 2. A specimen job description, job specification and person specification for a post of school-meals caterer/supervisor

Job Description

Title of Job	*School-meals caterer-supervisor*
Locations	1. Lord Nelson Comprehensive School, George Street, Westleigh, Midshire. (Main School) 2. North Street Annexe. 3. South Street Annexe.
Main purpose of job	To provide lunches daily (Monday to Friday) for 1300 pupils and 100 staff.
Tasks: (a) Key tasks	1. To produce meals, meeting criteria for a well-balanced diet within a prescribed budget in the required quantities at the required times. 2. To organise and supervise the resources provided to meet this objective, i.e. subordinate kitchen staff, materials, equipment, finances, etc. 3. To plan and evaluate menus. 4. To produce time and work-schedules for subordinate kitchen staff and to supervise their implementation. 5. To recruit and select kitchen staff when vacancies occur. 6. To give induction training to new staff and to develop the knowledge and skills of existing staff. 7. To ensure that all statutory requirements for food hygiene, health and safety at work, and terms and conditions of employment are strictly observed and implemented.
(b) Other tasks	8. To represent the school at monthly and other meetings of school-meals caterer/supervisors, convened by the County School-Meals Organiser/Adviser. 9. To represent the employer at local level in general liaison, meetings and negotiations with trade-union officials. 10. To fulfil additional, occasional catering needs of the school (e.g. sporting and social functions, special luncheons, etc.)

Hours of work	0830–1630 Mondays to Fridays inclusive.
	Breaks: lunch—1 hour; mid-morning and mid-afternoon—15 minutes each.

Responsible: (a) To	Deputy Head (as local line manager); County School-Meals Organiser/Adviser (as professional supervisor).
(b) For	
Staff:	supervision of work-performance, working conditions and welfare of 10 Subordinate Kitchen staff at main school and 6 at the two annexes.
Materials:	efficient maintenance and use of supplies and stocks of food, equipment, utensils and consumable items.
Finance:	efficient management of allocated funds; maintenance of accounts of expenditure, meals provided and stocks of materials and equipment.

Working Environment	The main school buildings are modern and very attractively planned. The kitchen is very modern in design, spacious and fitted throughout with modern equipment, including air conditioning. Both annexes are much older buildings. The kitchens, although fitted with modern equipment, are old-fashioned in design. It is planned to move out of these buildings in about five years' time. There is some noise and heat, inevitable in this kind of work, but they are not excessive, and do not cause serious discomfort.

Training and opportunities for advancement	The holder of the post will be expected to be adequately qualified professionally. Training is provided, however, in interpersonal skills, in employment legislation and negotiating with union officials. The LEA also arranges short courses on job-related subjects for purposes of up-dating professional knowledge and skills. The following opportunities for advancement currently exist: (a) transfer to a similar post with increased responsibility and remuneration. (b) promotion to one of four posts of Deputy County Organiser/Adviser of School-Meals. (c) promotion to one post of County Organiser/Adviser. These posts are filled whenever vacancies occur through open competition.
Terms and Conditions of Employment	*Salary:* Basic—£4000 per annum by annual increments of £200 to £6000. Overtime—payable at current rates for work outside prescribed working hours. Expenses—all expenses incurred in the course of authorised official duties are refundable. *Pension:* LEA's pension scheme for catering staff applies. *Holidays:* taken at the same time as school holidays—4 weeks (summer); 1 week at Easter and 1 week at Christmas, plus normal public holidays. *Amenities:* all welfare, sports, recreational, social facilities, etc., available to school staff and pupils, are also available to catering staff. *Clothing:* normal protective clothing used by catering staff is provided and maintained free of charge.

Job Specification

Note: The example quoted below is a specimen task taken from the total list of tasks, included in the job description. All tasks would be described in a similar way.

Task	Knowledge	Skills	Attitudes
Planning and evaluating menus	1. Nutritional values of foods. 2. Availability of foods and sources of supply. 3. Costing and bulk-purchasing of supplies. 4. Implications of the menus planned in terms of human and material resources, preparation and cooking required. 5. Prevalent food preferences of school-children and the associated problems. 6. Variety of uses of foods. 7. Potential health hazards in food-preparation.	1. Professional competence in all aspects of the practical application of menus, i.e. preparation, cooking, use of equipment, etc. 2. Administrative ability in the systematic planning and economic use of resources. 3. Interpersonal skills in dealing with a very wide range of people of varying status and age, i.e., kitchen staff, pupils and parents, school staff and external officials.	Imagination. Initiative. Diplomacy. Resourcefulness. Resilience.

Requirements	Essential	Desirable
1. Physical	Between 25 and 50 years of age. Excellent health with no history of serious or recurring illness. Neat, tidy and clean in personal appearance. Good-mannered and well-spoken.	
2. Attainments	At least five years' catering experience in schools or similar establishments. City and Guilds Catering Certificate (706), or Ordinary National Diploma in Institutional Housekeeping and Catering or acceptable equivalents.	Sound general education (i.e. a broad range of GCE 'O' level subjects including English language and mathematical subjects).
3. Intelligence	General common sense. Ability to think clearly and to react sensibly in emergencies.	
4. Aptitudes	Practical ability and manual dexterity. Calculative ability. Creative ability.	
5. Interests		Artistic and social
6. Disposition	Calm and equable temperament. Patient and Diplomatic. Able to command respect.	
7. Circumstances	Free from domestic problems and commitments which would affect work requirements or performance of duties.	Ability to drive a car.

4. Key requirements in terms of knowledge, skills, attitudes and personal traits.

5. Any special conditions (e.g. travel, unsocial hours etc.).

Two models have become widely known and used in practice as bases for producing comprehensive person specifications i.e. Rodger's 7-point plan and Munro-Fraser's 5-fold grading system. These methods are described below:

The 7 point plan

1. **Physical**	health, physique, age, appearance, bearing, speech.
2. **Attainments**	academic attainments, training received, experience and skills and knowledge already acquired.
3. **Intelligence**	the general intelligence, specific abilities and means for assessing these.
4. **Special Aptitudes**	special aptitudes (e.g. manual, mechanical, verbal, numerical, artistic, etc.).
5. **Interests**	personal interests as possible indicators of aptitudes, abilities or personal traits (e.g. intellectual, practical/constructional, physically active, social, artistic).
6. **Disposition**	personality characteristics needed (e.g. equability, dependability, self-reliance, assertiveness, drive, energy, perseverance, initiative, motivation).
7. **Circumstances**	personal and domestic circumstances (e.g. mobility, commitments, family circumstances and occupations).

The 5-fold grading system

1. **Impact on others**	general demeanour, appearance, speech.
2. **Qualifications**	education, training, work-experience.
3. **Innate abilities**	mental alertness, aptitude for learning.
4. **Motivation**	consistence, persistency, success in achieving goals.
5. **Adjustment**	stability, reaction to stress, relationships with others.

JOB ANALYSIS IN PRACTICE

We now need to consider who should carry out the job analysis and how it should be done. The first question is very much concerned with the skills and problems of the task and the second with specific methods. Job analysis calls for special knowledge and skills and could be carried out by external or internal agents. There are arguments for and against the use of either. For example, external agents may bring greater objectivity to their task, but may lack intimate knowledge of the organisation and its culture. They may also have problems of credibility. Internal agents, on the other hand, could be too subjective in their approach, but should have fewer problems in acquaintance with the organisation. Because of interdepartmental rivalries and suspicions they too could have difficulties of acceptability. In the normal circumstances, this task falls naturally within the scope of the personnel staff, who are already responsible for co-ordinating the various personnel processes which depend upon job analysis. Above all, they need the closest possible knowledge of the jobs in the organisation, if they are to perform their work effectively.

THE SKILLS OF JOB ANALYSIS

The task requires very careful forethought and preparation, based on an awareness of the psychological factors affecting the performance and perception of jobs and the possible problems that these may create. Since these are fundamentally important in determining the general approach, specific methods and possible achievement of job analysis, we need to begin by examining these factors.

1. The analysis of jobs is very different from the analysis of, say, inanimate matter. Jobs only come to life when they are filled and interpreted by people.

2. Different individuals, i.e. the job holders and their role sets of superiors, peers and subordinates will all have their own personal perceptions of the nature and requirements of the same jobs. There will also be differences of views between past and present holders of the same jobs.

3. Job situations are in a state of constant flux and changing inter-relationships with the environment. Analysis is not unlike the charting of sandbanks that are ever changing with wind and tide. Regular reviews are, therefore, essential.

4. Jobs invariably come to be regarded as the personal possessions of job holders, and this factor together with the inevitable egocentricity of perceptions means that job holders may well regard the analysis of their jobs as a territorial intrusion, no matter how carefully the analysis is prepared and approached.

5. Job analysis may imply the possibility of management's intentions to make changes. Changes at work are regularly resisted both overtly and covertly because of fear, distrust or misunderstanding of intentions.

THE METHODS OF JOB ANALYSIS

From the factors and possible problems examined above it can be seen that the skills of job analysis are essentially communicational, and that these have to be the foundation for the general approach and specific methods described below:

1. The first phase in job analysis is preparatory and educational. Initially, job analysts need to have consultations with managers, supervisors and union officials at all levels for the following purposes:

(*i*) To familiarise themselves with the organisational structure and climate.

(*ii*) To explain very carefully and sensitively the purposes of the job analysis.

(*iii*) To discuss possible methods in detail.

(*iv*) To demonstrate from the very outset to those whose jobs are to be analysed that the general approach to the task is based on foresight, frankness, understanding and co-operation.

2. The second phase is the actual process itself for which the following specific methods are commonly used:

(*i*) **Direct observation:** Here the analyst observes actual work in progress and makes notes as necessary under the various headings of the job description. These notes can be used as a basis for subsequent questions that the analyst may wish to raise. The advantages of seeing a job performed for oneself are obvious, but the method has the following limitations:

(*a*) It is very time-consuming. Much time would be needed adequately to observe a number of jobs. All jobs need to be observed with very close concentration over a period of time in order to appreciate the fluctuations between, for example, the quieter and busier periods. A brief observation can very easily produce a distorted view.

(*b*) There is no substitute for personal experience of the job and the evidence of observations can be very misleading. Special skills expertly applied may make jobs seem easier. Skilled workers could make jobs seem more difficult if they chose to do so.

(*c*) Behaviour which is formally observed is inevitably influenced by the act of observation, unless this is done without the knowledge of those being observed. All the research data confirm this phenomenon (often described as the Hawthorne Effect from the studies carried out at the Hawthorne Plant of the Western Electric Company USA by Elton Mayo and colleagues).

(*d*) There is a great difference between observation of manual and managerial jobs. There is often no way in which an observer can obtain any kind of accurate picture or evaluation of the mental energy expended, personal pressures, contemplative and planning activities or the subtleties of interpersonal relationships, which form a large part of the managers' and supervisors' work.

(*ii*) **Interviews:** These should be carried out with the job holders themselves, their immediate superiors and any others who can give useful information. The interview is a necessary and potentially useful method in job analysis, enabling the job analyst to raise questions to elucidate the evidence of observation and to compare the perception of one job holder with others. The caveats that need to be made about the use of the interview in job analysis are these:

(*a*) As in all other interview situations considerable skill is needed. The interview has to be systematic and purposeful and conducted with particular sympathy, tact and sensitivity.

(*b*) For reasons already explained, however co-operative the job holders may be, the job analyst has always to deal with personal biases and perceptions of jobs.

(*c*) The interviewer needs to be careful to distinguish fact from opinion.

(*iii*) **Diaries:** Using this method, the job analyst provides job holders with the areas of the job description about which information is required. Job holders then analyse their own work over a period of time recording information systematically in diary form under the required headings and the time spent on each item. The advantages and disadvantages of the diary method are these:

(*a*) Self-recorded data of this kind can be made over a longer period and thus provide a more reliable picture of the nature of the job.

(*b*) They can be used as valuable bases on which to conduct interviews.

(*c*) They are an obvious means of saving some of the time which prolonged direct observation of jobs requires.

(*d*) Like the other methods diaries are inevitably affected by factors of subjectivity. Moreover, because the information is self-recorded there is no means of verifying accuracy.

(*e*) To be of real value the diary has to be kept accurately, conscientiously and regularly, if it is to be of any real value. The task can soon become a chore, especially if job holders are not in sympathy with the job. It may, therefore, be perfunctorily fulfilled or neglected.

(*iv*) **Questionnaires:** Here the job analyst compiles a series of questions designed to elicit the maximum possible, useful information about the jobs under analysis, and distributes these

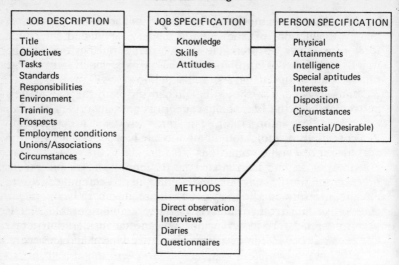

JOB DESCRIPTION	JOB SPECIFICATION	PERSON SPECIFICATION
Title	Knowledge	Physical
Objectives	Skills	Attainments
Tasks	Attitudes	Intelligence
Standards		Special aptitudes
Responsibilities		Interests
Environment		Disposition
Training		Circumstances
Prospects		
Employment conditions		(Essential/Desirable)
Unions/Associations		
Circumstances		

METHODS
Direct observation
Interviews
Diaries
Questionnaires

Fig. 6. Summary of the main elements of job analysis.

with careful instructions about the completion of the form. The advantages and disadvantages of questionnaires are these:

(a) They enable the job analyst to put standard questions to all the job holders taking part in the survey.

(b) Specialised skill is needed in devising the questionnaire and framing the questions. For example, attractive as the prospect of open questions may seem to be, it is probably better to require the respondent to choose from a range of answers that best fit particular situations. Similar skill is also required in the interpretation and evaluation of replies.

It is unlikely that any one of these methods will be adequate by itself. In practice, therefore, a combination of techniques is usually employed and adapted to meet the needs of particular situations.

THE PROBLEM OF EFFECTIVE PERFORMANCE

The analysis of jobs has little or no meaning unless the required standards and criteria for effective performance are also taken into account. This question has to be faced every day somewhere in the management of people at work. It is fundamental to decisions affecting, for example, the selection of personnel, training, performance appraisal, promotion and job evaluation. At the same time it is an abiding problem because the definition depends on human judgement. The question seems to be easier to handle in the analysis of more mechanical and manual types of work, as compared with jobs that are mainly managerial, supervisory or intellectual in content. In the former category, tasks are easier to observe and performance can usually be defined precisely and measured in terms of output levels required and achieved in prescribed conditions (e.g. time). Whilst this is generally true, there is still an assumption here that effective performance is to be assessed only in the light of achievement of output objectives. For example, is the coal-miner whose personal productivity is consistently above the required output levels, but who is also a very disruptive influence in his work-group, to be assessed as an effective performer? The debate could be endless, but in the end each organisation must consider and define its requirements for the effective performance of jobs. Otherwise it can only operate by guess-work. Since research data is regularly reminding us that effective performance at work has to include a balanced consideration of tasks and people, a broad framework may be derived from this evidence as a basis for comprehensive specifications of job requirements, conditions and standards, and for assessing achievement, i.e.:

1. **The task:** the achievement of specified outputs and objectives.
2. **The group:** the achievement of productive relationships within the group and with other groups and elements in the external environment.
3. **The individual:** achievement of personal, specified outputs and objectives, and contributions to the cohesiveness of the group.

QUESTIONS

1. Name and briefly describe the main elements of job analysis.

2. What items should be included in a job description, job specification and person specification?

3. Take one of the tasks in your own job and describe it in terms of the skills, knowledge, personal attributes and attitudes required.

4. What are the seven- and five-point plans and their relevance to job analysis?

5. Name and briefly describe the main headings in the seven-point plan.

6. What are the significant factors that influence the general approach to job analysis?

7. Name and describe the commonly used methods in job analysis; briefly evaluate each.

8. Why is the definition of effective performance an abiding problem in management.

8

Recruitment

ITS NATURE AND PURPOSE

Recruitment is the phase which immediately precedes selection. Its purpose is to pave the way for the selection procedures by producing, ideally, the smallest number of candidates who appear to be capable either of performing the required tasks of the job from the outset, or of developing the ability to do so within a period of time acceptable to the employing organisation. The smallest number of potentially suitable candidates can in theory, of course, be any number. The main point that needs to be made about the recruitment task is that the employing organisation should not waste time and money examining the credentials of people whose qualifications do not match the requirements of the job. A primary task of the recruitment phase is to help would-be applicants to decide whether they are likely to be suitable to fill the job vacancy. This is clearly in the interests of both the employing organisation and the applicants. But no matter how efficient an organisation may be in the preparation and publication of details of jobs or in the general administration of its recruitment procedures, it still has to deal with problems of the self-perception of people and has no control over applicants' perceptions of their own suitability to fill jobs. Thus, Manchester United Football Club can do nothing to prevent any number of cranks or eccentrics who see themselves as a potential team-manager from applying for the post when it falls vacant and wasting some of the employing organisation's time, at least, in dealing with applications of this kind. But apart from such extreme or bizarre examples, all advertised vacancies may regularly attract some applicants whose potential suitability is much more apparent to themselves than it is to the employing organisation. In practice, then, the objective of a recruitment procedure, is to attract genuinely suitable candidates and carefully examine their credentials in order to produce a short-list for further investigation in the selection procedures. Apart from the methods used and the general administration of the task, the achievement of the objective will depend very much in the end on how efficiently the basic tasks of manpower planning and job analysis have been carried out and applied. In short, efficient recruitment of staff may be described as knowing what resources you want, what resources are available, where and how they may be found. For purposes of studying the main details and requirements of an efficient, systematic recruitment-process the task may conveniently be examined under the following headings:

1. Determining the vacancies.
2. Considering the sources.
3. Preparing and publishing information.
4. Processing and assessing applications.
5. Notifying applicants.

DETERMINING THE VACANCIES

The first stage in the procedure is concerned with the question, what resources are needed, i.e. the demand. Determining vacancies to be filled will depend on the aim and objectives of the organisation and the needs for human resources which these engender. Details of requirements will emerge from the compilation and regular revision of the manpower plan. In practice, job vacancies may occur when an organisation or work-unit is set up *ab initio*, when any re-organisation takes place through changes of policy, technology or location or, most commonly, when employees leave the organisation and need to be replaced. Because of the subtle changes which are continuously taking place in work organisations, the existence and nature of job vacancies should not be accepted without question. Sound manpower planning and job analysis, regularly and systematically reviewed, should ensure that this does not happen.

CONSIDERING THE SOURCES

This stage is concerned with general questions about the supply and availability of resources and the particular avenues through which these are likely to be obtained. The manpower plan is designed to provide general information about the kinds of factors which influence the supply of labour at macro- and micro-levels. Here the situation is similar to that which the manufacturer has to face in ascertaining in advance what the limits of the available market are, what competition and other constraints obtain and what, therefore, the share of the market is likely to be. In considering possible sources of recruiting employees, it is easy to assume that these are inevitably external. Certainly, on the vast majority of occasions when jobs have to be filled, the employing organisation uses the resources of the external population. Even when it is possible and feasible to fill job vacancies from within the organisation, the transfers and promotions which this usually involves will more often than not produce a vacancy at the end of a chain-reaction, necessitating external recruitment. Nevertheless, the possibility of filling vacancies internally should always be given very careful consideration for the following reasons:

1. Existing employees are known to the organisation and are generally familiar with its customs and practices.

2. The costs and the time that recruitment, selection and induction procedures consume can be significantly reduced.

3. Internal recruitment to fill vacancies may be used as a means of career development, widening opportunities and stimulating motivation amongst existing employees.

When the organisation has to use external sources—and this is the normal situation—there are two main means of conducting the search for employees:

1. Through employment agencies—governmental, institutional and private-commercial.

2. By contacting the public directly through advertisements in newspapers and journals.

It may, of course, use a combination of these media. The main avenues available are described and evaluated below:

1. **Governmental Agencies:** Central government has played an important role in the employment field. Because of growing problems and pressures produced by economic, social and technological factors, central government has taken on ever-increasing responsibilities for co-ordinating and supervising the employment and development of the nation's manpower resources. This work is supported by a mass of statistical data, produced by the Department of Employment about the kinds of factors on which information is required for manpower planning, and by the comprehensive current legislation covering employment. Under the aegis of the DOE there is now a network of Job Centres and regional offices of the Professional and Executive Register (PER), which act as agents for potential employers and employees. Job Centres are concerned mainly with manual, clerical and junior administrative and shop staff; the PER deals with the managerial and professional/specialist fields. For young persons under 18 years of age and school-leavers, there is a special Careers Service which maintains a regular liaison between employers and local schools.

2. **Institutional Agencies:** Several different kinds of agencies are included under this heading. The features that they have in common are that they are all agencies set up by particular organisations to help their own members or ex-members find employment and that they are

generally non-profit making. The agencies of this kind that employers are likely to need and use most regularly are these:

(*i*) **Career services of academic institutions:** Universities and similar institutions maintain a full-time careers advisory service, known in the universities as University Appointments Boards. They serve as an employment agency for graduating or recently-graduated students and are centres of information for graduates about employment opportunities, and for employers who are seeking potential managers or professional specialists.

(*ii*) **Employment services of professional institutions and trade unions:** A number of professional institutions, such as those representing lawyers, doctors, accountants, engineers, linguists, etc., and a number of trade unions have an employment advisory service whereby a register is kept of members seeking employment and information is collected from employers seeking staff in particular professions and trades.

(*iii*) **Resettlement services of the armed forces:** All three services have full-time officer and NCO staffs with a specialised knowledge of employment opportunities liaising with government agencies, professional institutions, trade unions or directly with organisations to arrange employment for men and women who are returning to civilian occupations after periods of service of varying length. There are two main agencies working exclusively on behalf of the services: the Officers' Association and the Regular Forces Employment Association. The latter organisation caters mainly for the needs of non-commissioned personnel and has a network of regional offices.

3. **Private Employment Agencies:** These agencies have proliferated in recent years and are now quite well known to most people from personal experience of local offices and advertisements in the press. Local employment agencies deal mainly with clerical, typing, junior administrative, shop staff, etc. The other type of agency concentrates on recruitment and sometimes the initial stages of selection of middle and senior managers or of professional and specialist staff in fields such as medicine, law, accountancy, engineering, etc. Private agencies may, no doubt, provide at times a very valuable service especially in recruiting staff in situations where there is shortage of the particular kinds of employees required. However, since they exist to make a profit, employers have to pay for any employees they may recruit in this way. There are also pros and cons which have to be carefully weighed, especially whenever these agencies are used to assist in the selection of managerial or professional staff. The advantages are the specialist knowledge that an agency can acquire of the employment conditions and requirements in particular fields, objectivity of view, and skill in conducting the selection procedure. The main possible

disadvantage in using external assistance for recruitment–selection purposes is the agent's lack of first-hand experience of the cultural and environmental aspects of the organisation's work and life.

In recent times there has been a growth of so-called 'head-hunters'. As the term suggests, these are private firms and agencies of recruitment consultants who earn fees by meeting the needs of organisations for specialist and senior managerial staff. Much of their work is carried on by means of an informal network of contacts, whereby they keep records of career profiles of people likely to be in constant demand, and obtain information about the needs of employers for appointments to be filled. This method has proved its value to the employer and employee clientele of these agencies. However, there is sometimes a possibility that money could have more influence than ethics.

4. **Advertisements in the Press:** This is the commonest method by which employers carry out their search for suitable staff. Apart from the use of the national and local press and, to a limited extent, television and radio, an important source of recruitment by this means are professional and trade journals. When specialist staff are needed this is a very convenient and appropriate method for attracting the attention of those most likely to be suitable. The same basic information about the job has to be produced for publication whether the organisation uses an agency or places its own advertisements.

There is little point in any attempt to survey the sources of recruitment in terms of advantages or disadvantages. These have already been briefly mentioned, where any of these may be generally applicable. In practice, each organisation has to know what sources are available and then to ascertain which appear to be the most fruitful. The task of recruitment is likely to benefit greatly from regular personal contacts with recruitment agencies and sections of the population in which employees are most likely to be found. There are a number of ways in which contacts may be developed, e.g. regular meetings between the recruitment representatives of the work organisation and the employment agencies; regular visits by representatives of the employment agencies or potential applicants to the work organisation to acquire first-hand knowledge about the nature of jobs, facilities and working environment; conventions designed to bring employers, agencies and potential employees together to explain, discuss and ascertain employment opportunities. Meetings of this kind are especially useful for people entering full-time employment for the first time either from school or from university and similar institutions.

PREPARING AND PUBLISHING INFORMATION

This aspect of the recruitment process requires very special attention and skill. Its objective is to publish information which fulfils the following conditions.

1. It is succinct and yet gives a comprehensive and accurate description of the job and its requirements.
2. It is likely to attract the attention of the maximum number of potentially suitable candidates (i.e. is published through the right media).
3. It gives a favourable image of the organisation in terms of efficiency and its attitudes towards people.

The preparation and publication of this information is based on two simple questions that any applicant would normally ask:

1. What are the details of the job in terms of duties, rewards, conditions and special circumstances?
2. How should applications be presented?

The preparation of the information needed to answer the first question is based on the data produced by the job analysis and in particular by the various headings of the job description. Some of the items covered in the job and person specifications may also be included. This is a matter for the discretion of individual organisations, but, in general, there is not much point in waxing eloquently, as some job advertisements do, about the personal qualities needed. This is best left to the assessment of the personnel selectors. To ask members of the general public in effect whether they possess intelligence, drive, initiative, i.e. to make an assessment of themselves, is a futile exercise. On the other hand, it could well be relevant to mention any special features, such as aptitudes or personal circumstances that are important to the job, e.g. 'ability to read music at sight is desirable', or 'extensive travel throughout the UK and some evening or week-end work is an essential part of the job'.

The example of the job description in Chapter 7 was purposely comprehensive, so that it might be adapted to suit varying circumstances. This is the starting point for preparing and systematically structuring a job advertisement, for deciding what headings have to be included and what amount of detail is necessary. This part of the advertisement is, therefore, an abstract of the job description plus any significant elements from the job and person specifications.

The second part of the advertisement, advising applicants on the presentation of their applications, varies in practice. Sometimes a personal letter covering the applicant's curriculum vitae is the only form of application required. More frequently, the employer provides an application form together with information on requirements for testimonials and referees' reports. There is no point in making prescriptions for a wide variety of situations, but there are some useful, general observations which may be made about arrangements for applications. A letter of application or a curriculum vitae is sometimes used as a kind of selection device. Occasionally personal applications of this kind may even be passed to graphologists for a personality assessment. In effect, with this method applicants are being invited to sell themselves on paper, i.e. to argue their claims for appointment to the advertised post. There is certainly something to be said for giving applicants a free hand to state their own cases without inhibition, but there are some important caveats which have to be made about this method. Firstly, there is much evidence from those who work professionally in the field of careers advice and employment consultancy that very many people are unable systematically and concisely to prepare a relevant account of their general and employment records. Employers using this method must be prepared, therefore, to receive a number of lengthy irrelevant and perhaps boring self-reports which protracts the recruitment process. Secondly, a strong case can be made against the use of personally planned applications as a form of suitability test. The assessment of suitability for employment is difficult enough during the selection procedures. It certainly cannot be carried out either effectively or with justice on paper evidence alone.

The use of an application form has the particular advantage that employers can ensure that the information provided by applicants is on the whole relevant to the job requirements. At the same time, some flexibility and common sense are needed in the use of the form. No form, however carefully designed, can cover every possible contingency. Ample space should be included, therefore, for any additional, special points that applicants may wish to raise.

The Job Advertisement

The advertisement needs to cover information, derived from the job description, job and person specifications in six broad areas, namely:

1. The work organisation: its main occupation and location.

2. The job: its title; main duties (location, if varying from main centre).

3. Qualifications, and experience (both necessary and desirable): personal requirements; specifically professional qualifications, experience, aptitudes, etc.

4. Rewards and opportunities: basic salary and other emoluments; any other benefits; opportunities for personal development.

5. Conditions: any special factors and circumstances affecting the job.

Midshire County Council Education Authority
requires a
SCHOOL–MEALS CATERER/SUPERVISOR
at the
LORD NELSON COMPREHENSIVE SCHOOL, WESTLEIGH, MIDSHIRE.

Main duties
* providing school–meals for 1300 pupils and staff daily at the main school and two annexes.
* supervising the resources to meet this objective, i.e. 16 kitchen–staff, finances, materials and equipment.
* planning menus and ordering the necessary supplies.
* maintaining appropriate accounts and records.
* recruitment and selection of new staff.
* training staff.
* fulfilling statutory requirements for health and safety, employment conditions, etc.

Qualifications and Experience
* City and Guilds Catering Certificate (706), or Ordinary National Diploma in Institutional Housekeeping and Catering, or acceptable equivalents.
* At least 5 years in the school–meals service or similar catering employment.
* Age range 25–50 years.

Rewards
* Salary scale starting at £6000 and rising by annual increments of £200 to £8000 (starting point on the scale will be determined by qualifications and experience).
* LEA's pension scheme for catering staff.
* Annual paid holidays — 6 weeks, taken during school–holiday closures.

Opportunities
* Promotion to Deputy School-Meals Organizer/Adviser and County School-Meals Organizer/Adviser is on merit by open competition when vacancies occur.
* Training is given in personnel management and industrial relations. Short courses are also held in professional subjects to up-date knowledge and skills.

Applications
Write to Chief Education Officer, Midshire County Council (Dept P4), Midchester, for application forms and further details (marking envelope School-Meals Caterer/Supervisor).

Fig. 7. Specimen recruitment advertisement.

6. Applications: form of application; closing date; address for forwarding.

The Application Form

The design of an appropriate application form will clearly depend on particular situations and needs, but there are some basic principles which are universally relevant. Generalisations are often unsound but, on balance, it seems that public authorities often do not perform this task as competently as private companies—possibly because of misdirected efforts to economise. It is not unusual, for example, to find that the same form or very similar forms are being used for the appointment of a head of a school or department as for a clerical post. It is difficult and irritating for applicants for senior posts, where academic and professional qualifications and experience are important, to be asked to squeeze a quantity of significant information, perhaps covering many years, into a box of minute dimensions. If economy or any other reasons require the use of a general form for all appointments, then the form has to be sufficiently comprehensive and flexible to cover all possible situations. For all appointments the same general background details will be needed, for which a standard format is possible. Additional sheets can be added, specifically designed to cover the whole range of jobs from the town clerk to the officer in charge of refuse collection. Furthermore, there is no reason why these have necessarily to incur the expense of commercial printing. A well-typed form, carefully designed and adapted to cover the job vacancy in question, providing adequate space for the information required, is surely much better than a beautifully and expensively printed form, which attempts unsuccessfully to serve a variety of purposes. The items which will normally need to be included in application forms are:

1. Job title.
2. Applicant's full names.
3. Date of birth.
4. Nationality.
5. Marital circumstances.
6. Family circumstances (e.g. children and ages).
7. Education (full-time, part-time training courses).
8. Academic qualifications.
9. Professional qualifications.
10. Present employment.
11. Previous employment in chronological order.
12. Main current interests, pursuits and achievements outside work.
13. Health (including any serious illness or disability, past or present).

14. Court convictions (convictions other than for minor offences, e.g. car-parking, etc.).

15. Additional information (any information not covered in the form which the applicant considers significant to the application).

16. Referees.

17. Source of information about the vacancy.

PROCESSING AND ASSESSING APPLICATIONS

When all the applications have been received by the due date, the next task is to select those applicants who, on the evidence available, appear to be the most suitable as future employees of the organisation, and, therefore, worth the time and cost of further examination in the selection procedures. This task will be based on the published requirements for the job and involves a painstaking and scrupulous study of the information provided by applicants, a comparison of this information with those job requirements, and finally a decision whether to accept or reject at this stage. To systematise the process, it is normally useful to carry out a preliminary sift to produce three categories of applicants, namely; suitable; not suitable; marginal. With this method the main effort can then be concentrated on deciding which of the doubtful applicants should be accepted and which rejected. When there are constraints on acceptable numbers, and this is the normal circumstance, and a choice has to be made between applicants of apparently more or less equal merits in terms of the essential requirements, a careful consideration of the list of desirable requirements may provide the weighting needed to assist the final decision. A simple description of the sifting task such as this could make it seem a disarmingly mechanical process. It is, in fact, anything but this, and a number of important points need to be made about the general approach to the task and methods used.

To start with the general approach, those responsible for processing applications need to be very aware throughout firstly that they have a responsibility to their employers to be as careful and thorough as possible in selecting the most suitable of the applicants and, secondly, that they have a responsibility to the applicants themselves to examine their applications conscientiously and fairly. In this situation, applicants are entirely in the hands of those who carry out this task and seldom, if ever, have any chance of query or redress. It is also very important to realise that this is the link-stage between the recruitment and selection procedures. It is the first hurdle that the applicant has to overcome in obtaining employment with an organisation, and is, in effect, the first stage in the selection procedure. The assessment of suitable employees is difficult enough in the face-to-face situations of the selection interview and other selection methods. In deciding, therefore, that an applicant is unsuitable entirely on documentary evidence, the employing organisation needs to be as certain as it can be about its reasons for rejection at this stage. In short, the task must never be approached as a routine post-office exercise in which junior clerks are told to weed out all applications who, say, do not have five GCSE passes, or are over thirty-nine years of age. Since the task is virtually part of the selection procedure, it has very important implications for the choice of staff to perform the task. Junior clerical staff may be, and sometimes are, employed in the initial sifting task, and this method can save some time. However, if it is used, then it has to be done according to strict conditions. Firstly, any junior staff employed in this way must receive very careful and thorough instructions about their duties. Secondly, the resultant batches of applicants need finally to be carefully vetted by a responsible senior member of staff—especially those selected for rejection. It is most unjust and inefficient to delegate a very important, decision-making responsibility to junior staff.

A further important point that has to be made concerns the need for flexibility in making the final decisions about acceptance or rejection. This relates to the previous comment on the problems of making decisions on the basis solely of documentary information. To illustrate by example—if a job demands an HGV licence as an essential requirement, then all the applicants who do not have this qualification could be reasonably rejected immediately, no matter what their other qualifications may be; but if, say, at least five years' experience in the type of job in question were included as an essential requirement, it might be very shortsighted to rule out an apparently otherwise excellent candidate whose experience happened to be four years. There is no way of confirming from paper evidence whether the four years' experience of this applicant is not, in truth superior in quality and value to the longer experience of other applicants. It is best not to be stubbornly inflexible or over-precise about matters such as length of experience, age, etc. in the very first place. When job requirements are being established, room must always be left to decide individual cases on their merits.

Finally, a word needs to be said about the use of testimonials and referees' reports. Reports of this kind will regularly be used as evidence to assist in the final decisions of the selection procedures, but they also play some part in this phase of the recruitment procedure. Testimonials, despite some obvious limitations, are not always quite as useless as they are sometimes thought to be. For example, in the assessment of the merits and suitability of an application a brief attached report from a present or previous employer may at least confirm the applicant's experience and ability effectively to perform a job. Referees' reports, which are invariably confidential, will not normally be sought until a short-list of applicants has been produced. There is no point in incurring the time, trouble and expense in calling for referees' reports for all candidates, when a proportion of these will be rejected during the processing of applications. Referees' reports are, therefore, usually required as supplementary evidence for use in the assessment of candidates during the selection procedure.

NOTIFYING APPLICANTS

The final step is to notify the chosen applicants of the arrangements for the selection procedures, and the rejected applicants that they have not been chosen. The letter to the successful applicants will need to

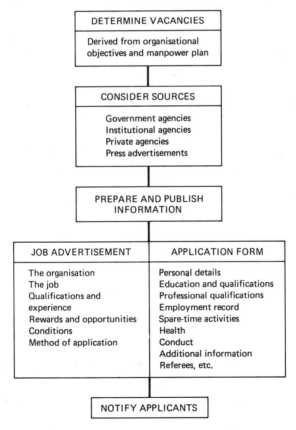

Fig. 8. An outline of the recruitment process.

give full details about the arrangements for the selection procedures, i.e. time and place together with other administrative information such as travel, expenses, etc. At the same time it is often very helpful to include any available literature about the organisation and its work. In this way a number of questions that candidates might otherwise wish to ask, for example, about locations, opportunities to travel, career opportunities in general, educational, training, social, sporting, welfare facilities, etc. can be anticipated. There is not much that can usefully be said about letters to rejected applicants, which is not already obvious. These should be briefly sympathetic, but not curt. All letters informing applicants of the results of applications should be sent as soon as possible. Apart from the natural tensions and anxieties that most people experience when waiting for the post to bring them news of any decisions that affect them personally, they have a special need for speedy information that concerns the planning of their working lives.

ADMINISTRATION OF THE RECRUITMENT PROCESS

The responsibility for administering and supervising the task of recruitment belongs to the personnel staff. They act as the representatives or agents of their employers and are a link between the managers of the organisation who require staff, the external sources for finding employees and the people who respond to the advertisements and apply for employment. The main elements of the task are:

1. Acting as the focal point for co-ordinating the organisation's needs for staff: in this function they use the data of the manpower plan and job analysis.

2. Providing specialist knowledge about manpower factors affecting the availability of required staff, and of current legislation affecting recruitment for employment: in this context they may also make recommendations about recruitment policies that the organisation should adopt.

3. Using specialist knowledge to decide what sources are likely to be most fruitful in the search for suitable staff: here it is particularly important that the personnel staff establish and maintain harmonious and profitable relationships with those agencies which are most likely to satisfy the recruitment needs of the organisation.

4. Formulating and administering the details of the recruitment procedures, related to the publication of information, processing of applications and notifying applicants: personnel staff need to liaise closely with line managers in the various stages of the recruitment process. The phases of the recruitment procedure when consultation between personnel staff and line management is most likely to occur

are the publication of the advertisement of the job vacancy and the processing of applications. Line managers may well be asked to verify that advertisements accurately reflect requirements before they are finally released for publication. They may often be consulted when a shortlist of candidates is being produced. There are some situations where consultation of this kind is essential, e.g. the appointment of managerial/supervisory staff reporting directly to the line manager, a personal assistant, etc.

5. Maintaining records and data on the value in practice of the various recruitment sources used by the organisation: this is an important source of feedback to the system in order to ascertain limitations in the supply of human resources and to ensure that the organisation obtains the best possible supply and quality of required employees.

Organisations need to take account of significant changes that have occurred in the labour market in recent times in their approach to recruitment. Because of rapidly changing technological, economic and social forces, present and future trends are, and will, be very different from the relatively static situation that once existed. Increasingly, organisations need to consider employing people with contracts that depart from convention e.g. short-time, part-time, job-sharing, working from home etc. At the same time franchise operations and sub-contracting arrangements provide opportunities for work to be carried out without the employer bearing the costs and risks of traditional recruitment and employment methods.

QUESTIONS

1. What should be the aim of an effective system of recruitment?

2. What are the five stages of a systematic process of recruitment?

3. What are the main sources of recruitment available to an organisation? Briefly describe and assess each of these sources.

4. Name the main headings that normally need to be included in a job advertisement.

5. Name the headings that normally need to be included in an application form.

6. What actions need to be taken to ensure that the processing of applications is as systematic, effective and fair as possible?

7. What are the main responsibilities of the personnel department in the recruitment process?

9

Selection of New Employees

ITS NATURE, PURPOSE AND PROBLEMS

The term personnel selection is mostly used to mean the acquisition of new staff from external sources. In fact, personnel selection or employment selection, as it is sometimes called, should cover the whole range of possible situations where a person is being selected for a new job, i.e. the initial recruitment and placement of new staff or the transfer and promotion of existing staff. The basic principles are the same for each. Here, we are concerned with the first stage in the process, the initial selection of employees from outside the organisation.

If the success of a work organisation ultimately depends on its employees, then the task of initial selection is one of the most important of all the decision-making processes that employers have to undertake. The essence of the task is to examine the qualifications of people of whom they usually have no personal knowledge and to choose those who appear to be potentially suitable for employment in the organisation. The possible penalties for mistakes can be very costly. If people are employed who cannot satisfactorily carry out required tasks or cannot collaborate with their work colleagues, then employers will be sowing the seeds for a future harvest of problems which may be far-reaching in the gravity of the consequences. Furthermore, because the root-cause of these problems, i.e. faulty selection methods, may not be recognised, they will continue and multiply, and an incalculable amount of time, effort, money and other resources may be wasted in futile attempts to deal with symptoms rather than causes. Thus, the organisation may fail to attain its objectives; employees may suffer from a variety of forms of bad management; communication may be poor; there may be conflict and low morale; rates of absence, sickness and turn-over may be high, leading in turn to regular losses in trained staff and repetitious recruitment and training of new employees. There is abundant evidence that the crucial importance of recruiting suitable staff is often not truly appreciated and, consequently, the selection process is unmethodical and inefficient. Since effective management depends firstly on an awareness of the nature and scope of the task or problem, and then on a systematic approach in practice, it is necessary to begin by asking what the task of selection entails, and then to consider what methods are available and which are likely to be the most effective.

The task has been described above as a decision-making process, in which those responsible for selecting new staff have to identify from a group of unknown people those who seem to be suitable for employment. The decision of suitability will normally need to be based on the potential of prospective employees to satisfy three broad basic conditions, namely:

1. To perform alloted tasks to standards of effective performance, as defined by the employing organisation.

2. To develop knowledge and skills in the job in order to be able to assume wider responsibilities for work and the management of others.

3. To settle successfully into the life of the organisation in personal and interpersonal terms, and hence to work co-operatively and productively with colleagues of all levels and occupations within the organisation.

If the main task of selectors is to identify those who will perform effectively in the organisation in these terms, they need to begin by asking and answering as precisely as possible what effective performance means and how it is to be recognised and assessed. Neglect of this essential stage is, in practice, perhaps the commonest and most serious fault which typifies unmethodical selection procedures. It stems, it seems, from assumptions by the selector representatives of the organisation that because of their experience or seniority they have a clear view of the requirements for effective performance in their organisation, that there are no significant discrepancies of views amongst the selectors, and that these views do not need to be made explicit. In fact, selectors may differ more widely about the requirements for the same job than they realise.

The starting point for the task of defining effective performance is thoroughly to analyse the job in question and on this basis to produce a job description, a job specification and a person specification. This process has already been discussed in detail in Chapter 7. However, the crucial importance of this stage cannot be too strongly emphasised, for it is the foundation stone on which the whole selection structure is built. At the same time, it is also necessary to consider the criteria which indicate that required standards have been achieved. To illustrate with a simple example—a job described as Technical Translator (European Languages) might include a requirement such as 'all-round competence and accuracy'. The criterion for assessing achievement of this requirement might be described as 'able to translate without error texts on all engineering subjects from the journals of learned societies and institutions from and into French and

German and one other language'. Knowing the requirement and the criterion for evaluating successful performance, we could produce a test to measure the capabilities of candidates for the job. The determination of criteria is seldom easy and it becomes especially difficult in occupations which are complex, such as management, and which can only be assessed on the basis of behaviour observed in a variety of situations over a period of time. Furthermore, there can be no absolute criteria for assessing effective performance in work organisations, because assessments depend on individual interpretations, which in turn depend on what the combined effects of heredity and environment have uniquely produced in each individual assessor in terms of attitudes, values, assumptions and expectations. This is why it is essential that selectors do not assume that they all agree about what they are looking for, and that they do not need to discuss and to specify the requirements for effective performance of the job.

Finally, there is one further complication in an already difficult task. There is invariably a difference in the standards of performance that an employer would require from a fully effective, experienced employee and a new recruit. This performance gap would be closed in time by training and job experience, but selectors have to consider this situation very carefully and to determine also how this difference will affect the selection process.

SELECTION METHODS

The second major task with which selectors must deal is to determine by what methods they can best identify candidates' potentiality to fulfil the prescribed conditions for effective performance. In essence, this is a problem of prediction and it is an inescapable dilemma of the selection process. Prediction by its very nature connotes uncertainty, but nothing could be less certain than forecasting human behaviour in a new work environment. Ideally, there is only one method whereby we could be reasonably sure whether unknown persons would be able to fulfil all of the main requirements for effective employment within an organisation. We should need actually to employ them and, after an appropriate period of time, make an assessment of their abilities in terms of the criteria for the effective performance of work. But this is clearly not practicable and selectors are compelled to devise methods which are inevitably predictive. It is worth noting, incidentally, that the practice of an initial probationary period before final confirmation of an appointment is to some extent a recognition of this basic dilemma and an attempt to produce the best available compromise. Organisations which use and properly apply this practice are, in a sense, admitting the inherent limitations of the predictive elements of the selection process, and are virtually extending the process over a much longer period to include an evaluation of actual performance of the job. Whilst probationary employment may be the best available means for revealing and remedying initial mistakes in selecting unsuitable people, it still offers no help in revealing and remedying the opposite form of mistake, namely the rejection of those who could, in fact, have been suitable employees, had they been selected. Although the method is undoubtedly valuable and may well save the organisation from the harm that an initially bad selection decision might have produced, we are still left with the central problem of predicting future human behaviour in specific terms of effective performance within a work organisation. The principal problem that faces selectors, therefore, in choosing methods is to reduce the inevitable uncertainty of prediction as much as possible. In effect, this means that they need to find predictive methods which are:

1. Practicable enough to be used in the short duration and restricted environment of the selection process.
2. Most likely to produce people who will prove suitable in the job.

In terms of psychology, this means that there needs to be the closest possible correlation between the predictor and the criterion for effective performance.

The main question, therefore, that has to be faced in choosing selection methods is this: in the absence of direct evidence, what predictive methods will provide the next best evidence of suitability for employment? Before discussing selection methods themselves, however, there is a fundamental general comment that has to be made about all selection tests. To be fully effective they need to satisfy the conditions of reliability and validity. A reliable test is one that gives consistent measurements at different times and in different circumstances with different subjects. Thus, for example, a ruler can be relied upon to give consistent measurements of length whether it is measuring string or cheese, in summer or winter, in Africa or Russia. A valid test is one that in fact measures what it purports to measure. Thus, for example, the litmus test purports to indicate acidity or alkalinity of substances and can be shown by the evidence of other data consistently to do this. But if, for example, a group of immigrants recently arrived in Britain were given a test written in the English language designed to test their knowledge of chemistry, the test might well be, in fact, as much a test of English as of chemistry. From the requirements of these conditions it follows that any predictive tests which depend on human judgement as a measure cannot be fully reliable and valid and may fall well short in satisfying these conditions. Therefore, before any selection methods are used, selectors need to know firstly what kind of methods are available and secondly what these can and cannot do. Above all, they need to be aware of the importance of reliability and validity in the use of selection tests and of the particular limitations of any methods that they may have to use *faute de mieux*. All the important data about selection methods have come mainly from the continuous research and study over a long period by psychologists with special experience in this field. If standards of personnel selection are to be improved, it is essential that personnel selectors, who are often line managers occasionally performing this duty, should receive training in the use of selection methods from experienced specialists, and should be advised and guided by them in the design and application of selection procedures in practice.

The search for methods that may improve the quality of selection decisions has produced a very wide variety of tests. These tests could be categorised in various ways, but in very broad terms they may be conveniently divided into two main types according to their purpose. They are designed to assess candidates' potential to fulfil the requirements of the job in terms of:

1. Knowledge, skills and attitudes which already exist;
2. Knowledge, skills and attitudes which might be developed after training and experience in the job.

In other words in a comparison between the test situations and those actually occurring in the job, prediction may be based on evidence derived from actual past behaviour, or from a calculation of potential future behaviour. To illustrate the difference with a simple example, let us suppose that a particular job requires the ability to speak Japanese fluently. Having first determined what we mean by speaking fluent Japanese and the criteria by which it is to be assessed, we could make a direct test of all the candidates who claim to speak the language fluently and then assess their abilities against our predetermined standards. By if there were a shortage of easily recruitable Japanese speakers, we might decide to invest in training suitable candidates to the standards required. In this situation, we should need to devise some test designed to show whether candidates with no knowledge of Japanese have the latent ability to learn to speak the language fluently in a given period of time. This alternative test clearly could not be a test in Japanese itself, but it would have to be some kind of aptitude-revealing test. We might decide, for example, that proven ability in other languages would be a sufficient indicator of the skills required, but to assume a correlation between, say, the ability to speak French fluently and a potential ability to speak Japanese fluently would be unwarranted. This is also an illustration of the need for specialist guidance, because any aptitude test devised would have to be based on a very careful analysis of the factors that seem to be important in speaking Japanese fluently. Furthermore, the reliability and validity of the test would need to be proved by confirming that an acceptable number of people chosen by this method have, in fact, become fluent speakers of Japanese. This kind of proof takes time, and the original test may well need regular modifications before the employing organisation is finally satisfied with its predictive qualities.

In the practice of personnel selection the methods which may be used are these:

1. **Ability tests of achievement:** These are designed to test what the candidate already knows or can do, relative to the requirements of the job (e.g. skills in driving, typing, foreign languages; knowledge of the law, antique furniture, etc.).

2. **Ability tests of aptitude:** These are designed to predict latent potential to meet job requirements which can be developed to required standards by training and experience. Aptitude tests may include intelligence tests, designed to measure a broad range of generally applicable abilities, or more specialised tests designed to indicate particular aptitudes, e.g. mechanical skills. The ability tests included under this heading are too numerous and varied in purpose to enumerate. Nevertheless, a well-known example of the use of these kinds of tests is worth quoting to illustrate their practical applicability and potential efficacy. Because the training of pilots to fly aircraft is enormously expensive, it is particularly important that selectors should make the fewest mistakes in selecting potential pilots. However, because they are faced with the central problem of predicting future success, they need predictors which are as reliable and valid as they can be, i.e. where the test data has the highest possible correlation with the performance criteria for flying. Over a number of years a number of aptitude tests have been developed which have been validated in practice and can be shown to be very sound predictors in terms of the success rates in flying training. When tests of this kind are used in combination, as they are in selecting aircrew, they are known as a test battery.

3. **Tests of personality:** Traits of personality undoubtedly have a very important effect on performance of work, and especially any kind of managerial work, where judgement, and influence on and relationships with others are crucial. A number of tests have been developed and used by psychologists over the years in an attempt to determine personality characteristics as a basis for predicting likely future behaviour in work. Various methods have been designed e.g.

(i) **Projective tests:** a method in which the subject is required to react freely and spontaneously, usually to visual stimuli. Reactions are then interpreted by the tester as indicators of personality traits, interests, etc. The best known examples of this kind of test are probably the Rorschach Ink-Blot Test (interpreting responses to ink-blot shapes) and the Thematic Apperception Test (interpreting responses to a series of pictures). The interpretation of the results of these tests is a task for specialists.

(ii) **Inventories:** with this method subjects are required to respond to questionnaires normally concerned with how they feel about certain subjects and situations. Well known examples of these kinds of tests have been produced by Cattell (16 PF), Eysenck and Myers Briggs. Some inventories are designed to be administered and scored by anyone using the instructions and key provided. With others the tests have to be administered by people trained in their application and interpretation.

4. **Group situational tests:** In these tests, candidates are observed by the selectors over a period of time as they perform a variety of tasks as a team, sometimes with and sometimes without an appointed leader. Tests of this kind first became well-known during the Second World War. They began in the UK with the War Office Selection Boards (WOSB) and are now widely used by the armed forces, governmental and industrial organisations for the selection of potential leaders. The tests are designed to reveal data about the personality traits and interpersonal skills required in managing or co-operating with others in the performance of actual tasks. They undoubtedly provide useful insight into candidates' behaviour as members of groups in a way that no other individual selection method can do. Nevertheless, in essence they represent behaviour measured by the personal, subjective interpretations of human observers in artificial circumstances, and are, therefore, open to question in terms of their reliability and validity.

5. **Interviews:** Whatever other tests may be used, the selection process invariably includes an interview. Quite often it is the only method used. It may be used in various ways. There may be several interviews covering general and specialist aspects of the job; interviews may be conducted by individual interviewers or by a board of interviewers. Apart from the information obtained at the interview itself interviewers also make use of accounts provided by candidates themselves in the form of completed application forms, curricula vitae, letters, etc., and by others competent to comment on the candidates in the form of open testimonials or confidential reference reports. The interview is by far the commonest method used in personnel selection. At the same time it is an entirely subjective method and, thus, of dubious efficacy. Moreover, any value that it can have may be still further reduced because of lack of skills on the part of the interviewers. Since it plays such a significant part in the selection process, it needs a separate and detailed examination by itself.

THE SELECTION INTERVIEW

For many years the selection interview has been the subject of research in order to determine its value as a method. In general, the research has produced a pessimistic evaluation of the selection interview, but has also indicated that its value may be significantly enhanced when interviewers have been trained. If the interview is analysed in the light of the general problem of human communication and of the particular requirements for reliability and validity, it is not difficult to see why it has inherent barriers to success as a selection method. The selection interview is not reliable for the following reasons:

1. The instrument of measure is human.
2. No two interviewers will interpret and assess information in the same way.
3. The same interviewer will reveal fluctuations in interpretations of data and assessments over a period of time.

The interview cannot be a valid test of candidates' suitability for employment for the following reasons:

1. It is a contrived, interrogative conversation, involving a meeting invariably between strangers and seldom lasting for more than about an hour. It is, therefore, an artificially distorted and entirely stressful situation, no matter what efforts the interviewers may make to reduce the tension. The larger the number of interviewers the greater the tension is likely to be.
2. It cannot possibly test the important areas that add up to suitability for employment, i.e. competence effectively to perform the professional requirements of a job over a period of time; the personal disposition to relate co-operatively with future work colleagues in smaller groups and within the organisation as a whole; the capacity for self-development and the potential to assume wider responsibilities.
3. The interview may indicate that a candidate is presentable, fluent or quick-thinking under the conditions of the interview, but to suppose that the pattern of interview behaviour would be repeated in the very different circumstances of work over a long period of time would be a quite unwarranted assumption.

The only kind of validity that the interview can confidently be said to have is to test whether people can cope with the special and unusual conditions of the interview. Nevertheless, it is often very difficult to persuade selection interviewers that much of the evidence that they require about a candidate's potential for effective performance of work cannot be properly tested by the interview.

It is pertinent to ask why the interview is so widely and prominently used if it is a method of such demonstrable limitations. The reasons are these:

1. It has a high face-validity, i.e. both selectors and candidates have long been accustomed to its use and appear to have much greater faith in its efficacy than the research evidence warrants.

2. Sooner or later there has to be a meeting between the employer and prospective employee, if only so that a number of routine checks may be made on both sides and to give the employer an opportunity to amplify and clarify information provided by application forms and any other documents.

3. Despite continuous research and the introduction of possibly promising advances in new directions (e.g. personality tests), a method that will solve the basic dilemma of accurately forecasting future behaviour in employment has yet to be found.

Since the interview is likely to continue to play a major role in the selection process, it seems sensible to adopt a realistic approach, which means making the best possible use of the interview. This is the really important question to which attention needs to be given. As the research data has shown, anyone who is likely to have responsibilities for personnel selection needs to be trained. At the same time the following caveats have to be made about interview training.

1. Because of its innate limitations the total attainable efficiency of the interview as a selection method can never be any more than moderate. Therefore, any improvement produced by training can only be relative.

2. Trainees need to be made fully aware of these limitations. Otherwise they may be led to believe that if only they can learn to apply in practice conventional maxims about sound interviewing (essential though this is) then all will be well.

3. There is sometimes a particular problem in training senior managers. Having interviewed without any formal training perhaps for many years, they inevitably develop confidence in their own styles and methods and often come to believe that seniority and experience are the main requirements for making decisions on suitability for employment. They may find it very hard to accept that the selection method that they have been using for so long is a very fallible instrument, or that they lack system and skills. Training courses can have a particular value in helping to overcome problems of insight and sensitivity in unskilled interviewers. Trainees can participate in selection interviews that are very close to reality. Discussion with observers and tutors, supported by video-tape replays of the interview, can demonstrate the inherent problems of the interview itself and the methods that are likely to be effective in practice, in ways which no amount of lecturing or reading could ever achieve.

A well-planned course should include the following main areas of study:

1. The general nature and problems of personnel selection.
2. The particular limitations of the interview as a selection method.
3. The application of systematic interviewing through practice interviews as a means of making the best use of the interview.

The emphasis of the course needs to be laid almost entirely in interview practice in small groups as a basis for a structural analysis of the interview itself. In this connection, it is worth noting that the views and feelings of the interviewees should be used to provide a very valuable and powerful feed-back to the interviewers—a learning experience which they can never have in real life.

Using the Interview Effectively

A systematic interview is based on three interdependent chronological phases:

1. The pre-interview preparatory phase.
2. The interview itself.
3. The post-interview assessment and decision phase.

Each of these elements contributes vitally to the effectiveness of the total operation and weakness in any one element will adversely affect the other parts. For example, if the essential pre-interview preparatory work is unsound, then no matter how well the interview itself may be conducted, the quality of the final decision will inevitably suffer.

The main requirements for a sound interview can now be considered under these headings.

Pre-interview Preparatory Phase

1. Use the data of job analysis to determine the requirements for effective performance of the job and the criteria by which these may be identified and assessed. These data provide the foundation for the whole selection process.
2. Determine acceptable entry-levels for new staff *vis-à-vis* the job requirements for fully effective performance.
3. Consider and, whenever practicable, use other tests and information to supplement the evidence provided by the interview. Any other selection methods used need to be validated, i.e. shown to improve the predictive quality of the process.
4. Decide on the number of interviewers. When an interview board is used, the membership should be the smallest number necessary to fulfil the task.

5. Pay particular attention to all important environmental details such as time, place and setting to enable candidates to feel as comfortable as possible.

6. Produce a coverage plan designed to provide the maximum possible significant information. The plan that is the simplest and likely to be most effective is a systematic, chronological survey of the important areas of the life-history. The coverage plan is not the same as the seven- or five-point plans, whose applicability to selection interviews is described below.

7. When interview boards are held, discuss and agree the objectives, criteria, the coverage plan and the areas that each board member will cover. The leadership of this discussion is a major responsibility of the chairman.

Interview-Coverage plan

The criteria for assessing applicants' suitability for employment are contained in the Person Specification, which is a definition of the knowledge, skills and personal attributes needed for effective performance. Applicants may already possess some of the required qualifications or have the latent ability to develop others with training and work experience.

Within its known limitations the interview is used to ascertain what qualifications candidates already have in terms of the Person Specification and what potential they may have for further development. As we have already seen, specific tests may be used to ascertain existing and latent abilities. When the interview is used for these purposes information on which to base judgements about either existing or latent abilities can only come from the evidence of past achievements and behaviour. It follows that the broad plan for the interview that is most likely to provide the required information is a systematic, chronological investigation of the main areas of a life-history. A comprehensive interview-coverage plan should, therefore, take the following form:

1. Introductions and brief explanation of purpose and scope of the interview.
2. General and domestic background.
3. Education (full and part-time).
4. Work (full and part-time) and training.
5. Spare-time interests and activities.
6. Knowledge of and interest in the job.
7. Opportunity for applicant to
   (a) add any further information.
   (b) ask any questions.

The investigation of these areas should aim to reveal the maximum possible relevant information i.e. it should be directed towards the requirements of the Person Specification. For example, the discussion of spare-time pursuits may reveal valuable information about ability to organise, sociability, initiative etc. It should aim to reveal not only factual information about actions, decisions and achievements, but also as much as possible about reasons for decisions, motives, values, attitudes and personal attributes.

The Interview

1. Concentrate initially on establishing a sympathetic, productive atmosphere to encourage candidates to talk freely.

2. Begin with introductions and brief explanation of the purpose and scope of the interview.

3. Follow the broad chronological, systematic coverage—plan throughout in order to ensure a comprehensive coverage. Deviations are likely to create gaps in the information obtained.

4. In board interviews arrange for each interviewer to interview in turn. If the situation is allowed to become a free-for-all, then control is lost, the coverage plan cannot be methodically followed and candidates are likely to become unsettled and confused.

5. Pay the utmost attention to the form of question, i.e.

 (i) Concentrate on acquiring as much solid evidence as possible of potential ability to do the required job, based on the facts of past behaviour and achievements;

 (ii) In general, avoid hypothetical questions, especially those which have no bearing on the job. They can only produce hypothetical answers;

(iii) Use a simple, open question form which does not imply answers, make unwarranted assumptions or influence candidates in any way (e.g. why? what? where? when? who? etc.).

6. Be constantly alert to the possible effects of the interviewers' non-verbal behaviour and manner and the possibility of the misinterpretation of intentions by candidates. In general, a demeanour which is sympathetic and avoids extremes of bonhomie or coldness is the most appropriate.

7. Place information in perspective. The fact, for example, that a candidate was in charge of a section would be of little value, unless the important circumstantial details were also ascertained, such as: the work objectives; whether they were achieved or not; if not achieved, what the reasons were; what remedial actions were taken; other problems and how they were handled; responsibilities for staff in numbers and types; other responsibilities. To discover that a

competitor came third in a race only makes sense if we know how many were competing, in what conditions, at what level, etc.

Post-interview Assessment and Decision

1. Systematically assess the evidence obtained in the light of the job requirements. For this purpose, the discipline implied in the seven- and five-point plans is invaluable.

2. In assessing evidence concentrate on solid facts of past behaviour as indicators of motivation, attitudes, values, personal qualities and abilities and, in sum, of potential to do the required job. Behaviour in the highly artificial situation of the interview itself should be treated with extreme caution. There is little correlation between this behaviour and likely behaviour in the actual environment and conditions of work.

3. In the assessment process take account of all available evidence. When the interview is the only method used, the other main sources of information are usually referees' reports and testimonials. These documents can be very useful when written by authorities competent to confirm the facts of past performance. They are of much more doubtful value when they purport to assess suitability for employment, because of the likelihood of bias and the writers' probable lack of direct knowledge of the job-requirements.

The Use of Seven- and Five-Point Plans for Selection Interviews

These plans, discussed in Chapter 7 on Job Analysis, are especially useful in selection interviewing. The various headings are not intended to be followed sequentially during the interview as a framework for a coverage plan. Their purpose is comprehensively to cover the main items of information required in a person specification. Applied to the selection of new employees, the particular advantages of such plans are:

1. They systematically specify the evidence that the selectors need and thus unify all three phases of the interviewing process.

2. They induce interviewers to prepare and plan the interview to cover all areas of the life-history as the important, potential sources of significant information.

3. They help to focus attention on what is truly discoverable about candidates and hence to discourage tendencies to try to test the untestable or to set up irrelevant quiz-games.

4. They are invaluable in the final assessment phase as a check list, disciplining interviewers to move systematically through the main job requirements and the evidence obtained in each area.

Table 3. The Seven-Point Plan as a Model for a Selection Procedure for Potential Aircraft Pilots

	Essential	Desirable	How identified
Physical	100% fitness.	—	Comprehensive range of medical tests.
Attainments	Specified subjects and grades in GCE 'A' and 'O' levels.	Degree or equivalent qualifications.	Documentary evidence, amplified by interview.
General intelligence	Levels specified in terms of psychometric tests.	—	Ability tests of education/intelligence, supplemented by interview data.
Special aptitudes	Co-ordination. Mechanical comprehension. Speed of reaction. Handling rapidly changing information.	—	Special ability tests of aptitude related to success in flying training.
Interests	Aviation and related subjects.	World affairs.	Documentary evidence, amplified by interview.
Disposition	Equable temperament, sociable and co-operative.	—	Documentary evidence amplified by interview.
Circumstances	Mobility.	Initially free from heavy domestic/family commitments.	Documentary evidence, amplified by interview.

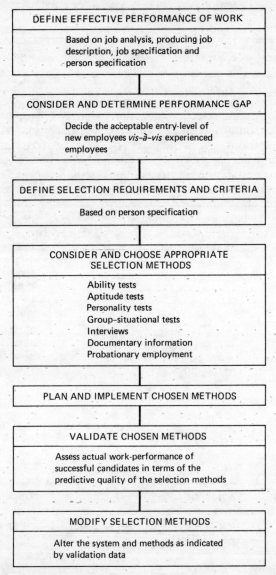

Fig. 9. Summary of the main elements of a system for the selection of new employees.

Employment Law and Personnel Selection

Employment law is discussed in detail in Chapter 23. However, we need to stress here the importance of recent legislation about discrimination on grounds of race or sex in personnel selection. Current legislation and codes of practice require employers to take all possible measures to ensure that there is no direct or indirect discrimination in their job descriptions, person specifications, advertisements and selection procedures. Direct discrimination (e.g. white males only) is blatant. Indirect discrimination (e.g. asking women questions about effects of domestic commitments on employability but not men) is more difficult to combat. It is usually the result of long established attitudes and selectors are often not alert to their own unfair discriminatory practices.

To reduce and eliminate discriminatory behaviour which is particularly likely to be unfair to candidates who are female, from ethnic minorities or physically handicapped, positive action is needed by work-organisations. They need to publish and distribute the relevant sections of employment law and to produce their own codes of practice, and to train their personnel selectors with particular emphasis on the requirements of employment law in this context and on the need to guard against unfair, discriminatory practices.

QUESTIONS

1. What is the first essential stage in an effective system of personnel selection?

2. Describe the various methods by which selectors might identify suitable employees.

3. What is the significance of reliability and validity in the use of selection methods? Give examples to illustrate these terms.

4. What are the limitations of the interview as a selection method?

5. How may the interview be used to best effect?

6. Describe the main areas that need to be included in an effective interview-coverage plan.

7. What significance does employment law have in the process of personnel selection?

8. How may the seven- and five-point plans be used for the purposes of personnel selection?

FURTHER READING: PART 3

Agrell, T., *Recruitment Techniques*, Thorsons, Wellingborough, 1977.

Boydell, T., *A Guide to Job Analysis*, BACIE, London, 1970.

HMSO, *Company Manpower Planning*, 1974.

Jessup, G. and Jessup, H., *Selection and Assessment at Work*, Essential Psychology, Methuen, London, 1975.

Munro Frazer, J., *Employment Interviewing*, Macdonald & Evans, Plymouth, 1966.

Nunnally, J., *Introduction to Psychological Measurement*, McGraw-Hill, Maidenhead, 1970.

Plumbley, P., *Recruitment and Selection*, IPM, London, 1971.

Rodger, A., *The Seven-point Plan*, N11P (Paper No. 5), 1973.

Rott, H. and Watson, T., *Job Analysis*, IPM, London, 1967.

Sidney, E. and Brown, M., *The Skills of Interviewing*, Tavistock, London, 1961.

Stainer, G., *Manpower Planning*, Heinemann, London, 1971.

Ungerson, B., *Recruitment Handbook*, Gower Press, Epping, 1970.

PART 4

The Effective Employment and Development of Human Resources

Having expended a considerable outlay in its efforts to obtain suitable employees, a work organisation has a very strong vested interest in ensuring that these human resources are employed as effectively as possible. The weight of research data and the continuing reports of industrial problems provide convincing evidence that some organisations are clearly falling far short in making effective use of the people they employ. To do this an organisation has to start by recognising that people are its most valuable asset, that they are not simply another factor of production for the achievement of short-term objectives, and that they are a reservoir of knowledge and skills, which must be nurtured and developed for the survival and growth of the organisation in a constantly changing and increasingly complex environment. An enlightened, long-term view such as this needs to be based on a psychological insight and awareness of the complexities of individual needs and motivation, and hence the potential, inherent conflict between the needs and objectives of the organisation and those of its employees. Here, the main problem that the organisation has to face is how to create a working environment that enables its objectives to be achieved and at the same time is able to motivate people by providing meaningful and satisfactory work.

This part of the book describes the necessity for a systematic approach to the employment and development of staff in general, and in particular, to the induction period of employment, to the assessment of work performance and potential as a basis for determining needs for work-experience and training, and to the maintenance of the personnel records that provide the essential information on which the whole system depends.

10

A System for the Employment and Development of Human Resources

THE BASIS OF A SYSTEM

Since people are the most valuable of the resources available to organisations, they need to be employed as effectively as possible. At the same time people are not simply just another factor of production. All the literature of this century on the treatment of people at work emphasises how crucially important it is that employers should understand the psychological needs of their employees and should treat them humanely and sensitively.

Although the first priority of any work organisation is the achievement of its operational objectives, at the same time it must create opportunities for the use and development of the knowledge and skills of its employees to the mutual advantage of both. In practice this objective can be achieved in two ways, i.e.

1. By planning work experience so that knowledge skills and attitudes needed for effective performance of work may be developed through a continuing variety of work situations and through appointments to jobs of wider responsibilities, i.e. what is generally described as career development. It is important that this approach should apply generally to all employees, but it is especially important for management succession planning to ensure that senior managers have acquired appropriate experience.

2. By training in the wide interpretation described in Chapter 13, whereby learning situations are purposefully structured in a variety of ways at the work place or on formal courses so that job-related knowledge, skills and attitudes may be developed.

To employ people effectively in these ways requires organisation and system i.e. there needs to be:

(*i*) A definition and publication of personnel policy, objectives, methods and responsibilities.

(*ii*) Formal methods that enable the various agents in the system to communicate and to provide the necessary information as a basis for decisions about employment and training i.e. formal arrangements for performance appraisal, potential and reward reviews, assessments of training and developmental needs, career-development interviews, promotion etc.

(*iii*) Comprehensive, accurate and relevant records for all employees, covering work-history, assessments of performance, reviews of potential and rewards, career interviews, training and promotion.

Obviously the Personnel Department has the main responsibilities for the day-to-day effective operation of this system, but line management, training staff and individual employees themselves also have important roles to play.

THE ROLE OF THE PERSONNEL DEPARTMENT

A system for the employment and development of an organisation's human resources cannot be either operationally effective or fair if there are wide divergences of practices and standards between the various units of the organisation. The central administration and control of the system is, therefore, a crucially important function. How the Personnel Department is organised to carry out its role will naturally vary according to work-organisations' functional differences, but in general the organisation of the Personnel Department must provide for the supervision of two broad areas i.e.

1. The specialist functions that fall within its province and professional competence i.e. manpower planning, job analysis, recruitment and selection, induction, performance appraisal, potential review, career development, promotion, discipline and in-efficiency, health and safety, welfare, industrial relations and employment law, retirement and redundancy, job evaluation, pay and conditions of service. In these areas the Personnel Department will be responsible for formulation of policy, approved by senior management, and the daily implementation of this policy and the monitoring of its effectiveness.

2. The employment and career development of all individual employees in the organisation. In this way every employee will be allocated to a particular personnel manager to whom he or she may refer and who is responsible for supervising his or her career path. Allocations of groups of staff may be made in various ways e.g. types of employment—administrative or technical grades, geographical areas and so on.

Figure 10 is an imaginary example of a Personnel Department in a large organisation, showing how the heads of various divisions are

Personnel Department

Chief Personnel Manager

P1	P2	P3	P4	P5	P6
Manpower planning, job analysis	Recruitment and selection	Performance and potential appraisal, Career development, Promotion	Discipline and inefficiency	Industrial relations, Employment law, Health and safety and welfare	Job evaluation, Pay and conditions, Retirement and redundancy

P4 A

Employment of all admin staff Grades 1–3

P4 A(1)	P4 A(2)	P4 A(3)	P4 A(4)
(North)	(South)	(East)	(West)

Fig. 10. Organisation of the Personnel Department.

responsible for specific functions. At the same time, they are the line managers for the personnel staff in their divisions and sub-divisions, who share responsibilities for certain types of staff in certain locations. Thus, the Head of Division P4 is responsible for policy and practices for sub-divisions e.g. P4 A, B, C, D etc. As Figure 10 shows, sub-division P4 A looks after all administrative staff of grades 1 to 3 and is further sub-divided into branches which are responsible for geographical areas.

In carrying out the responsibility to see that the organisation is properly staffed with the employees that it needs and that the organisation's human resources are properly developed, personnel managers may fulfil executive and consultative roles. Their executive role is concerned mainly with the movement of staff i.e. initial placements of newly recruited employees, internal movements to fill vacancies and for purposes of individual development and arranging for staff to attend training and educational courses. Their consultative work involves discussions with, and advice to, line managers and individual employees about proposed movements, i.e. changes of jobs, promotions, training, terms and conditions of service, welfare, discipline etc.

The work of the personnel staff has a number of inherent problems that arise from the nature of their co-ordinating role and affect relationships with line managers and individuals.

It is not uncommon for managers to develop possessive feeling about their own employees and to be sensitive about any relationships that members of their staff may have outside the work group and, therefore, to some extent perhaps outside the manager's control. This explains the antipathy that some line managers may show towards personnel and training staffs. Inevitably, some managers are not as competent as others and personnel managers may sometimes have to deal with the consequences of managerial deficiencies such as poor standards of reporting, badly conducted appraisal interviews, neglect of subordinates' training and developmental needs etc.

Problems may regularly occur in dealing with individuals who inevitably have egocentric perceptions and naturally find it difficult to see the implications of the employment and development of human resources from the broader, organisational standpoint that the personnel manager has to take. The objectives of individuals and the organisation often do not coincide. Individuals may have different views of their own performance, potential and work from those held by organisational representatives. Because of the traditional concept of a career ladder individuals may have expectations that are impracticable, unrealistic and beyond the capacity of the organisation to satisfy. Personnel managers may experience some role conflict or ambiguity in carrying out their responsibilities as executive representatives of the employing organisation and, at the same time, being counsellors to individuals.

In order that the personnel department may carry out its responsibilities as effectively as possible, and thus minimise the kinds of problems described above, there are a number of basic requirements that need to be met in terms of the organisation of its work and the knowledge, skills and attitudes of its staff, i.e.

1. A hierarchical organisation of personnel staff, so that each is responsible for a group of employees, representing particular grades or employment types.

2. A manageable span of responsibility and control, enabling personnel staff to familiarise themselves with the personal details of the employees for whom they are responsible. Ideally, they should be able to know these individuals and their line managers personally. The system cannot be effective if a personnel manager has to look after very large numbers of employees who are little more than names on cards.

3. Full information about organisational policies and intentions and their implications for manpower planning.

4. Comprehensive and up-to-date information provided by job analysis in terms of job descriptions, job specifications and person specifications.

5. A comprehensive and accurate system of immediately retrievable information, including work histories, qualifications and aptitudes, terms and conditions of service, pay records, staff reports, performance appraisals, potential reviews, reward reviews, etc.

6. A policy and plan for providing career-development interviews, potential reviews, reward reviews, etc.

7. Close personal liaison with the line managers and their staffs. Personnel staff can best gain the credibility and respect that they need to do their work effectively through regular visits to work sites to gain first-hand information about people, their jobs and their problems.

8. Close personal liaison with the various union representatives in the organisation. Apart from their principal concern with pay and conditions, unions also have a strong interest in the development of the employees that they represent.

9. Specialist knowledge and skills, e.g.

(*i*) Employment legislation: an up-to-date knowledge of all recent statutes affecting employment and staff development.

(*ii*) Training: an extensive knowledge of all facilities provided by the employing organisation, external authorities and Industrial Training boards.

(*iii*) Interpersonal skills: personnel staff require a very high level of interpersonal skills in their informal relationships with a very wide variety of line managers and their staffs and in formal situations, such as those concerned with job analysis, recruitment and selection procedures, counselling interviews, career development and potential reviews.

THE ROLE OF TRAINING STAFF

Training and the role of trainers is described in detail in Chapter 13. Because of the crucial importance of training for developing an organisation's human resources, the training staff must obviously work in very close liaison with personnel staff. In some organisations the training staff are included as a branch of the Personnel Department, and the Head of the Training Division reports directly to the Chief Personnel Manager.

In short, the principal responsibility of the training staff is to supervise an effective system for:

1. Identifying the training needs of the organisation.

2. Seeing that those needs are met in a variety of ways by training at the work-place, by formal courses organised within the organisation or by formal courses arranged outside the organisation.

3. Acting as the organisation's link with external agencies and institutes in order to keep up to date with current best practice.

4. Acting as a focal point for ideas, and providing a means for exchanging ideas between the various divisions and branches of the organisation.

5. Providing advice and assistance to line managers in the design and implementation of work-place training e.g. coaching, open distance methods etc.

6. Providing centrally organised training for the organisation in subjects of common need e.g. management training, training of trainers.

7. Assessing the effectiveness of training and instituting the formal procedures for this to happen.

8. Initiating any changes that the assessment of effectiveness shows to be needed.

As with the personnel staff there are certain prerequisites for an effective contribution by the training staff to the employment and development of the organisation's human resources, i.e.

1. A high degree of professional knowledge based on work experience and specialist training. The training task should not be given to any employee in the organisation as a routine job, although this may occur because some organisations are short sighted in giving a low priority to this very important function.

2. Continuation training for training staff, especially in subjects such as the identification of needs, course-design, training methods, the use of resources and the validation and evaluation of training effectiveness.

3. Close liaison with line managers and personnel staff to identify the training and educational needs of the department to provide the necessary programmes and courses and to evaluate the effectiveness of these programmes and courses.

4. Close liaison with external authorities and institutions, where applicable, in order to maintain a continuous flow of information on training subjects, legislation, etc.

5. Comprehensive and up-to-date information provided by job analysis about job descriptions and job specifications. These are essential data for training staff as a basis for determining the job-related knowledge, skills and attitudes which need to be learned through training.

6. Accurate records showing the training courses taken by employees and their achievements.

THE ROLE OF LINE MANAGERS

The primary task of line managers is the achievement of the objectives and work output for which they are responsible. Since they can only do this by means of the collaborative knowledge and skills of their subordinate staffs, excessive task orientation, as research has regularly shown, is likely to be counter-productive. Line managers can promote the development of their employees in two ways: firstly, within their own work environment they should seek to provide as many opportunities as possible for individual growth by means of job experience and on-job training: secondly, within the larger environment inside and outside the organisation they need to encourage their subordinates to pursue all available opportunities for self-development. This requires liberal and far-sighted attitudes which are sometimes difficult to reconcile with the many pressures to fulfil short-term objectives.

Nevertheless, since line managers have a direct and immediate influence on all employees, they necessarily bear a major responsibility for the effective employment and development of an organisation's human resources. They can take certain positive steps to promote the achievement of this goal, i.e.

1. Creating an open, trusting (Theory Y) type of climate that encourages rather than hinders the effective employment and development of subordinates.

2. Delegating as much responsibility as possible to allow subordinates to learn from their own mistakes, to mature and to develop self-confidence.

3. Consulting regularly with subordinates about objectives and methods of improving the effectiveness of work and its environment.

4. Approaching the formal tasks of staff reporting and performance appraisal with the utmost preparation, care and conscientiousness.

5. Liaising continually with the personnel and training staffs to inform them of developments affecting jobs, employees, training and educational needs.

6. Being personally alert to current developments in managerial training and education and constantly developing their own knowledge and skills as managers.

THE ROLE OF INDIVIDUALS

So much attention is given to the importance of the roles of the personnel staff, line managers and training staff in the development of human resources that the responsibilities of the individual tend to be overlooked or not even acknowledged. Traditional attitudes have relegated individual employees to a passive state, in which they are seen mainly as material to be manipulated by the organisation's representatives. As a result, employees themselves have tended to become conditioned to this state. Evidence of this kind of conditioning is regularly reflected during counselling interviews when individual employees may reveal assumptions and expectations that the organisation is wholly responsible for their development.

However, conventional thinking which casts the organisation and its specialist representatives in the role of developers and the mass of employees as malleable material requires revision. A number of leading commentators on the management of people at work have made similar comments about this question. It is implicit in Douglas McGregor's Theory Y, and the same author has spoken elsewhere of the need for organisations to adopt what he describes as an 'agricultural' (i.e. growth) rather than a 'manufacturing' approach. Peter Drucker maintains that development can only be achieved through individual responsibility and initiative. What these and other authors are, in effect, saying is this: development, or learning, can only be achieved by individuals themselves.

The responsibility of the organisation is, therefore, similar to that of a good teacher in creating the right climate for growth and providing scope and opportunity for the self-development of its employees.

The model system which has been described above is applicable to the large organisations of the public and private sectors. It would

Line management	Personnel staff	Training staff
Supervision of work experience and on-job training. Conduct of performance appraisal and identification of employees' needs (experience and training). Recommendations for promotion, future employment and training. Conduct of reward reviews. Liaison with personnel and training staffs.	Supervision of policy and practice for: Manpower planning. Job analysis. Recruitment and selection. Induction. Performance appraisal Potential assessment. Reward reviews. Job evaluation. Pay and conditions. Retirement and redundancy. Discipline and inefficiency. Health and safety. Industrial relations. Employment law. Supervision of effective employment, career development of recruited staff, and promotion system. Liaison with line management and training staff.	Supervision and implementation of the training system, i.e. identification of needs, provision of required training (centrally, at workplace and externally), assessment of cost-effectiveness, coordination of organisational training effort, liaison with external training agencies, liaison with line management and personnel staff.

Fig. 11. Summary of main agents and responsibilities in a system for the employment and development of human resources.

necessarily be modified for smaller organisations where, for example, the personnel and training functions might be combined. Nevertheless, the basic principles of the system in terms of its elemental instruments and agents are generally valid. However, a sound framework can do no more than make effectiveness possible. Whether this is achieved in practice will always ultimately depend on the agents themselves, their understanding of its purpose, their commitment, conscientiousness and communication.

EMPLOYMENT AND DEVELOPMENT OF HUMAN RESOURCES IN PRACTICE

As we stated at the beginning of this chapter, the employment and development of human resources in practice is achieved by planned employment to enable employees to acquire the knowledge, skills and attitudes they require to perform work effectively through direct experience of various situations and by formal courses.

We have emphasised the importance of organisation and system to achieve this objective and we have indicated the roles and responsibilities of personnel managers, training staff, line managers and individual employees.

The development of staff by means of training will be discussed in detail in Chapter 13. We need now to consider the development of staff through employment and to discuss career development, management development and succession planning.

CAREER DEVELOPMENT

Much of the work of line managers, personnel and training staff to employ and develop the human resources of the organisation through a variety of job experiences and training is described as career development. However, the interaction of rapidly changing economic, technological and social forces is producing clearly visible effects upon working life, the most obvious of which is the change from the comparative stability of the old order to conditions which are much less certain or predictable. These changes are especially significant in their influence on ideas about careers in organisations.

The traditional view of a career rooted in earlier, more settled times and strongly reinforced by the educational system, is of a planned progression in working life, often within one organisation and always following, it seems, an upwards direction towards a summit which only a chosen few are destined to reach. In this process, the personnel staff are often seen as playing a role something like that of a guardian angel, and are expected to watch benevolently over the careers of each individual in the organisation. To many people, and especially those who work in bureaucratic organisations with rank-gradations, career development is very closely associated with promotion. Lack of promotion, therefore, is easily interpreted by employees as a failure or a lack of esteem on the part of their employers. Reassuring comments by line managers or personnel staff during counselling interviews that an individual's contributions are highly valued tend to cut little ice, unless accompanied by more tangible evidence of appreciation. There is convincing evidence from the data of research into career development schemes that the difficulties which arise from employees' expectations, based on the traditional concept, are further aggravated by the use of the term 'career development', which is commonly used in many organisations.

No single term can be entirely satisfactory, but the term 'Human Resources Development' seems as suitable as any as an indication of an organisation's intentions to provide opportunities for developing for all of its employees.

Contemporary forces of change and instability are affecting the traditional concept of an organisational career from two points of view. The economic and technological influences on the uses of requirements for manpower are making it increasingly difficult for organisations to make predictions and plans about careers in the traditional sense. At the same time, younger generations are tending to show much more mobility in their attitudes to employment. The thought of a gold watch at the end of forty or fifty years' service with one employer has become a daunting or even ludicrous prospect. It is becoming more and more evident that organisations need a radical revision of thinking about career paths. Because of the uncertainty of the future, an unprecedented level of imagination and flexibility will be required to break with long-established traditions in order to plan careers and staff-development programmes that are appropriate to the conditions of rapid and fundamental change. The subject has already begun to attract serious study and a number of interesting ideas are being proposed, for example: career patterns may be planned that follow horizontal as well as upward-vertical directions and do not imply promotion to managerial responsibilities as the main means of reward; the possibilities of much more interchange of staff between departments and organisations and of crossing hitherto sacrosanct professional boundaries need to be explored and imaginatively considered; staff-development programmes need to concentrate more than ever on providing a broad basis that will equip people to cope with the problems of rapid change and with the unforeseen complexities of an unstable future.

MANAGEMENT DEVELOPMENT AND SUCCESSION PLANNING

We have emphasised throughout that organisational effectiveness greatly depends on human resources and the planning and practices needed to make the best use of these resources in the interests of employers and employees alike. However, managerial staff need particular attention because of their obvious importance to the ultimate effectiveness of organisations. Organisations need, there-fore, to take conscious measures to ensure that managerial talents are constantly developed and the stream of managerial ability leading to the senior posts does not dry up.

The point has already been made that people are trained and developed at work in two ways—by work experience and by formal training. For the moment it is enough to say that, although formal training, provided that it is properly designed, is initially important for developing managerial abilities, people learn to manage mainly through actual practice i.e. through the experience of varying situations, from mistakes and from observing and internalising the behaviour of others. The organisation cannot control individual learning, which depends upon a range of difficult personal factors, but it can and should take conscious measures to ensure that its managers are provided through career planning with as much variety of learning experience and opportunities as are compatible with organisational needs to fulfil specific tasks.

Apart from the general need to train and develop managers in this way, organisations need to plan for succession. There will always be a constant flow of managers out of the organisation caused by retirements as planned, premature retirements, unexpected deaths and, of course, by people leaving to join other organisations. Other vacancies may occur when new managerial positions are created because of changes in policy and objectives or by expansion of activities.

The Glossary of Training Terms issued by the ministry of Labour in 1967 provides a useful and comprehensive definition of management development i.e. 'the systematic process of developing effective managers at all levels to meet the requirements of an organisation, involving the analysis of present and future management needs, assessing the existing and potential skills of managers, and devising the best means to meet these requirements.' The particular value of this definition lies in its emphasis on the need for a system and all that this implies in terms of positive action to develop managerial staff and to plan for succession i.e.

1. Commitment by senior management and the formulation of policy.

2. Effective manpower planning.

3. Effective formal schemes for career development, and the assessment of performance and potential.

4. Effective training based on the concept of a Systems Approach to Training.

5. The collaboration of managerial, personnel and training staffs.

QUESTIONS

1. How may work-organisations make best use of their human resources?

2. (a) Who are the main agents in the process of employing and developing human resources?
   (b) What are the responsibilities of each?

3. In broad terms how should the Personnel Department be organised to carry out the task of effectively employing and developing human resources?

4. (a) How would you define management development and succession planning?
   (b) What are the requirements for an effective system?

11

Induction

THE INDUCTION CRISIS

Its Nature

The induction of new employees into an organisation is such an important part of the management of people at work that it merits separate and special consideration. There is good evidence that the subject seldom receives the very careful attention that it truly needs by employing organisations. Regular analyses of the statistics of labour turnover often show losses during the first year of employment that should be considered alarming. The wastage in financial and human terms needs no elaboration. Undoubtedly, a portion of the blame can be attributed to faulty recruitment and selection procedures. Equally certainly, the reasons why so many people leave organisations shortly after joining them are connected with the treatment they receive from their employers during this initial phase of employment. This is not to say that too many organisations are treating newly recruited employees badly. The sin is more one of omission than commission. In other words, the problems of social adjustment that newcomers have to face are simply not always appreciated or sympathetically handled. This may seem surprising since all human beings at some time in their lives experience loneliness and a sense of disorientation when finding themselves in a new and unfamiliar environment. It starts at a very early age when we face the first day at school and continues throughout life, whenever we move from one place of learning or from one job to another. Age and maturity do not necessarily make the experience progressively easier.

Because of the rigours of contemporary living, stress has become a subject that is receiving increasing attention. It is interesting to note that where research has produced data on the various factors that cause stress, a change of job receives a high weighting. Thus, the early phase in a new job is well known to be a stressful period both from personal experience and from the evidence of research data, and yet organisations continue to tolerate high rates of labour turnover and often do not seem to be able to deal effectively with a problem which sociologists have described as 'the induction crisis'. Apart from the effect that a lack of attention to new staff has upon turnover, the effect on those who remain is by no means negligible in terms of motivation. If employers wish to develop well-motivated staffs, it is most important that they should demonstrate by their actions from the very outset of their employees' engagements that they are caring organisations, who place a very high value on their human resources.

Its causes

It could be said that the assistance of the behavioural sciences is not necessary to understand why people have a problem when they join new work organisations. The cause can readily be ascribed to the strangeness of a new environment, which is an inevitable discomfort that everybody has to face and accept, and which will pass with time. It is probably this kind of reasoning that lies behind the failure of many organisations to pursue the causes of the problem more deeply and to find effective remedies. People taking up new employment are clearly in a position of particular insecurity. The continuity of their lives has been broken for the moment and they are making a fresh start in a situation in which they have no previous history. In general, their past achievements tend to count for little in the new work environment and they have to prove themselves anew professionally and socially. Most of these difficulties stem from well-established phenomena of group and organisational behaviour, and especially from factors of the following kind:

1. Organisations and groups develop norms of acceptable and expected behaviour of their members. Newcomers have to learn what these are and to accept and internalise them before they become accepted members of groups. These norms may be very different from those of the previous groups which the newcomers have recently left and may make the process of adaptation more difficult.

2. Group cohesiveness does not always operate in productive directions. It may also be employed antagonistically towards other groups or individuals who are perceived as non-conformist or deviant. Newcomers may be perceived as threats to groups for various reasons and they may experience difficulties in gaining acceptance.

3. The psychological contract may often be a source of difficulty in the induction phase. As we have seen earlier, apart from the formal contract agreed between employing organisations and individual employees about the hire and rewarding of labour, both have expectations about each others' behaviour that are not formally prescribed. For example, new employees may regard a sympathetic, democratic style of management as their basic right. If, however, they encounter unexpectedly authoritarian styles, they may believe that they have been somehow deceived by their new employers, although

there is nothing in the formal contract about the styles of management that may be adopted.

THE ORGANISATION'S RESPONSIBILITIES FOR INDUCTION

To mitigate the induction crisis, to help new employees to adjust to their new surroundings, to gain their confidence and commitment and to avoid costly levels of labour turnover require positive attitudes and actions on the part of employing organisations, based on an awareness that:

1. The induction phase is much more critical and stressful than it is often recognised to be.

2. The length of the critical phase will naturally vary and depend on the adaptability of each individual, but it may well last for many months.

3. The causes contributing to the general problem may be found in the psychological and sociological factors affecting organisational and group behaviour, as described above.

4. The induction phase needs to be very carefully planned and supervised, as the first stage in staff development.

THE INDUCTION PROGRAMME

The induction of new employees has to be regarded as a comprehensive and systematic programme continuously monitored and evaluated. Too often it has come to mean little more than a day or two set aside, during which time new employees may have interviews, attend short courses, listen to talks about the organisation, receive a quantity of literature, be taken on quick guided tours to glimpse the various sections of the organisation and to meet a variety of people. This is the kind of programme that might be prepared for visitors with limited time available, rather than for people who presumably are expected to stay with the organisation for several years. Induction arrangements of this kind could well do as much, if not more, harm than good. When a mass of information—much of which may be unnecessary—is crammed into a very short space of time, and many of the questions on which newcomers need reassurance are left unanswered, it is likely that initial feelings of confusion, inadequacy and insecurity will be increased rather than allayed.

For the induction programme to be comprehensive and effective the employing organisation has to begin with a clear view of what it intends to achieve as a basis for designing the programme. This means that an aim and a set of objectives have to be produced similar to the example described below.

Aim

That new employees become integrated as soon as possible functionally and socially into the organisation and its environment.

Objectives

1. That they should understand the function, aim and objectives of the organisation as a whole.

2. That they should understand the specific objectives to be achieved by their sections and their personal responsibilities and expected contributions to the achievement of these objectives.

3. That the necessary initial training and work experience should be planned to enable them to fulfil these responsibilities.

4. That comprehensive information should be provided on the following subjects: conditions of employment; working arrangements; the system of personnel management and especially the arrangements and opportunities for staff development; the whole range of facilities provided for the benefit, welfare and recreation of employees.

5. That positive measures should be taken to facilitate the social adaptation of new employees.

6. That the induction programme should be continuously monitored and its total effectiveness assessed.

The main responsibility for implementing, supervising and evaluating induction lies with the responsible line and personnel managers. In fact, the induction phase should be regarded as the first stage in the process of staff development in which line and personnel managers have complementary parts to play. The contents and methods of induction programmes will necessarily vary considerably in their details, but will need to include the following main elements in order to meet the prescribed objectives:

Interviews

New employees need to be formally interviewed by the responsible line and personnel managers at the beginning and end of the induction programme. Initial interviews serve the following purposes:

1. To explain the aim, objectives and plan of the induction programme itself.

2. To provide the comprehensive information indicated in the programme objectives.

3. To inform new employees where and how they may obtain assistance whenever this is needed.

4. To encourage them to consult their supervisors, line managers or personnel managers if any problems arise.

5. To ascertain whether there are any initial problems or queries that need to be dealt with and generally to reassure.

In some organisations, the specific jobs to which new employees will be assigned are covered in the recruitment selection process. In others, this is left for individual departments, branches or sections to decide. In those situations, a placement interview will be needed in which the line or personnel manager will discuss in detail with new employees the question of the jobs to which they should be allocated.

The next formal interview that is required in the induction programme will probably take place towards the end of the first year of employment, when line and personnel managers assess progress to date, prospects for the future and the need for any changes in existing arrangements. Apart from the formal interviews, informal discussions may take place between management representatives and new employees at any time as required to check progress or to deal with difficulties that may arise. It is especially important that the employees themselves should not feel inhibited in discussing any problems that they may encounter with their superiors or responsible line or personnel managers.

Training

Induction training is mainly vocational and designed in order to give new employees the skills and knowledge required for productive employment. It may take the form of short full-time courses or very much longer programmes where a high level of performance is essential, such as, for example, engineering apprenticeships, flying training, etc. Sometimes induction training is given on the job itself. More often than not the programme is a combination of both forms of training.

Work Experience

This covers a very wide range of possibilities and is a matter for each organisation to decide. Whether new employees remain with one occupation or are rotated to meet particular requirements of experience, an imaginative approach is necessary to widen new employees' knowledge of their organisational environment as much as possible. This could include, for example, a schedule of visits or short attachments to other units. Increased knowledge of the organisation will help to develop confidence and is a significant means of stimulating interest and motivation.

Social Adaptation

As we have already seen, this is a particular source of difficulty in the induction phase. Managers cannot expect to control the subtle interplay of intra-group relationships, but they need to develop a psychological awareness of group and individual behaviour in order to assist their new staffs to settle down. This requires a close knowledge of the individual members of their groups, the ability to anticipate where inter-personal difficulties could arise and how the social forces within the group could be used to advantage. In this way, the varied experience and strengths of the different members of the group may be used skilfully to help newcomers to adapt. The more members of the group that can be usefully involved in this process the better.

Finally, because of the complexity and variability of the initial phase of employment from the individual's point of view, employers cannot

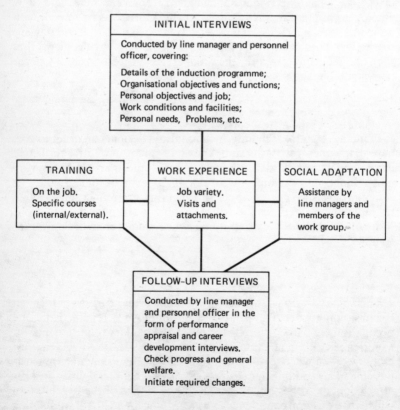

Fig. 12. Summary of the main elements in an induction system.

naively assume that a formally planned induction programme coincides with each individual employee's induction phase, as though the programme covers a fixed period at the end of which new employees cross, as it were, a boundary that separates the novitiate from full membership. The process of socialisation is infinitely subtle and varies with each individual. Although new employees may often undertake parts of an induction programme together, such as, for example, formal courses, their induction into the organisation still has to be regarded as an essentially individual process. Programmes, therefore, need to be very flexible and to take full account of individual differences and needs.

QUESTIONS

1. What is meant by the induction crisis?

2. What are its causes?

3. What steps can an organisation take to mitigate the induction crisis?

4. What should be the aim and objectives of an induction programme?

5. What are the main elements that should be included in an induction programme? Give a brief description of each.

12

Staff Assessment

THE BASIS OF A SYSTEM

Assessing the work of employees is a key function in personnel management. It is needed for the following purposes:

1. To determine how far people are meeting the requirements of their jobs and whether any changes or action are indicated for the future.
2. To determine developmental needs in terms of work experience and training.
3. To identify people who have potential to take on wider responsibilities.
4. To provide a basis for assessing and allocating pay increments and similar rewards.
5. Generally to improve communication between managers and their staff.
6. Generally to develop motivation and commitment by providing regular and scheduled opportunities for feedback on performance and discussions of work, problems, suggestions for improvement, prospects etc.

Because assessments of this kind involve human judgement in which the last word invariably rests with the management, problems are inherent in any system for assessing the work of employees, e.g. the basic subjectivity of human judgement, the natural reluctance of people to be judged by others, feelings of injustice and so on. Much depends, therefore, on the system and the underlying philosophy that work-organisations reveal in their approach to this very important task. Details of systems will naturally vary with different organisations, but the following requirements for effectiveness are general. The systems should:

1. Aim to improve the total effectiveness of the organisation.
2. Be comprehensive, covering all aspects of work performance and needs for work experience, training, development, advancement and fair rewards.
3. Be uniformly and fairly applied throughout the organisation.
4. Be published in detail in unequivocal language so that all

employees understand exactly what is intended and required, and hopefully may accept the system as fair.

5. Be based on formal arrangements, designed to achieve the effective collaboration of personnel staff, line managers and their staffs.

6. Include provisions for scheduled, open and constructive discussions between managerial staff and individual employees.

7. Include provisions for regular review and possible revision of the system.

8. Include provisions for training all personnel staff and line managers in the administrative and interpersonal knowledge, skills and attitudes, needed to make the system effective.

In practice, the assessment of the work of employees involves three types of review i.e. performance appraisal, potential and reward reviews. These reviews are closely inter-related and linked by the main theme, but in detail they serve different purposes, require different methods and cannot be undertaken by one manager. Assessing work performance of an employee in a particular job is clearly the responsibility of the line manager concerned. Reviewing potential has long-term implications. It needs to take into account all available information about performance over a period of time in a variety of jobs and may require the use of specialist techniques and methods for the assessment of potential. It has to be seen in an organisational context, related to organisational needs, objectives and opportunities. For these reasons it is a task to be organised by the personnel staff, who by definition have an overall view of the organisational personnel function. Reward reviews would normally be carried out by line management, but could well involve personnel staff.

We can now discuss in turn and in detail these three aspects of the assessments of staff.

PERFORMANCE APPRAISAL

Performance appraisal will now be discussed in detail on the basis of the following related questions—what is performance appraisal and why is it necessary? In what form has performance appraisal developed in organisational practice and what has been learned from this experience? What are the general requirements for an effective system in practice? What are the problems of performance appraisal and why is training essential to mitigate them?

The 'what and why' of performance appraisal

Performance appraisal is a periodic, formal assessment of work achievement as a basis for future actions and decisions. Formal schemes of performance appraisal are sometimes regarded with suspicion or disdain by both managers and their staffs.

Managers sometimes object to formal schemes, claiming that they are continuously appraising their staffs and that valuable time is wasted in implementing schemes imposed by the personnel department, which invariably necessitate much paperwork and scheduled interviewing. Employees and their union representatives may sometimes object to formal schemes of performance appraisal on the grounds that they are another means for furthering the exercise of management prerogative. As we shall be discussing later, it all depends on the underlying philosophy and approach that is applied in practice.

However, there can surely be no tenable arguments against performance appraisal in principle. It is an essential stage in the general process of systematic management, which is based on fundamental questions, such as:

What aim has to be achieved?
How can the aim be best achieved?
Has the aim been achieved?
If not why not?
What changes and actions need to be made and taken in the future?

These questions apply to organisations as a whole, sub-groups and individual employees alike. The last three questions describe performance appraisal and are essential elements of any work-system. Appraisal of performance is taking place informally all the time. Managers are assessing their staffs; individuals are assessing themselves and their colleagues. Continuous appraisal of performance by managers and by individuals of themselves is essential to effectiveness. Formal systems of appraisal are not intended to replace, but to complement the informal process. They are also essential for the following reasons:

1. Periodically to take stock of progress and needs, and to make positive plans for the future.
2. To ensure that all appraisers of performance in the organisation have a similarly disciplined approach to the task.
3. To ensure that all employees receive similar treatment and opportunities, provided by a formal, organisational system of performance appraisal.

The development of performance appraisal in practice

Historically, performance appraisal in this country originated mainly in the public sector of employment—the Armed Forces and the Civil Service. Now, formal schemes of performance appraisal are widely used in the majority of work-organisations in both public and private sectors. The details of these formal schemes vary considerably depending on the purposes and preferences of individual work-organisations. These differences are reflected in terms of the format of reports, degrees of confidentiality and openness, the appraisers, the level of participation by those being appraised, and the nature of appraisal discussions between those appraising and those being appraised.

In the development of schemes of performance appraisal two broad approaches are discernible. For convenience of description and comparison we may label them as Theory X and Theory Y, after McGregor's thesis on managerial attitudes. The essential difference between the two is this: in a Theory X scheme managers produce assessment reports on their subordinates; in a Theory Y scheme the assessment report is the product of joint discussion between managers and their sub ordinates. A Theory X performance appraisal scheme has the following typical features:

1. Managers are the sole judges of work-performance.

2. There is an apparent confidence in the manager's ability and authority to judge and, therefore, no training is given to appraisers for this task.

3. Assessments are based on numerical ratings of abstract qualities e.g. initiative, drive, energy, reliability, intelligence, loyalty, integrity etc.

4. The appraisal includes a narrative report made by the manager not divulged to the appraised subordinate and open to personal bias, to misunderstandings of meanings and sometimes even to sarcasm.

5. There are no formal provisions for feedback to, or discussions with, those being appraised.

6. The main purpose of the appraisal is to identify those seen by management as good or bad performers.

7. There is little or no attention paid to the developmental needs of employees.

A Theory Y form of performance appraisal has objectives which are quite different from the Theory X approach i.e.

1. Identification and remedying of problems in the job itself.

2. Identification of strengths and weaknesses in performance as a basis for future action.

3. Identification of needs for training, development, further work experience, suitability for advancement.

4. Development of constructive manager/subordinate relationships.

5. Development of individuals' capacity for self-assessment and

self-awareness, for seeking ways to solve their own problems and to find ways for self-improvement.

The Theory X approach to performance appraisal in its extreme form, as described above, was prevalent in earlier times when styles of management were generally more authoritarian than they are now. In recent years there has been a visible move towards the Theory Y end of the continuum. Nevertheless, vestiges of a Theory X approach to performance appraisal still survive. In some organisations it remains very much in its traditional form. In others, whilst their schemes may reveal noticeable changes in the direction of a Theory Y approach, e.g. more openness in discussion between managers and their subordinates, they still retain some of the essential features of Theory X attitudes. For example, in spite of the demonstrable and proven problems of defining and measuring abstract qualities and the obvious advantages of concentrating on the objectives and tasks of the job, some managers are still required in some schemes to give marks for abstract traits (e.g. initiative, reliability etc.). Again, although open discussions may be held between managers and their subordinates, these may in practice amount to little more than attempts by managers to justify their own views and marks, which have already been written into reports and are not likely to be affected by anything that appraised subordinates may say during discussions.

When all is said and done, the main difference between these extremes is the limitations of the one and the opportunities afforded by the other. All the evidence of academic research and practical experience strongly emphasises the advantages and potential effectiveness of performance appraisal schemes based on a Theory Y approach. We can now examine in more detail the general requirements for an effective scheme, which applies this philosophy in practice.

The requirements for an effective system of performance appraisal

1. The first step is to define the requirements for effective performance of the job, which need to be discussed and agreed by managers and their staffs. This is an essential prerequisite, without which performance appraisal has no point.

2. In the course of work managers and their staffs should regularly discuss the job and make informal appraisals of progress and needs. There is no need to make copious notes, but it is very important for both to keep a record of main events, issues raised, problems, decisions etc.

3. When the time comes for the formal periodic appraisal, the

manager and member of staff being appraised need to meet to
determine the time and place and the agenda of the discussion.

4. The details of the agenda will naturally vary with different
situations, but the broad outlines for the performance appraisal should
cover the following headings and questions:

(a) *The job*

The job description, objectives, component tasks, methods and
resources.

Are these satisfactory?

If not, why not?

What changes are indicated?

What precise action is recommended by whom, how and why?

(b) *Job performance*

What are the objectives that have to be met and the tasks to be
fulfilled?

Have these been achieved?

What is the actual evidence from work-performance, indicating
success or failure?

What are the reasons for success or failure?

How far have any failures been within or outside the job-holder's
control?

What does the evidence of past performance show about
strengths and weaknesses in the knowledge, skills and attitudes
of the job holder?

What precise action is recommended—by whom, how and
when—to build on strengths, to remedy weaknesses and to
develop the individual by means of training and further work
experience?

(c) *Summary of action proposed*

What action has been agreed to be taken by whom, how and
when?

5. Before the appraisal discussion takes place the manager and
individual member of staff separately work through these headings to
answer the main questions, using any notes that they have made
throughout the period under review. This exercise is the crux of the
process and of the philosophy underlying this approach, because it
emphasises and concentrates on:

(*i*) Joint-assessment, involving both managers and their staffs.

(*ii*) The key issues—the job, performance and future needs.

(*iii*) Observable, measurable evidence from actual work rather than
abstract qualities.

6. Having made their separate notes and assessments, the manager
and the individual meet to compare their views, to find out how far
they agree or disagree, to explore reasons for any disagreement, to try
to find constructive solutions and to decide what action is needed for

the future to resolve problems in the job and to meet the individual's development needs.

7. The manager leads the discussion and is, therefore, responsible for seeing that it systematically follows the agenda in order to achieve its purpose. At the same time, it is very important that it should be conducted in an atmosphere which is as informal and relaxed as possible. The manner in which the discussion is conducted is extremely important. The manager is 'in the chair', but if performance appraisal is intended to help to improve performance, to develop individuals and to improve communication, then the discussion needs to be an open exchange of perceptions and not a managerial monologue. Thus managers should try to find out how far perceptions coincide, where and how they differ, and what any differences of views might imply; they need to stimulate people to think, to encourage them to analyse, to become more self-aware and to put forward constructive proposals. In practice this requires managers to start by asking questions and listening. Having noted what those being appraised have to say, they are then better placed to make helpful comments, to give their own views and any advice or instructions that they think appropriate.

8. At the end of the discussion the main points covered and the action agreed need to be summarised, recorded and above all, followed up. These decisions will be the first items on the agenda of any subsequent appraisal discussions.

Forms for performance appraisal

The headings and questions described above need to be incorporated in an official appraisal form so that everybody in the organisation understands the requirements of the system and follows a similar approach and standards in practice. The details of the form used for performance appraisal are a matter for each organisation to decide for itself. In general, this form should be simple, easy to understand and accompanied as necessary by notes explaining organisational policy, purpose and practice.

Problems of performance appraisal

Whatever scheme of performance appraisal is used there will always be fundamental, inevitable problems. In essence, performance appraisal is a human judgement which, as we have already seen when considering personal selection, suffers from problems of reliability and validity. Human judgement depends on the unique genetic and environmental influences that form each individual's values, attitudes, expectations and perceptions. Inevitably, therefore, there may be differences of view of each of the basic questions of performance appraisal, and this complicates the whole process from start to finish, i.e.:

What does the job require?

What does the job holder have to do to perform effectively?

What evidence from work performance would indicate effective performance?

What does the assessment of evidence of performance indicate about future action required?

These questions are systematically interdependent. Each requires a judgement that affects the next question in the sequence.

The major criticism of the Theory X approach is that it exacerbates the fundamental problems by requiring managers to judge in isolation, to give numerical assessments of abstract qualities and produce subjective narrative reports. But a Theory Y approach cannot eradicate these fundamental problems. Its virtue is that it may mitigate some of the worst effects, because it concentrates on the evidence of actual performance, requires a systematic, disciplined approach and opens up judgements to analysis and discussion.

Although the mechanism for an open discussion and frank exchange of views is established by the use of a Theory Y approach, this still does not mean that all kinds of problems may not occur because of personality differences and conflicts, emotions and a lack of communicational and interpersonal skills. Because these problems are essentially human, they cannot be eliminated but they can be better understood and reduced by means of training.

The need for training

Because a system is only as good as the people who operate it, managerial staff of all levels need training in performance appraisal to make it effective in practice.

The objectives of training should be:

1. To standardise practice.

2. To explain the organisation's system and give opportunities for staff to discuss and question.

3. To identify general requirements for effective practice.

4. To provide practice in the important skills, i.e. assessing and discussing performance, as a basis for further individual development.

Details of potentially effective training exercises are outside the scope of this chapter. However, they should simulate reality as closely as possible in the following ways by requiring trainee managers:

1. To make assessments of real, but unidentified job-holders, so that the discipline of the appraiser's approach may be analysed, i.e. defining criteria for effective performance, making sound and fair conclusions.

2. To carry out role-play discussions, based on credible scripts, in

order to practise the general performance appraisal agenda described earlier and the necessary communicational skills.

The learning opportunities provided by simulated role-play exercises will be significantly enhanced by the use of CCTV recordings for purposes of analysis and discussion.

THE ASSESSMENT OF POTENTIAL

In practice, the review of potential serves two main purposes, namely, the identification of those who appear to be suitable for promotion, and the assessment of the general potential of individuals in order to decide how their abilities may best be employed in the interests of the organisation and of the individuals themselves.

Identifying Staff for Promotion

The selection of staff for promotion is, in essence, the same process as the selection of new employees. Everything that has already been said about the problems of selecting new employees, the limitations of predictive methods and especially the interview, apply equally here and need not be repeated in detail. A job vacancy has to be filled and there is usually a field of several candidates; the requirements and criteria for effective performance in the higher level need to be defined in exactly the same way as for recruitment selection; the task of the selectors is to predict likely behaviour in a new job situation. However, there are some significant differences between the recruitment and promotion situations. In the former situation the employing organisation is dealing with unknown people. When selecting staff for promotion, it already has a store of information both formal and informal about candidates. Furthermore, there are important areas in which prediction is not necessary, namely compatibility with the organisational culture and relationships with colleagues. Nevertheless, examples regularly occur of employees who are very effective at one level, but prove to be far less successful at a higher level, as if to confirm the well known Peter Principle that people eventually find their own level of competence/incompetence. Such promotional failures seem to be rather more frequent in situations where a capable specialist transfers to what is essentially a managerial job. The problem is noticeable, for example, in educational and academic posts, where appointing authorities seem to be prone to converting able teachers into incompetent heads of departments, because apparently they fail to understand that managerial skills are just as important in these posts as professional knowledge and ability.

The methods adopted by organisations for the promotion of staff vary considerably. In some, promotions may be made virtually by the unilateral decision of heads of companies or departments on the basis of demonstrated work competence. This method is more likely to occur in a business enterprise. In the public sector of employment and a number of large industrial and commercial concerns there are formal procedures for selecting candidates for promotion. Since most of these also have a system of formal periodic staff reports, these are used as the basis for decisions about promotion. They provide a total picture derived from a series of reports on performance in a variety of jobs and situations by a range of managers. Since staff reports also suffer from the same difficulties of subjectivity as the selection procedures themselves, the problem is, in fact, compounded—hence the importance of ensuring that the system of staff reporting is as sound as it can humanely be.

When staff reports are used as the basis of a formal process of promotion, two methods are possible. Some organisations hold promotion boards, which select candidates by interview in a process very similar to the recruitment-selection procedures. Others convene promotion boards which select candidates on the evidence of reports without interviewing candidates. The interview method is claimed to be fairer, because candidates are subjected to a further examination of their worth by a panel of experienced managers and are given a chance at the same time to advance their own claims for promotion personally. Nevertheless, cogent arguments can be put forward against the use of the interview for promotion-selection purposes. In this situation, it can very easily be misused as a form of examination, purporting to test areas such as presence of mind, reasoning powers, appearance and bearing, knowledge of current affairs, etc., despite the fact that the invalidity of the interview for tests of this kind has been well established. This explains why some candidates, extremely well rated by their managers, still fail to be promoted because 'they are unimpressive in front of the board'. Thus, a mythology is created about the kind of interview behaviour that is likely to be successful with boards. But organisations already have all the available evidence about work performance of their employees from the accumulated records of past performance. There is little that an interview can add to this information except subjective impressions about the way the candidates behave at an interview. What is to be said of a situation where a series of managers have independently rated a particular employee as fit for promotion on the evidence of several years' continuously competent performance, who is then rated as unfit by a promotion board on the evidence of a forty-five minute interview? It is perfectly true, of course, that rejection by a promotion board does not necessarily mean that a candidate is not fit for promotion. More often than not there are more candidates than there are vacancies to be filled, so that one of a board's main tasks is to produce an order of merit. Inevitably, some suitable candidates will not be promoted. Nevertheless, some organisations have shown that the task of assessment can just as easily be carried out by a panel of managers, chosen to provide as fair a cross-section of views as possible, without interviewing the candidates themselves. As with the recruitment-selection interview, if an organisation decides that further, predictive evidence is needed to assess their employees' suitability to fill posts of higher responsibility beyond what is already available from personnel records, then it needs to devise job-related tests which can be shown to be reliable and valid in providing this additional information.

Assessing General Potential

The essence of this task is to assess the types and levels of work that employees have the potential to perform. This assessment has to be based on the evidence available from personnel records, staff reports, performance reviews, training and education records, which are centrally maintained and co-ordinated by the personnel staff. These records cover a period of several years and extend beyond the confines of the present job. Since the assessment of the general potential of employees is set in the wider organisational context, it is a task which is especially appropriate to the personnel managers responsible for supervising the career paths of individual employees. In some organisations, the review is carried out jointly by the responsible personnel and line managers. This method is not only feasible, but could also be seen as a logical and sensible method. However, much depends upon the nature and culture of the organisation.

Attention has already been drawn to the responsibilities of individuals for self-development, but people cannot take a detached view of their own potential. They may easily overestimate or underestimate their own capabilities. Personal interests, past conditioning or narrowness of experience may also play a part in restricting individuals' capacities to assess their own potential. Nevertheless, it is very important that individual employees be fully consulted in any review of their potential in order to help them to see themselves as the organisation sees them, to enable them to put forward their own views and wishes, and to develop their commitment to any plans for their future employment. This can be achieved by means of a schedule of career-development interviews, in which personnel staff use the history of past assessments and the career record to date as a basis for joint consultation with employees about their potential and the opportunities for employment and development that are or may become available.

The Potential Review/Career-Development Interview

This interview is very similar to the performance-appraisal interview in terms of the basic framework and general approach that are appropriate to the situation. The three phases of the interview should be planned and conducted in the following way.

Pre-Interview Preparation

1. As with the performance appraisal, members of staff to be interviewed need to prepare themselves by considering their personal career objectives and by analysing their own strengths and weaknesses, training and educational needs and employment preferences.

2. Personnel managers conducting the interviews need to study the relevant personnel records, i.e. career histories, staff reports, performance-appraisal summaries, and training records. They will usually need to consult responsible line managers to ascertain whether any changes have occurred since the last report and generally to amplify information about current performance and potential.

3. Finally, they will need to determine the specific objectives to be achieved in each particular situation.

The Interview

1. The interview should be based on the following broad plan:
   (*i*) Explanation of the general purpose and scope of the interview.
  (*ii*) Discussion of the individual's career to date in terms of perceived strengths and weaknesses, likes and dislikes, employment preferences.
 (*iii*) Discussion of the future in terms of the potential revealed by past performance, the opportunities that the organisation is able to provide, and the individual's needs for training and education.
  (*iv*) Summary of agreements about action required.

2. Like the performance appraisal this is essentially a problem-solving, counselling situation and the prerequisites for its successful conduct are basically the same. However, there are some special aspects of this interview which are worth stressing:
   (*i*) Because of the fundamental problems associated with the egocentricity of human perception and individuals' natural pursuit of personal objectives, the essential task of the personnel staff in this review is not only to assess potential, but also to help to reconcile organisational and individual perspectives.
  (*ii*) Therefore, because a joint commitment and agreement between employer and employee is necessary for success, the general

purpose to be pursued by personnel staff in this kind of review is to help individuals in the following ways: to make as realistic an assessment as possible of themselves and their own potential; to adopt realistic expectations of what is achievable and available; to understand that, whilst the organisation has a duty and a vested interest to provide all possible opportunities for growth, individuals must accept responsibility for personal development.

Post-Interview Action

1. Immediately after the interview personnel managers should produce a brief summarised report of the interview, the main points of discussion and agreements reached for retention in the personnel records.

2. Line managers should be consulted on points arising from the interview that may affect them, e.g. misperceptions revealed by their subordinate staffs, firm proposals for their career development in terms of employment experience, training, education, etc.

3. Any action promised by personnel managers must be conscientiously fulfilled.

Assessment Centres

In recent times, increasing use has been made of assessment centres for assessing the potential of staff. They have been used rather more in the USA than elsewhere and especially for identifying younger managers with the apparent potential effectively to fill senior appointments, the so-called 'high-flyers'. In large organisations these centres may be internal units. More often they are external, independent and used by a variety of organisations. They are staffed by trained assessors, who are usually psychologists specialising in this field. The methods used for assessment include group and individual psychometric tests, similar to those introduced into personnel selection by the War Office Selection Boards. Assessment centres have the advantage that they are more objective than conventional methods and are supervised by specialists. There are possible disadvantages, however, in their detachment from the work situation and organisational culture, and in any early predictions about the potential of young managers to rise to the top, because assessments of this kind tend to become self-fulfilling prophecies. Nevertheless, the basic idea is promising and needs to be developed, because it represents an attempt to assess the potential of employees with much more system and skill than is customary. At the same time, such centres should be concerned with the potential of all staff or at least all managerial and supervisory staff. If they are seen as a system for the early identification of an elitist band of 'crown princes', then the ultimate loss to the organisation through the establishment of win-lose groups and the possible demotivation and disaffection of the majority of its employees could far outweigh any benefits.

REWARD REVIEWS

Reward Reviews are used when salary increments, bonuses and similar forms of additional incentives are awarded on the basis of an individual's performance. Although, in the main, the same basic information is used in all forms of performance appraisal reviews, performance and reward reviews serve different purposes and should be regarded, therefore, as distinct processes, separated in time. If the two were to be combined, then the purpose of the performance appraisal will inevitably become influenced and confused by considerations of evaluating performance in financial terms.

In the reward review, managers should concentrate on quantitatively assessing the amount of increment or bonus that they consider the work of their subordinates deserves. Because of its nature and purpose, the reward review will not require the same kind of counselling approach as performance and potential reviews. At the same time, it needs to be something more than a straightforward announcement of a reward decision by a manager to a subordinate. If this were so, then the information could just as well be passed on in writing.

To be effective the reward review needs to be conducted according to the pattern described below:

Pre-Review Preparation

1. Information should be collected on which to base reward decisions that are within the manager's personal discretion, such as, for example, the distribution of a particular type of reward amongst similar groups, the numbers of other employees receiving a particular type of reward and the basic considerations that influence decisions (e.g. age, length of service, nature of duties, other reasons).

2. Each individual subordinate's salary and reward cards should be studied to ascertain what has been awarded in the past, reasons for awards and other special considerations to be taken into account.

3. An individual's performance should be compared with other members of the group performing similar work in order to decide levels of awards.

4. The personnel department should be consulted for any specialist advice required or in any cases of difficulty.

The Interview

1. The interview should begin with an explanation of the purpose and scope of the interview.

2. The next step is to ascertain the subordinate's expectations, needs and feelings about rewards, taking into account the wide possible range of individual differences on this question.

3. The rationale of the reward should be discussed and explained to prepare the subordinate for the reward decision.

4. The manager should ensure that as far as possible the subordinate understands and accepts the reasons for the reward decisions.

Finally, the need for a flexible approach to the reward review is very important. For example, on occasions, because of the information gained during the exchange of views with subordinates, managers should be ready if necessary to delay their final decision on recommended rewards pending a reconsideration of the situation.

QUESTIONS

1. What are the main purposes of assessing staff?

2. What are the three main types of review that are commonly carried out and who is responsible for each?

3. (a) What is performance appraisal?
   (b) What fundamental problems does it involve?
   (c) How may they be mitigated?
   (d) What are the characteristics of 'Theory X' and 'Theory Y' approaches to performance appraisal?

4. Describe the main requirements for carrying out an effective appraisal of performance and the subsequent review.

5. How may potential be assessed?

6. What is an assessment centre?

7. What are the requirements for conducting an effective reward review?

MAIN ELEMENTS OF THE SYSTEM

PURPOSES

Assessing achievements of objectives.
Determining needs for staff development.
Establishing basis for rewards.

Performance appraisal.
Potential review.
Reward review.
Training staff to apply the system effectively.

PERFORMANCE APPRAISAL (Line Manager)	CAREER DEVELOPMENT/ POTENTIAL REVIEW (Personnel Manager)	REWARD REVIEW (Line Manager)
Managers and staffs: Define and agree job requirements. Maintain separate records. Regularly discuss performance. Managers and staffs: 1. Prepare for performance by arranging meeting and agenda i.e. (a) Objectives, job description, methods etc. (b) Actual performance. (c) Action for future. 2. Hold discussion. 3. Agree action plan. 4. Record discussion.	Personnel Manager and individuals: 1. Review work history to date e.g. strengths, weaknesses, preferences etc. 2. Assess potential in light of past performance and opportunities available. 3. Summarise discussion (advice and action agreed). 4. Reward discussion.	Manager prepares by: 1. Collecting information e.g. rewards for similar work. 2. Studying work record. 3. Comparing individual performances of work. 4. Consulting Personnel Dept. Manager conducts reward review by: (a) Explaining purpose. (b) Ascertaining expectations and feelings. (c) Ascertaining that individuals understand reasoning and accept. (d) Be prepared to revise decision if necessary.

Fig. 13. Summary of the main elements of a system of staff assessment.

13

Training

DEFINITION—THE FOUNDATION FOR EFFECTIVE PRACTICE

Helping employees to become effective in their jobs is one of the fundamentally important tasks in personnel management that any work organisation has to undertake. Employers depend on the quality of their employees' performance to achieve organisational aims and objectives; employees have motivational needs for development, recognition, status, achievement etc. that can and should be met through job-satisfaction. The initiative for providing this help must come mainly from the employers. The vocabulary to describe this kind of help in the context of work includes terms such as training, development, education and, more recently, human resources development. Attempts are made by some authors to separate these terms by differential definitions. For example, 'training aims to achieve short-term specific organisation objectives', 'education is directed towards the long-term development of individuals'. Definitions of this kind over-simplify a very complicated process. What, for example, is to be said about the universally accepted term 'teacher training'. This process is certainly not concerned with short-term objectives and certainly includes educational and developmental purposes. As the common denominator of all of these terms is learning, it is better to see the training as a learning process, as defined below, rather than to engage in debates about semantic differences.

There is no adequate, all-embracing term to describe this process. 'Work-directed learning' might be a candidate. In the meantime, the word 'training' will be used throughout in discussing the process in the widest possible context, starting with the following comprehensive definition as a foundation for effective practice.

'Training in a work organisation is essentially a learning process, in which learning opportunities are purposefully structured by the managerial, personnel and training staffs, working in collaboration, or by external agents, acting on their behalf. The aim of the process is to develop in the organisation's employees the knowledge, skills and attitudes that have been defined as necessary for the effective performance of their work and hence for the achievement of the organisational aim and objectives by the most cost-effective means available.'

The importance of using a comprehensive definition as a basis for practice is that it focuses attention on the main aim of training, i.e. effective performance, and leads logically to the following important conclusions that determine the design and provision of training in practice i.e.

1. Training is always a means to an end and not an end in itself i.e. training is of no use by itself. Unless it leads to the effective performance of work it inevitably incurs a waste of valuable resources.

2. Precise definition of the requirements for effective performance in terms of knowledge, skills and attitudes by means of job analysis is of fundamental importance.

3. Because it is directed towards effective performance of work, it must be seen as an integral and vital part of the whole work system. It is not, for example, an extraneous activity for which training staffs are largely responsible.

4. Since managers are responsible for the effective performance of work to achieve the organisational aim and objectives, they must logically have the responsibility for ensuring that employees are effectively trained for this purpose. Management must take the initiative in setting up, resourcing and monitoring the effectiveness of the training system and its provision in practice.

5. Whilst management bears the main responsibility, all staff in the organisation are involved in the training task. Effective practice requires the collaboration of managerial, personnel, and training staffs.

6. The purpose of training may be achieved by a variety of means e.g. by planned work experience in a series of different jobs, by planned experience within one job, by formal training at the work place or at training centres. The sole criterion for choice of method is whatever will cost-effectively achieve specific objectives.

7. The development of an organisation's human resources applies to all its employees from the most senior to the most junior. When training is defined in traditional narrow terms, it tends to be directed towards junior and middle grades of employees. But all employees are likely to need training of some kind throughout their working lives. It surely could not be assumed that senior staff, on whom so much ultimately depends, have no need for further learning—especially in view of the demands of economic, social and technological changes in the present times.

8. Because of the vital contribution that training makes to the development of human resources and the achievement of organisa- tions' aims and objectives, all those responsible for training in any

shape or form need themselves to be trained for the task. In particular, because training is essentially a learning process, they need to have a basic understanding of learning—what it is and how people learn.

9. To integrate training systematically with work it has to be based on a Systems Approach to Training (SAT), which is described and analysed below, as an essential foundation for effective training in practice.

A SYSTEMS APPROACH TO TRAINING

Practical experience of training in recent decades in many organisations has emphasised the crucial importance and efficacy of this approach. The SAT is no magic formula. It is based on the same principles that are required for effective management, i.e. defining aim and objectives, defining the requirements for effective performance by job analysis, planning, resourcing and implementing the means of achieving the aim and objectives, assessing achievement and initiating any necessary changes.

The SAT is so called because it involves a series of interdependent systems, functionally linked together and to the whole work-system, in order to achieve total effectiveness. The interdependence of the component systems is crucial, since the malfunction of one unit inevitably affects the other units and hence the whole main system. Above all, the SAT is a discipline and a problem-solving process that compels those responsible for design and provision to ask the right questions in a logical sequence as a prerequisite to finding the right answers i.e.

1. What are the requirements for the effective performance of work?
2. What knowledge, skills and attitudes have to be learned to meet these requirements?
3. How does the learning process affect the design and provision of training?
4. How should training be designed and provided in the light of identified work requirements and of the learning process, so that people may cost-effectively learn what is needed?
5. Have people learned what they needed to learn?
6. What changes, if any, need to be made to the system itself or in the design and provision of training in the light of the assessment of training effectiveness.

If training is not based on SAT principles, there is every chance that it will be determined more by trainers' preferences and prejudices than by the work-related needs of individuals and the organisation. The basic questions listed above provide a basic framework for discussing in detail the SAT in practice. Far and away the most important issue is the role of management in the SAT and especially of senior management. The commitment, involvement and initiative of senior management is essential to success. The SAT will not work if only the full-time trainers have been converted to the faith and try to practise it in the face of indifference, lack of support or even persecution. Management must take the lead in putting the SAT into effective practice and this requires some system of continuous central direction to ensure that it is applied throughout the organisation.

THE CENTRAL DIRECTION OF THE SAT

Because training permeates the whole organisation and is related directly to all its main functions, the central direction of the SAT must involve the collaboration of senior representatives of the organisation's central staff i.e. operations, finance, personnel, training etc. The details are a matter for each organisation to decide for itself. It could come from the Board of Directors or from an ad hoc body specially established for this purpose. The daily supervision of the SAT should be the responsibility of either the Director of Personnel or the Director of Training, depending on whether these are separate, but inter-related departments, or whether the training function is located as a sub-unit of the Personnel Department, in which the Director of Training reports to the Director of Personnel. Whatever form the central direction of the SAT may take, the general responsibilities for the staff concerned may be defined as follows:

1. To formulate and publish policy and plans for training.
2. To provide the human and material resources needed.
3. To set up all the formal apparatus needs to make the SAT work effectively, i.e. formal systems for:
 (*i*) identifying work-related training needs.
 (*ii*) designing work-related training to meet identified needs.
 (*iii*) assessing the effectiveness of training in terms of training objectives and actual work-performance.
4. To define the responsibilities of all staff responsible for implementing these systems i.e. line managers, personnel and training staff and individual employees.
5. To prescribe all the formal communicational methods needed for the effective functioning of these systems in practice i.e. scheduled meetings, interviews, forms, questionnaires etc.
6. To co-ordinate the training work of the various sub-units of the organisation.
7. To act as a focal point for the exchange and dissemination of ideas about training design and provision throughout the organisation.

8. To act as a link with the external world of training and to bring new ideas into the organisation to improve cost-effectiveness.

9. To monitor the effective functioning of the SAT and the cost-effectiveness of training in the organisation.

WHAT NEEDS TO BE LEARNED—IDENTIFYING TRAINING NEEDS

It is a primary requirement of cost-effective training that it must meet actual, rather than imagined, needs of work. Therefore, an analysis of these needs is an essential prerequisite to the design and provision of effective training. This is the first main stage in the problem-solving process that characterises the SAT i.e. the diagnosis that systematically precedes prescription. In simple terms, the purpose of this diagnosis is to determine whether there is a gap between what is required for effective performance and present levels of performance. If any deficiencies are revealed, the causes and remedies may be various, and training is only one of a number of possible solutions.

Training needs arise at three levels—organisational, sub-group and individual. They are interdependent because the corporate performance of an organisation ultimately depends on the performance of its individual employees and its sub-groups.

The corporate needs of the organisation and its sub-groups may be identified in the following ways:

1. *The evidence of manpower planning*: This provides information about the demand and supply of human resources and the possible implications for training needs. Thus, a forecast of a possible difficulty in recruiting people with required entry levels in knowledge and skills could affect recruitment and training policy, compelling the organisation to recruit at lower levels and then to provide compensatory training to fill the performance gap.

2. *The introduction of new methods*: Whenever new methods of work are introduced, e.g. computers, this changes the requirements for effective performance, creates a performance gap in knowledge and skills (and with new technology in attitudes also, perhaps), and hence a training need.

3. *Collective evidence from performance appraisal and formal methods for needs assessment*: Information emerging from the performance appraisal of individual employees or from formal methods such as meetings, interviews or questionnaires, in which line managers, personnel and training staffs and individual employees are involved, may reveal needs for training that are common throughout the organisation or to groups of employees.

This systematically acquired information is an essential basis for seeing that centrally provided training is what is really needed. Without this information it is very easy for central trainers to provide training in the basis of unsubstantiated views and personal preferences.

Accurately to diagnose the specific training needs for individuals requires the following system:

1. Job analysis to determine:
 (*i*) the objectives and component tasks of the job.
 (*ii*) the knowledge, skills and attitudes required for the effective performance of these tasks.

2. Assessment of the performance gap by line managers and individuals, based on a comparison of the required levels with present levels.

3. Specification of training needs indicated by this comparison.

4. Specification of the forms of training needed to satisfy the identified needs.

The joint participation of line managers and their individual members of staff to assess training needs is very important. It is more likely to produce a comprehensive and systematic analysis, and commitment on the part of the individual. It is also an opportunity to encourage individuals to assess their own needs and possible solutions as a part of their development.

It requires time and conscientious effort to make a thorough analysis of jobs and their specific requirements and then to set up formal arrangements for assessing needs, but there is no other basis for designing and providing the training that is really needed.

Specific training needs for individuals may arise at any time during their working careers. However, there are particular occasions when a formal assessment is needed, based on the system described above, i.e.

1. *Starting employment*: New employees will invariably need some kind of training to fill the gap between their present levels of knowledge and skills and those needed for effective performance of work.

2. *Appraising performance*: In performance appraisal recent performance is compared with required levels. The comparison regularly reveals deficiencies and needs, which have to be remedied by training.

3. *Changing jobs*: People changing jobs are in a similar situation to those starting employment. The requirements for the new job may well create a performance gap that needs to be filled by training.

Apart from the specific needs described above, individuals have continuing general needs for training in the broad developmental sense. They need to develop their experience within particular appointments. This is the responsibility of line managers, who must determine these needs by careful observation of performance and regular discussions with their staffs, and provide the necessary opportunities by informal methods such as delegation, job rotation etc. People also need the wider experience that comes with a variety of jobs. It is the responsibility of these Personnel Managers in their career development role to ascertain these developmental needs and to meet them by career planning as far as operational demands will permit.

HOW DOES LEARNING THEORY AFFECT THE DESIGN AND PROVISION OF TRAINING?

Since training is essentially a learning process, all those who are in any way involved in training need to have an understanding of learning and what needs to be taken into account in the design and provision of training. Because learning is a continuous human activity, it has always occupied an important position in psychological studies. The main questions to be discussed are what learning is and how people learn. There is a general consensus about the first question, but much more debate about the second.

Learning may be defined as a more or less permanent change in behaviour, which occurs as a result of the influence of external, environmental stimuli on the inherent, genetic disposition of the individual. In the context of training it is useful to consider learning and behavioural change in terms of knowledge, skills and attitudes needed for effective performance. In formal learning situations this change is required to be demonstrated and assessed by examinations or tests. In everyday life it is ascertained by observable changes in behaviour patterns e.g. a previously lazy employee demonstrating through behaviour that he is now hard working and conscientious. Since training is directed towards the effective performance of work, ultimately this is the point where learning or behavioural change really matters and needs to be demonstrated. There is no point in such changes being shown at the end of a training course, if they are not transferred into observable changes in practice in real work.

How people learn has been the subject of continuing discussion and some controversy for many decades. Various theories have been fashionable at different times. There is no need for training practitioners to become deeply immersed in the literature of learning theory. Nevertheless, from the wealth of practical experience acquired over many years, it is possible to distil some basic, simple general truths about learning which are fundamentally important to those responsible for the design and provision of training i.e.

1. People must be motivated to learn. They must see a beneficial outcome for themselves. They must see how training could help them to perform their work effectively. They must see a personal need for this to happen and to accept the methods chosen to achieve the training objectives.

2. Feedback is important to the motivational and learning progress. People need to have feedback on their learning-achievement.

3. Because learning depends on motivation, it is essentially an individual process. People will learn, if they want to, in their own preferred ways and at their own pace, depending on a variety of genetic and environmental factors and on age.

4. People learn from example and by imitation. In consequence they may demonstrate behaviour that could be regarded as socially unacceptable or not conducive to the effective performance of work. In other words, people may easily acquire bad habits and practices as good.

5. Learning can only take place through the human senses. All of these may contribute to the learning process, but the visual is the most powerful, and to a lesser degree, the auditory.

What implications does the individual orientation of the learning process have for trainers?

1. Training is a learner and not a trainer-orientated process.

2. The trainer is essentially a catalyst in the learning process. As Galileo is reputed to have said 'You cannot teach people anything. You can only help them to learn.'

3. In the practice of training trainers need, therefore:

 (*i*) To explain why people need to learn certain things, how it will help them, how their learning fits into a total picture and the relationship of parts to a whole (e.g. the rationale of a whole training programme or of a single subject in a course).

 (*ii*) To make training as experiential and active as possible i.e. using real work as the learning medium, or methods which relate to real work as closely as possible.

(*iii*) To see that people learn from good examples and practice as far as possible.

(*iv*) To use an imaginative approach, involving interesting, varied and stimulating methods for learning, supported by helpful audio-visual and similar aids.

 (*v*) To be interesting and stimulating themselves through their own presentational skills.

(*vi*) To structure learning so that people have regular assessments of their performance and achievement. Although tests are an obvious means of providing feedback, it can be given informally by the skilful choice of participative, active methods, CCTV recordings etc.

HOW SHOULD TRAINING BE DESIGNED AND PROVIDED

This question is the second stage of the problem-solving process. The first stage was diagnostic i.e. to determine what the needs are. The second stage is prescriptive i.e. to decide what action is most likely to meet the identified needs. This requires generating and analysing a range of options in the light of objectives to be achieved and the economic use of available resources. As we have already seen, options available to meet the requirements of work, i.e. to fill the performance gap, could well cover a wide range and training is only one of these possibilities. When training is, in fact, the selected option, the same problem-solving principle applies, i.e. the next step is to determine in detail what form of training is most likely to meet identified requirements cost-effectively. In the light of a broad interpretation of training the range of possible options is wide. Making these choices raises questions such as who should provide training, of what kind, where and by what methods. The answers to all of these questions will be determined by training objectives.

Training Objectives

The definition of training objectives is an essential prerequisite for designing and providing training. They will naturally vary according to the requirements of particular situations, but in general they must all point in the same direction, i.e. requiring that trainees should demonstrate that at the end of training they have learned, and can demonstrate that they have learned, whatever knowledge, skills and attitudes have been identified as necessary for effective work performance. Since learning needs to be demonstrated by measurable achievement, objectives should specify the performance that is required, the standards to be achieved and any attendant conditions. To illustrate the point by a simple example in writing objectives for training typists, we should need to define the required end-of-course performance in the following terms: what kind of documents have to be typed, for what purposes, in what formats, with what typing speeds, to what standards of accuracy, by what methods (e.g. copy and/or audio), and on what types of machines. On this basis we could meaningfully start to plan the details of a training course, whose objectives compel us to consider what methods will best enable the required learning to be achieved and provide us with criteria for significant assessment. In the absence of such objectives we are left only with guesswork in the design and provision of training and in the assessment of learning achievement.

It is a relatively straightforward task to define training objectives in performance-measurable terms for specific work activities such as typing, driving, flying, cooking, etc. It is much more difficult when the work-activity is complex, such as management and related areas. The essential problem here is that complex subjects of this kind cannot really be encompassed in short training courses, despite the attempts that are sometimes made to do this. The futility of these attempts is at once revealed by the insoluble problem of defining truly measurable training objectives. However, when managerial training is related to specific activities such as, for example, chairing meetings, public speaking, interviewing etc., then the learning requirements can be made specific; the course contents can provide opportunities to demonstrate learning; and the total learning achievement at the end of training can be meaningfully assessed.

Before we leave the subject of training objectives, an important point needs to be made which illustrates the essential nature of the SAT. The definition of training objectives as one system and the assessment of learning achievement and training effectiveness as another are totally interdependent. If objectives are not defined in terms of measurable performance, then obviously there is no basis for any significant assessment of achievement.

As we have seen, training objectives determine the details of design and provision. The next step is to plan and provide training that will enable objectives to be achieved, taking account of the basic principles of learning and giving the best value for money. A systematic discussion of the design and provision of training must necessarily include the people who design and provide training and the methods and locations that might be used in practice.

Training designers and providers

The thesis that training should be viewed as an integral part of work, requiring the involvement and collaboration of all employees leads to the logical conclusion that training concerns all the staff of an organisation. Organisational staff may be involved in providing training in the following ways:

1. Managers or their deputies, who provide or supervise on-job training, coaching or open and distance methods at the workplace.

2. Full-time training staff, who give formal training at training centres or assist line managers in the design, provision and supervision of training at the workplace.

3. Managers, specialists and other members of staff who give occasional inputs to training on particular subjects.

An analysis of the range of tasks that training might entail would reveal a variety of managerial and presentational tasks i.e.

1. Organising and supervising a total system (e.g. a Director of Training).

2. Directing training programmes and managing full-time training staff (e.g. Head of Training Department or Training Institute).

3. Designing and presenting training, lecturing and tutoring (e.g. a Course Director, full or part-time lecturer or tutor).

In practice, the managerial and presentational roles may be combined e.g. a Course Director, who also makes presentational contributions to the course.

It is generally claimed that full-time training or teaching requires particular qualifications, especially in human skills. This is undoubtedly true, but it also needs to be said that essentially there is no significant difference between the requirements for effectiveness in managers and in trainers. Both require the ability to identify, pursue and achieve work-related objectives, to manage human and material resources and time, to show qualities of leadership, interpersonal, communicational skills and presentational skills. The fundamental requirements are the same. The particular techniques can be learned by trainer-training and experience.

This proposition has important consequences for the selection, employment and training of trainers. Organisations need full-time training staff in the same way that they need specialists in other fields, to concentrate on the various human and material functions, to build up a store of expertise, to provide central training, to train the organisation's trainers both full-time and part-time. At the same time, very considerable benefits may be gained from a policy of exchanging staff between operational and training duties. A few years spent by managers during their careers in full-time training duties could provide invaluable experience and opportunities and develop their human skills. In this way they may return to managerial work the better for the experience and committed to the importance of training for the effective performance of work. In organisations where senior management shows a commitment to the fundamental importance of training, the temporary appointment of managers and other staff to full-time training duties would be seen as prestigious and as an important stage in career development. In organisations where attitudes are short-sighted or reactionary, appointments to training work may be regarded as a form of banishment or as a demotion. Interchanges also need to be made as a matter of policy in the other direction. Appointing permanent full-time training staff to temporary appointments in operational and other posts is also very important both for the organisation and for the individual's career development. In particular, this policy helps to prevent training centres from becoming ivory towers, which become out of touch with the realities of life at the sharp end of the organisation and lose credibility with their clients.

Traditionally, the training of trainers has been directed almost exclusively to permanent training staff. But if the need for employing managers, personnel managers and other staff in training roles is accepted and practised, then clearly they too should be trained for these tasks and given some basic training in the principles and practice of the SAT, in the use of various learning methods and in instructional and presentational skills. How can the integrated work and training systems be effective, unless all concerned share the same philosophy, speak the same language and apply the same principles in practice?

Training methods and locations

Training methods and locations can be discussed under three broad headings i.e. training at the workplace; training at organisational or external centres; a combination of training at the workplace and training centres. The choice will be determined by whatever is assessed as most likely to achieve the objectives of training and work by the most cost-effective means.

Training at the workplace: training at the workplace may take a variety of forms. In its very broadest sense it may be identified with career development and the acquisition of required knowledge, skills and attitudes from the continuous experience and opportunities provided by work itself. Here, the Personnel Department has the key role in the supervision and direction of career paths to enable employees to widen their horizons and to develop their capabilities to assume wider responsibilities for the future. Line managers also obviously have the main responsibility for training their own staffs at the workplace. They may do this in the course of normal work by delegation, job rotation, attachments and visits to related work units, placing individuals under the tutelage of selected, experienced employees or by the use of formal workplace methods such as coaching, open and distance learning.

In recent times as a result of the ever-increasing emphasis on cost-effectiveness there has been a noticeable tendency for much of the training that was formerly given at training centres to be now carried out at the workplace. This shift applies particularly to training related to individual proficiency i.e. what is sometimes described as trade or vocational training. It has been stimulated by recent developments in open and distance methods, often based on computer and video technology. It has also led to a change of emphasis in the central trainers' role. Nowadays they are tending to be increasingly employed as consultants to local managers in the design and provision of training at the workplace and less in their traditional presentational and instructional roles. The cost-effectiveness of this approach has already been demonstrated by a number of organisations in terms of saving the very high costs of central training and in improved performance.

Training at training centres: most people are familiar with formal methods of training centres and most organisations have permanent centres or hire accommodation for central training. Here the training is conducted by full-time training staffs, assisted as necessary by occasional lecturers and tutors. Trainers usually work in groups and the methods commonly employed are lectures, discussion groups, case studies, simulation, role play and exercises of various kinds, supported by films, CCTV, tape-slide projections and other audio-visual aids. Training usually covers subjects where needs are identified that are common to groups of employees of similar grades or jobs. The choice of methods and locations must be determined by the criterion of cost-effectiveness.

Whilst centrally-based training is costly and requires people to leave their places of work, it is necessary and essential for some forms of training, especially in managerial and related subjects. Here people need to work in groups and to learn from each other in a residential setting. Just as line managers need the assistance of central trainers to plan local programmes so the central trainers must design central training in collaboration with line managers to ensure that it provides what they and their staffs need for effective performance of work.

Some central courses, especially those provided by external centres, could be described as 'off-the-peg'. To avoid a mismatch between the trainee and the course it is most important that the training centre should publish specific details about the course i.e. aim, objectives, people for whom intended (target population), contents, methods and duration. This kind of problem is much less likely to occur when a particular organisation uses the external centre to provide specific forms of training for specific members of its staff. Here the organisational managers and the training staff of the centre can jointly plan a 'custom-built' course.

Combining workplace and central methods: the third general heading that needs to be considered is the combination of workplace and central methods, which gives the possibility of having the best of both worlds. The typical features of this approach to training are these:

1. Training is designed by central trainers and managers, and if necessary, subject specialists to ensure that it is work-related.
2. Training is designed as a series of separate, but interdependent modules, arranged in a logical sequence and often based on the principles of programmed learning.
3. The basic pattern of training is a series of short courses at the centre, interspersed with long periods of study at the workplace supervised by central trainers and local managerial staff.
4. Training at the workplace is prepared in a form that facilitates

locally supervised self-study e.g. programmed texts, video-films and computers.

5. Progressive and final tests of learning achievement are built into the programme.

This combination approach to training has a number of potentially significant advantages i.e.

1. It uses the advantages of the individually oriented workplace and the group-oriented central training methods.
2. It is very flexible.
3. There is no pressure to cram training into a short period of time because of the demands of work or the costs of central training. Training can be extended as long as is necessary, e.g. over several months, to cover subjects in the required depth and breadth.
4. There is a continuing achievement-oriented partnership between line managers, trainees and central trainers.
5. The crucial importance of line management and the integration of work and training is very apparent.
6. When training is extended over longer periods and is directly work-oriented, the assessment of learning achievement is more valid.
7. It is especially useful for management training, which can never be satisfactorily encompassed by short central courses.
8. It is likely to be more cost-effective than other methods.

Has the required learning been achieved—the assessment of effectiveness?

Assessing the effectiveness of training is the 'bottom line' of the SAT. It is the end of the road and the point when we have to ask whether the costly investment in analysing needs, designing and providing training has been justified by the results, i.e. the effects on work performance. In practice, two kinds of assessment are needed—individual and organisational. The information gained from this diagnosis not only comments on the soundness of the investment, it also provides feedback for any necessary modifications.

In assessing the effectiveness of individual training there are two main occasions when it is necessary to take stock i.e.

1. On the completion of training to determine whether training objectives have been achieved.
2. After a lapse of time following the completion of training in order to determine whether training has had the required effect on actual work performance.

The assessment of the effectiveness of training for individuals must be carried out jointly by trainers, trainees and line managers.

Moreover, it must be done by formal, scheduled arrangements as an essential system in the SAT, which are systematically linked to the definition of requirements for effective performance of work and to training objectives. Without a precise definition of learning that has to be demonstrated, what basis can there be for assessing the effect of training on work-performance?

There are two sources of information for assessing the effectiveness of training of individuals i.e. tests designed to measure learning achievement as objectively as possible, and subjective opinions. On completion of the typing training course, quoted earlier as an example, we can set up tests which will show, with little room for argument, to trainers and to trainees, whether trainees have actually learned to type the required documents, in the required formats, at the required speeds, with the required standards of accuracy, on the required machines, by the required methods. What cannot be objectively measured, however, either at this stage or subsequently are attitudes. Only time will tell whether ex-trainee typists are conscientious, co-operative and constructive. The judgement can only be made after experience of actual work and there it can only depend on the subjective opinions of line managers.

Apart from the evidence of objective tests both trainers and trainees will have opinions about the value of training. Such opinions are subjective and, therefore, limited. On formal central courses it is a well-known phenomenon for a course camaraderie to develop and an end-of-course euphoria, which clouds more sober judgements. People may leave a course aware of an enjoyable experience, but not very sure about what they have learned or of its possible usefulness. Nevertheless, the end-of-course exchange of opinions by trainers and trainees at central courses is important, but needs to be structured to produce the maximum benefit. Trainees must analyse the course in terms of their own needs and objectives, and assess what they think they have learned and its potential value to their future work. Central trainers need to make a careful note of trainees' comments to compare with comments made about previous courses and to take account of any strong consensus of views, when making modifications to training design and provision.

When trainees return to their work on the completion of a central training course, there also needs to be a constructive, systematic discussion with their line managers. The main purpose of this discussion is to ascertain the trainees' views of training, but especially to plan how line managers may help their staffs to develop through their jobs the knowledge and skills that they have learned in training. It is a very demotivating experience for trainees to return to work from a central or external training course with an awareness of their needs for improvement and stimulated to put their new learning into practice, only to be ignored and sometimes even discouraged by the attitudes of their line managers.

The second stage in the assessment of training effectiveness for individuals after a lapse of time is the ultimate verdict. It is very easy after a lapse of time, when people are caught up once more in the toils of work, to forget about recent training. A formal system is essential, therefore, to impose the necessary discipline for action and to standardise organisation practice. This assessment is of particular concern to line managers and ex-trainees and should be automatically included in a formal scheme for performance appraisal. When the training is provided centrally or externally, it is also very important for the training staff to receive feedback. The questions to which answers are needed are:

1. How far has training met the specific needs of work for which it was designed?
2. What changes need to be made, if any, in future training i.e.
 (i) Was any material included that has subsequently proved to be of limited or no value?
 (ii) Was any material omitted that has subsequently proved necessary?
(iii) How appropriate were the training methods for learning purposes?

There are mainly three ways by which central and external trainers may obtain the information they need i.e.

1. By sending questionnaires to all former trainees and their line managers.
2. By visiting a sample cross-section of former trainees and their line managers for direct discussions at their places of work.
3. By holding short (e.g. 1-2 day) conferences of former trainees for a collective comparison of post-training experience and assessment of training's ultimate effectiveness.

There is a very important postscript that has to be made to the discussion of the final stage of assessing training effectiveness for individuals. Judgements can only be made after a lapse of time, when line managers and former trainees have gained some perspective about work-performance after training. However, the fact that a lapse of time is necessary at once eliminates the possibility of a pure assessment. In the interval between the end of training and the point of assessment other influences will inevitably affect work performance for better or worse e.g. personal problems, managerial styles, working methods and conditions etc. There are many factors both inside and outside work, some hidden from view and not measurable, which may affect behaviour. The influence of training over a period of time cannot, therefore, be isolated as a single measurable factor.

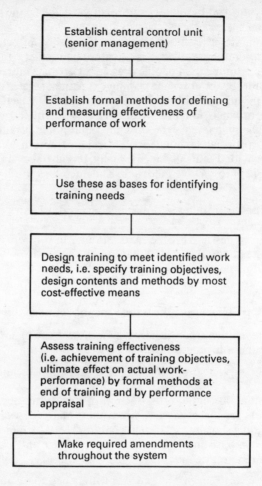

Fig. 14. Summary of the main elements of a training system.

The last word on the assessment of training effectiveness and the SAT in practice concerns the organisation as a whole unit. The performance of individuals is only important collectively as a means of achieving organisational aims and objectives. The final question, therefore, is whether the costs of all the human and material resources that are directed to training are justified in terms of their contribution to this purpose.

The problems that beset the assessment of the effectiveness of training for individuals are the same, but obviously much more complicated at organisational level. Here, we return to the starting point of the discussion of the SAT in practice—the crucial role of senior management and the central direction of the SAT. The assessment of the cost-effectiveness of training for the whole organisation is their primary responsibility. They can only do this if they have the best information available, and this can only be provided through the formal systems that are the essential components of the SAT. If there is no central direction for the SAT in practice to co-ordinate and account for the total organisational training effort, who is to ask the relevant questions about cost-effective training, to analyse the answers and to take any action that is indicated?

QUESTIONS

1. Define training and the main consequences that arise from the definition.

2. What is meant by the Systems Approach to Training?

3. What are the responsibilities of central senior staff?

4. What does the identification of training needs entail?

5. How does learning theory affect the design and provision of training?

6. What should training objectives attempt to achieve?

7. Who may be responsible for training?

8. Describe the various forms that training may take in terms of methods and locations.

9. How may the effectiveness of training be assessed?

14

Personnel Records and Statistics

THEIR NATURE AND PURPOSE

Personnel records and statistics provide a total store of information on which important decisions about the use of human resources are based. As with military intelligence, the future success of the organisation very much depends upon the quality of information on which it bases its decisions. This information is continuously needed for major organisational purposes and the day-to-day management of personnel. For example, statistical records may indicate a trend of increasing difficulty in recruiting certain key categories of employees, which needs to be taken into account in manpower planning; or it may be necessary to identify an employee with specific qualifications to fill a post at very short notice.

The essential requirements for a sound system of personnel records and statistics might seem to be too obvious to need stating, but there is enough evidence to indicate that they are sometimes, if not often, inadequately maintained. To fulfil their purposes records need to be

1. Accurate,
2. Relevant,
3. Comprehensive,
4. Simple,
5. Accessible.

Two broad categories of information need to be maintained; individual records, which provide all the personal information required about each employee; statistical information which describes the personnel situation in the whole organisation. Both kinds of information have the same general aim, i.e. to use past evidence for assessing the present stage and predicting likely future trends and requirements. The areas with which these assessments are mainly concerned and the uses of records for these purposes are summarised below.

INDIVIDUAL RECORDS

The main areas on which organisations need information for a variety of decisions on personnel matters are:

1. Contribution to the work of the organisation.
2. Types of employment for which the employee is best suited or in which experience is needed.
3. Needs for training and education.
4. State of health.
5. Pattern of conduct.
6. Entitlements for salary, other emoluments, pension, leave, etc.

The basis of all the information that the organisation maintains about its personnel is the records for each individual employee, which normally include the following items:

1. **Personal details**
Name, address, sex, date of birth, family, organisational identification number.
2. **Terms and conditions of employment**
Present occupation and grade, hours of work, pay and emoluments, retirement date and pension details, leave entitlement.
3. **Qualifications**
Academic and professional qualifications.
4. **Training and education**
Full-time and part-time education and training, courses attended, including details of contents and results obtained (if applicable).
5. **Work history**
Previous employment and record of employment with the organisation showing jobs, responsibilities, promotions and dates.
6. **Attendant circumstances**
Absence, health, accidents, conduct.
7. **Assessments of performance and potential**
Staff reports, performance-appraisal and potential reviews.
8. **Membership of associations**
Details of membership of unions, associations and societies, offices (if held).
9. **Termination of employment**
Date and reason, new employer (if known).

How this considerable quantity of varied information is organised will depend upon the requirements and practices of each organisation. Except for small, private organisations it will usually be necessary to use several documents, to decide what information, if any, is confidential, what is to be kept centrally, i.e. in the personnel department, what is to be kept by each department. The main, comprehensive records will certainly need to be kept centrally in the personnel department, but departments and branches will probably need some basic items for regular daily use. The amount of detail of

local records will depend on the availability of the central records and
the degree of co-ordination within the whole organisation to eliminate
unnecessary duplication. For some items it is easily possible for copy
documents to be kept by line managers for speed of reference.

In practice the mass of personnel information listed above can be
usefully arranged in the following way:

1. A personal file containing general information and correspondence with and about the individual employee. The first entries would
be the original application form and correspondence referring to
recruitment and the offer of employment, including the letter which
sets out terms and conditions of employment. It would also contain a
chronological record of the details of jobs held in the organisation.

2. A confidential file containing all documents relating to reviews of
performance and potential, staff reports, and promotion decisions.

3. A training and education record to provide a continuous history
of all training and educational courses attended with results of
achievement, where applicable.

4. A pay-record card containing a full-history of all pay received,
increments, bonuses, merit payments, etc.

5. An abstract which summarises by use of coded abbreviations,
signals, etc. the main items of information that the personnel
officers responsible for particular individuals might need to retrieve
immediately, e.g. job and training history to date and assessments.

ORGANISATIONAL STATISTICS

Organisational statistics serve two very important functions: they
provide essential information about main areas affecting the general
state of the organisation at a particular time; they also indicate trends
that need to be made apparent, so that timely measures may be taken
to improve conditions of work and performance. The main statistics
that normally need to be kept are briefly described below:

1. The state of the labour force, i.e. the number actually employed
as against the budget, or establishment, figure. This needs to be for a
specific period, and we will assume that this is *one year* in the ratios
under 2, 4, and 5 below.

2. Labour turnover

$$\text{Ratio:} \quad \frac{\text{Number of employees terminated}}{\text{Average number employed}} \times 100$$

3. Labour stability

Ratio:

$$\frac{\text{Number of current employees with more than 1 year's service}}{\text{Number of employees employed one year ago}} \times 100$$

Turnover is a general measure of the numbers moving through the organisation, whereas by calculating the stability index shown above it is possible to determine whether or not it is the same jobs which are subject to a high turnover, and therefore whether or not it is a widespread problem, or located in a particular occupation or department.

4. Time keeping/attendance

$$\text{Ratio:} \quad \frac{\text{Number of man-hours lost}}{\text{Total possible man-hours worked}} \times 100$$

5. Accidents (including types)

Ratio for frequency:

$$\frac{\text{Number of lost time accidents}}{\text{Number of man-hours worked}} \times 100,000$$

(100,000 = total of hours in an average working life)

6. Health (including types of illness)

These statistics need to be broken down into departments, locations, occupations, grades, sex, age-groups and, where applicable, causes.

In addition, statistics are regularly required for assessments of national situations and trends by external organisations, such as the Department of Employment, Health and Safety Executive, employers' associations, trade unions, Industrial Training Boards, British Institute of Management, Royal Society for the Prevention of Accidents.

METHODS OF RECORDING

The methods used to record personnel information depend on the answer to the following question: what methods will enable all the required information to be collected and retrieved with the minimum amount of labour and the minimum cost? Organisations have a choice between simple or more sophisticated manual methods and computerised methods. The former which include card-index and punch

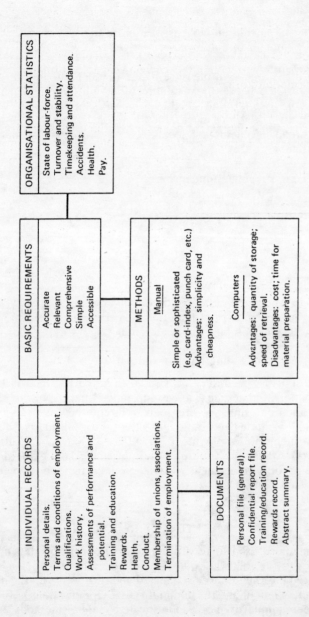

Fig. 15. Summary of the main elements of a personnel records and statistics system.

card systems are often perfectly adequate for most purposes, especially in smaller organisations. They have the particular advantages of cheapness and simplicity. The advantages of computers in terms of speed and ease of retrieval, and the quantity of data that can be processed, need no emphasis. There are, however, disadvantages that need to be taken into account, especially since it is tempting nowadays to regard computers as being capable of fulfilling all needs for information storage and retrieval. The first obvious disadvantage is the cost. Paradoxically it may also take up more time than the simpler methods because of the preparatory work involved in collecting and feeding accurate data to the computer and in up-dating information.

Whatever methods are used, there are some basic requirements that must be met or the entire system will inevitably be drastically reduced in its efficiency. All systems depend on a series of standardised forms which provide much of the essential information. These forms need to be designed with much forethought and care. Form design is a much more difficult technique than is often appreciated, and is not a task that anybody in an organisation can easily undertake. It is prudent, therefore, to use the professional advice and assistance of specialists in work study or management services for this purpose.

Finally, it is obvious, but nevertheless essential, that information be kept up to date. This involves constant attention, a methodical approach and an investment of time in personnel work that may sometimes appear to be tedious, but is likely to be more than repaid in the quality of decisions.

QUESTIONS

1. What are the main requirements that an effective record system should fulfil.

2. What main areas of information should individual records provide?

3. What headings should be included in the records of individual employees?

4. What are the main areas for which organisational statistics are normally maintained?

5. Name and briefly describe the separate documents that the personnel department might maintain for individual employees.

6. What is the most important consideration that should determine methods of recording information? Briefly describe and assess the main methods available.

FURTHER READING: PART 4

Anstey, E., Fletcher, C. and Walker, J., *Staff Reporting and Staff Development*, Allen and Unwin, London, 1976.

Burgoyne, J., Boydell, T. and Pedler, M., *A Manager's Guide to Self-Development*, McGraw-Hill, Maidenhead, 1978.

Fletcher, C. and Williams, R., *Performance Appraisal and Career Development,* Hutchinson 1985.

Hague, H., *Management Training for Real*, IPM, London, 1973.

Hall, D., *Careers in Organizations*, Goodyear, USA, 1976.

Hamblin, A., *Evaluation and Control and Training*, McGraw-Hill, London, 1974.

Kolb, D. A., Rubin, I. M. and McIntyre, J. M., *Organizational Psychology: An experimental approach*, Prentice-Hall, Englewood Cliffs, N.J., 1974.

Long, P., *Performance Appraisal Revisited*, IPM, London, 1987.

Pepper, A., *Managing the Training and Development Function*, Gower, 1984.

Rae, E., *How to Measure Training Effectiveness*, Gower, 1986.

Randell, G. et al., *Staff Appraisal*, IPM, London, 1974.

Stammers, R. and Patrick, J., *The Psychology of Training*, Methuen, London, 1975.

PART 5

The Reward and Conservation of Employees

Personnel managers are fond of a gardening analogy. According to this vision of managing people, provided the employee is given the conditions in which he can put down roots, has his needs tended carefully, and is given room to grow, he will bloom and prosper. It is perhaps not unreasonable that we should think in this way as it corresponds to how we often regard the development of children, and we may well have learned such attitudes from our own parents. In modern business life, however, a caring and helpful attitude is not enough. Although this attitude may be a very necessary motivation for managers, more than goodwill is required to cope with the pressing and serious issues of rewarding performance equitably and in accordance with a range of relativities which extend beyond the organisation.

The theories of motivation we outlined in Chapter 1 exhibited the complexity of reasons for working. The theory we considered by Porter and Lawler gives full weight to the different values which individuals place on rewards. Their model suggests that employees calculate the amount of effort required, and the probabilities that the accomplishment of the task will result in the achievement of rewards and satisfactions. Since the calculation of these probabilities is influenced by the individual's expectations about his role in the organisation, he is likely to have preconceived notions of the relative worth of different jobs and he will also match his own values against the norms of the organisation which he joins.

The reward and treatment of employees is bound up with the overall conditions under which the person works. Holidays, sick pay, pension and company car schemes, for example, provide a framework of benefits associated with salary and job level. Although Herzberg argues that 'hygiene factors' such as these are not positive motivators, he acknowledges that failures in these areas result in what might be termed 'demotivation' to work. The interdependence of 'hygiene factors' and 'motivators' makes the distinction between the two factors hard to see in the actions of people which relate to their working intentions. Apart from the obvious physical conditions of the work (such as the geographical location, surroundings, the danger, etc.) there are influences such as the style of supervision, the stress of some jobs and different decision-making habits which go to create the 'feel' of a job, and which are part of the 'culture' of the organisation. This 'feel' is as much a consequence of personnel policies as of the ways in which the job is regarded by the incumbent and his colleagues. The policies managers pursue towards employees carry implications for the kinds of relationships they create.

It is of prime importance, therefore, that managers understand how to evaluate jobs and how to construct systems for rewarding people as part of their employee relations strategy. The treatment of employees is underwritten in the UK by rights, the sources of which are in the various collective agreements between employers and unions and in the employment contract around which there is a framework of employment law. We will look at these in the chapters that follow.

The starting point for the manager is to design reward systems which take into account relativities and which represent the philosophy of management which his organisation has decided to adopt. There is then a need to control the wage and salary policies by systems which are flexible and which grant a place to the interest groups—managers and unions—who want to be represented. The personnel policies which go to form the general conditions of service are also related, since they contribute so much to the organisation's culture and the individual's sense of well-being. In the following chapters we will look at: job evaluation, in its many forms, how to design pay systems and salary administration. Finally, we will make an assessment of the policies which are, in the most general sense, for employees' welfare.

15

Job Evaluation

In this chapter we are concerned with the question how can the different forms of pay be developed for the organisation's economic efficiency? This leads us to look at job evaluation as a prerequisite of any reward structure.

DEFINITION

The purpose of job evaluation techniques is to measure the relative worth of jobs so that the relationship between the jobs can be expressed in salary and wage scales, based on a logical, ordered system. 'Job evaluation' is a term used in a general way for a number of techniques which are in different forms. These techniques entail analysing and assessing the content of jobs so that they may be classified in an order relating to one another.

COMMON FEATURES OF JOB EVALUATION TECHNIQUES

1. Job evaluation is concerned with differences in the work itself, not in differences which are found between people.
2. Reference is made to the 'content' of the job; i.e. what the work consists of, what is being done, and the actions which are performed. This is normally discovered by job analysis.
3. There are predetermined criteria, or factors against which each job is measured. These may be descriptions of the whole job, or of its component parts.
4. The practice of involving those who are to be subject to the job evaluation at an early stage helps to ensure both accuracy in job analysis and a commitment to the job evaluation scheme. At the very least, a committee with worker representatives should be responsible.
5. The outcome of a job evaluation should be wage and salary scales covering the range of evaluated jobs.
6. All systems need regular review and up-dating, and have to be flexible enough to be of use for different kinds of work, so that new jobs can be accommodated.

WHAT DO WE MEAN BY THE WORD 'JOB'?

This may seem to be a silly question to ask, but we must remember that 'jobs' have no physical bounded existence. There is no way of 'seeing' or using any of our senses to comprehend the 'whole' of a job. The idea of 'job' is an analytical one—it enables us to describe a set of actions which are associated with the execution of a range of tasks. 'Tasks' consist of a number of elements which are actions (i.e. intended behaviours) that are both observable and measurable. In thinking of tasks we have to think of people performing them, and therefore the major difficulty experienced by the job analyst who wishes to describe a 'job' is to be able to divorce the essential nature of the job from the people performing the job.

PROBLEMS OF MEASUREMENT

As people are at the centre of all 'jobs', either in the perceptions of others or in the written descriptions of jobs deriving from observations of how they are done, the evaluation is of human activity, not of some kind of impersonal act. This is our first problem of measurement. It is the problem of the inherent subjectivity contained in the discriminatory judgements of the work of others. Our second problem of measurement emerges here also—because the criteria or benchmarks on which evaluation will be made are based on aspects of human action. We may illustrate this last point by thinking about the amount of discretion involved in any job. People seem to want to make choices about their work, and typically seek to extend the areas of discretion they already possess. Even the most routine hourly rated job contains choices: sometimes about rest pauses, the amount of work, or its quality. Even if, according to the operator's manual, the sequence and timing of actions are pre-set, there are always other aspects of the total job (such as collecting materials, reading drawings, talking to the supervisor) when the worker can exercise some freedom of action.

Job evaluation requires the acceptance of the assumption that there is sufficient typicality in the way the work is performed to make comparisons between groups of jobs worthwhile. The differences between people and the consequences for the way the work is done may not be significant. It is not until job evaluation has been undertaken that we can see what the differences are. The changing activities of an organisation have to be put into an ordered context for pay purposes. Change emphasises the need to conduct evaluation on a continuous programme, to up-date rewards and keep the balance in our rewards in the direction which best suits the organisation's objectives. The problems and advantages of job evaluation can be summarised as follows:

The Problems of Job Evaluation:

1. Because of the problems of measurement, there may be bias, and the scheme may be more subjective than appears at first sight.

2. The measures that are selected determine the outcome. The decision of what to measure therefore partly pre-conditions where the job is to be placed in the hierarchy of jobs which is being constructed.

3. Job evaluation committees, where they exist to reconcile interest groups, have to reach compromises over what is 'politically' acceptable within the organisation. 'Trade-offs' between the interest groups occur.

The Advantages of Job Evaluation:

1. Some form of evaluation is necessary to introduce rationality into pay scales—enabling comparison to be made on an explicit basis. This reveals where the differences in rates are a consequence of tradition or custom rather than for economic reasons (see Chapter 23 on 'equal value' legislation).

2. Any inherent bias in the process can be recognised, and partly dealt with, by using committees to help in the evaluation, and perhaps outside analysts to describe the jobs.

3. Job evaluation can be applied to different situations—it is a technique which can be adjusted to the requirements of the organisation—its size, the kind of work, etc.

4. By involving employees at an early stage in establishing the system, it is possible to draw on their own feelings of fairness, their concepts of what should be rewarded, and to gain their commitment.

A job description and a person specification are essential first stages to job evaluation. The procedure is the same as we described in Chapter 7, the person specification being an outline of the qualifications, experience and other attributes which are needed to do a job. The person specification should show the job factors. Both the description and specification could be summarised into a 'job profile'.

DIFFERENT KINDS OF JOB EVALUATION SCHEMES

Broadly speaking, there are two main dimensions on which job evaluation schemes can be delineated: whether they are quantitative or qualitative in the treatment of job factors, and the extent to which they are analytical of a job's content.

A brief description of each of the most well-known schemes is given below.

Whole Job Ranking

This is a non-quantitative and non-analytical method. It is a technique in which jobs are placed in order of importance or value relative to each other. The main guide is usually the amount of responsibility in each job or the importance of the job to the organisation. This method looks at the whole job, not its component parts, and is concerned with the rank order of jobs, not differences in any absolute sense.

The procedure to be followed is:

1. 'Benchmark' jobs are identified. These are jobs which are 'yardsticks' or standards against which others can be compared. They should be chosen because they contain a wide range of job requirements, and there should be no controversy about their content, their value or importance.

2. The benchmark jobs should be drawn from various levels in the organisation.

3. Each job to be evaluated is compared with the benchmark job and a judgement is made to determine its relationship with the benchmark job.

4. As the number of ranked jobs increases, we can compare new jobs with those which have already been ranked.

5. In large organisations, we can use 'job families' where there are similarities, as finite populations—for example, accounts department staff.

6. It may be easier, administratively, to write the job descriptions on cards and to use assessors to achieve a consensus on the ranking by comparing evaluations at a meeting.

7. A further refinement is the paired comparison method, where each job is compared with all the others in turn, until a consensus is reached amongst the assessors on the ranking. This should improve the reliability of the ranking.

Generally, the whole job ranking method is thought to be appropriate for small organisations. There are problems in getting agreement amongst the assessors if the number of jobs is larger. It is difficult also, to choose benchmark jobs which do not have some flaw as yardsticks, if a number of different departments and specialisms are involved.

Classification or Grading Scheme

This is also a qualitative and non-analytical method. It is a centralised approach which may best be seen as part of the design of the organisation to which it is applied.

This approach requires the examination of jobs in the light of predetermined definitions of the grades, as part of a planned organisation structure, where the level of work in each grade is founded on what is thought to be appropriate, functionally. New jobs are then compared with the predefined grade descriptions to indicate the placing of the job in a relationship with other graded jobs.

Assuming that the grading scheme is to be integrated with the design of the organisation, the following steps should take place:

1. The shape and size of the organisation's hierarchy has to be determined. This becomes a question of how many levels there should be in the hierarchy, and the span of control (the numbers reporting to each supervisor) at each level.

2. The job hierarchy is divided into a number of grades, with written definitions for each.

3. The definitive grade descriptions are associated by outside analogues with appropriate pay rates, and effectively become the benchmarks against which other jobs are graded.

4. The broad differences that management wish to apply are written into the grade descriptions, often being in terms of the level of skill or responsibility.

5. Jobs are fitted into the structure by evaluation committees, who arrive at a consensus by comparing the ungraded jobs with the grade descriptions.

There are similarities between whole job ranking and grading schemes in that jobs are taken as wholes. The hope with a classification system is that it will produce a planned organisation. There are benefits in the approach for manpower budgeting and career planning. There are problems in making comparisons where an 'in house scheme' is used. If the categories or grades contain a wide range of skills or job requirements this reduces the usefulness in discriminating between jobs.

Points Rating

Points rating technique entails the analysis and comparison of jobs according to common factors, which are represented by a number of points, the amount depending on the degree of each factor present. Jobs are then placed in order of their total points rating. Pay is usually determined by reference to benchmark jobs. Points rating is therefore both a quantitative and an analytical technique.

The technique requires a number of steps which must be undertaken with care:

1. 'Job factors' are discovered by an examination of the most essential elements in the job. Job factors need to be present in all the jobs to be evaluated. This is accomplished by taking a significant sample of jobs for which complete job descriptions and person specifications should be prepared. The factors which are selected from the descriptions and specifications should be those which are critical for differentiation between jobs.

2. The factors—which may be such categories as 'engineering knowledge' required to do the job, or 'physical effort', are sometimes taken to be at a broad level—and can be termed 'generic factors'. There are then a number of specific sub-factors which comprise the 'generic' factor—for example, 'engineering knowledge' could be broken down to different aspects of mechanical engineering, or in the case of 'physical effort' the physical demands can be qualified more precisely.

3. The sub-factors should then be weighted according to the degree of importance they have in each job. This is done by dividing each sub-factor into a number of 'degrees'.

4. In order to resolve the problem of how to award points to each factor, and degree, it is useful to begin by assuming that the value of all factors present in any job will add up to 100%. The evaluation committee can then give relative values of each factor in each benchmark job so that the generic factors are given a percentage which totals 100%, and each sub-factor a percentage which adds up to 100% of the generic factor. The evaluation is of each sub-factor, so that each sub-factor should be broken down into degrees. At this stage we have an indication of the relative importance of each generic factor and each sub-factor. The number of degrees used should not go beyond what is likely to be recognisable, up to 5 degrees of a sub-factor being the maximum for most purposes. Definitions of each degree used for each sub-factor are required.

The total number of points can be any number; but the maximum number for all factors must add up to this total, and therefore the number of points is dependent on the number of factors, and evaluators should allow room for the maximum combination of points. A popular number is 500 points.

Table 4 illustrates this part of the process.

Since acquired 'skill and knowledge' is rated relatively high in the example, and training and previous experience is rated high on this, we may grant the highest degree of this sub-factor, 100 points, of the 500 points total possible (i.e. 40% of 500 = 200, 50% of 200 = 100). The number of points in each degree can be an arithmetic or a geometric progression, and the sub-factor's degrees need definitions. For example: 'Experience'

1st Degree (up to one month) 2nd Degree (over 1 and up to 4 months)
   20 Points   40 Points
3rd Degree (over 4 months but less than 12)
   60 points
4th Degree (1 yr–18 months)   5th Degree (over 18 months)
   80 Points   100 Points

using an arithmetic progression.

Table 4. Points rating scheme
(The factors are drawn from the BIM 'Job Evaluation', 1970)

Generic factor	Importance %	Specific sub-factors	Importance %	Maximum points
Acquired skill and knowledge	40	Training and previous experience	50	100
		General reasoning ability	20	40
		Complexity of process	20	40
		Dexterity and motor accuracy	10	20
Responsibilities and mental requirements	30	For material or equipment	15	7.5
		Effect on other operations	40	60
		Attention needed to orders	40	60
		Alertness to details	10	15
		Monotony	5	7.5
Physical requirements	20	Abnormal position	60	60
		Abnormal effort	40	40
Conditions of work	10	Disagreeableness	90	45
		Danger	10	5
				500

5. A chart should then be drawn up, which shows the values for each sub-factor, broken down into degrees present, with clear, agreed definitions of the sub-factors and degrees.

6. Each job is then evaluated, preferably by a committee which will

arrive at a consensus on the total number of points for the individual jobs being evaluated. Out of this the jobs may be placed on a range or scale.

Although the points scheme may seem complicated, this technique has been widely used since its invention in the 1920s, in Britain and the USA.

There are a number of variations on the method outlined here which indicates the flexibility of the points scheme. The use of 'points' should not be seen as a sign of scientific objectivity, as the points system relies on judgements by evaluation committees. Nevertheless, the technique is useful in comparing many different jobs which contain the same job factors and has been developed into tailor-made schemes to fit the specific requirements of companies.

Factor Comparison

Factor comparison is another analytical technique which uses some of the ideas of both the points rating and the ranking methods. One version of factor comparison, illustrated here, is a 'direct to money' approach. This system entails evaluating jobs in terms of each other, on a basis of a certain limited number of factors, and reconciling these rankings with money values for each factor derived from benchmark jobs. Out of the first stages of the exercise comes a table of factor rates for the benchmark jobs against which all the other jobs can be evaluated. There are two parts to the early stages therefore: factor ranking, and factor evaluation.

The method is more involved than the others described, as there are difficult judgements to be made at each juncture.

1. The first step is to agree on the factors which are found in each of the jobs to be evaluated, so that these can be defined. The number of factors chosen is usually limited to a few broad factors, not less than four or more than seven.

2. Early studies suggested: mental requirements, skill requirements, physical requirements, responsibility, and working conditions, but the factors chosen will need to be those which are appropriate for the jobs.

3. The next stage is to choose benchmark jobs, which must contain all these broad, generic factors. These benchmark jobs must clearly be representative of the factors, and in addition, there should be an unambiguous wage or salary for the job in question.

4. The payment for the benchmark jobs can be either the current rate, (if this is thought correct) or the intended rate for the job, based on evidence from salary surveys, or negotiated agreements.

5. The evaluation committee then rank the factors contained in each benchmark job. Taking the four generic factors we used in our

Table 5. Factor comparison

Generic factor	Rank order for: Word processor operator (£125 total)		Data input clerk (£95 total)	
Acquired skill and knowledge	1	£45	2	£28
Responsibility and mental requirements	2	£35	1	£35
Physical requirements	3	£30	4	£12
Conditions of work	4	£15	3	£20

previous example (Table 4), we can follow the factor comparison procedure for two jobs, say a word processor operator, and a routine clerk concerned with computer input. It must be appreciated that full job descriptions and person specifications would be needed for these two jobs before evaluation, and we will assume for the sake of simplicity that these have been prepared.

6. The committee must approach the benchmark jobs also from the perspective of factor evaluation, when money values are given to each factor. Given that the total job is worth 100% of the composite wage, a percentage of the wage can be attributed to each factor on a basis of its importance in the job. In Table 5, we have shown money values against each factor.

7. The reconciliation between the factor rankings and the factor evaluation is a crucial stage for resolving any differences. Because two different scales are being applied and there are not necessarily equal intervals, it is possible that there could be wide variations. Thus 'acquired knowledge or skill' is worth much less for the data input clerk than for the word processor operator, although there is only one difference in rank. Problems such as these would need some compromise solution by the committee.

8. A pilot study would help to resolve any serious difficulties in reconciling the factor rankings with the money evaluation, and, should the factors or benchmark jobs prove unsuitable, then the whole process must be restarted.

9. The remainder of the jobs to be evaluated can be dealt with more speedily, once this early work has been done and as each job factor is ranked, and then evaluated, the network of values and rankings should reveal a pattern on which decisions can be reached more easily. Full descriptions of all the other jobs to be evaluated need to be prepared, of course, and the pay for each factor after the job has been analysed

can be settled by reference to this table of rates for the key jobs, which has been constructed.

Factor comparisons schemes are often treated with suspicion by employees, and are not as popular in the UK as the other three methods we have outlined so far.

The benefits of the scheme are that, in the early stages, when benchmark jobs are being evaluated, two different approaches to the same job are reconciled to produce a practical compromise on the relative value of the job. This is likely to result in greater accuracy than the ranking method, as far as management or the evaluation committee is concerned.

Time Span of Discretion

This is still a somewhat theoretical approach to job evaluation, developed by Elliott Jaques. It borders on being a social philosophy. The assumption is made that individuals have a subconscious awareness when their work, payment and capacity are all approximately at an acceptable level of demands and rewards. When a person's work and capacity are equally matched, there is, according to the theory, an amount of payment (including salary and benefits) of which the individual is aware which matches the work and capacity level. Thus people can feel under- or over-paid, worked or utilised.

A second aspect of Jaques' theory is the view that the discretionary work activities which an individual performs can be measured in terms of the time that elapses before a manager is aware that his subordinate has performed this discretionary element satisfactorily—in balancing the pace and quality of his work.

These two aspects of the theory are related, in that what people feel is 'fair' pay is understood by individuals in conformity with the time span of discretion that their work demanded. The pay norms which are felt to be fair are intuitive understandings by people of the rates which others receive for similar work, their own standard of living, and conceptions of equity, all conditioned by their feeling of the extent to which their capacity is being used, or developed.

Research in the UK and the USA has indicated that there is a high correlation between felt fair pay and time span measures. The implications are that at each level in the organisation there are time span measures which should therefore correspond to pay levels. Jaques also claims that individuals have 'capacity growth curves', these being the rates at which an individual expects his capacity to grow in the future and therefore the salary progressions he would anticipate. Salary scales could be constructed, therefore, using this information.

The theory has aroused a lot of interest, and has informed discussions on rates of pay, and questions of social justice. However,

its practicality as a proposal for the evaluation of jobs remains in
doubt. There is disagreement over the validity of the research where
such vague concepts as subconsciously held pay norms are used, and
where there are different interpretations of what is discretionary.
Because of the tendency for people to draw on their own experience,
there must be a bias towards maintaining the status quo, in any
organisation, i.e. the time span approach does not make clear which is
the dependent variable. Do people believe that they have a certain
time span of discretion because they are paid at a certain level in
relation to others? If so, the theory becomes a self-fulfilling prophecy.
Finally, there are difficulties in obtaining acceptance of these ideas by
those in industry.

Decision Banding
This method starts with the premise that all organisations tend to
reward their members in terms of the decisions they make. This is
similar to the time span of discretion, where the quality of the decision
varies at each level of the organisation. Paterson, who invented the
decision-banding method, postulates six basic kinds of decision:

Bands			
	E	Policy-making decisions	(Top management)
	D	Programming decisions	(Senior management)
	C	Interpretative decisions	(Middle management)
	B	Routine decisions	(Skilled workmen)
	A	Automatic decisions	(Semi-skilled)
	O	Vegetative decisions	(defined by others—unskilled workers)

All bands, except O can be divided into two grades, upper and lower,
thus giving 11 grades.
   The stages recommended by Paterson are:

1. The establishment of job bands according to the kinds of
decisions.
2. An analysis of the content of the jobs, from which jobs can be put
into the appropriate subgrade for Band B, using points rating, and by
ranking for Bands C and D into the agreed Band.
3. Monetary values are assigned to each level. The increase
between grades for pay rates is exponential, requiring equal distances
between the mid points.

Paterson claims that his method can be used for all jobs in the
company, and that given proper consultation it is possible to achieve a
consensus on the difficult question of differentials. Amongst the
possible problems one can envisage with the decision banding
approach are the rigidity of the bands, the reliance on the job analysts'

descriptions, and the difficulty of convincing employees that this rather perplexing scheme has initiated an accurate rate of pay.

Direct Consensus Method

The direct consensus method is another derivative of the time span of discretion theory. Again there is an assumption that a consensus of opinion will be found in any working group concerning the relationship between jobs. It is argued that a wages structure will be acceptable to employees if it embodies their conventional wisdom.

The method is simple, but for most practical purposes requires the use of a computer both to produce the ranking of jobs and to calculate the variations of assessors' opinions.

1. Job descriptions are prepared from a representative sample of jobs. The number of jobs should be a 'prime number' between 11 and 79.

2. A representative committee is established with a sufficient number of assessors to make it possible for each one to rank an equal number of jobs, using a standard form for the computer input.

3. The jobs are ranked as 'wholes' using the question how important (presumably to the organisation) is the job, in relation to each other job.

4. Jobs are ranked using the paired comparison method. All possible pairs of jobs are compared; the total number of comparisons is $N[N - 1))/2]$ where $N =$ the number of jobs.

5. Reconciliation between job rankings is usually left to a computer which will also calculate the variation between the assessor's ratings.

Ranking jobs as wholes can lead to rather difficult ranking decisions, and it is possible that, given computer facilities, jobs could be ranked under the broad factor headings which is one variation of this approach. The direct consensus method is expensive in the time of assessors, and the use of hardware. Since job content is likely to change, a comparison of factors would probably help to make the method flexible. Multiple regression can be used to weight factors relative to what is thought appropriate.

Guide Chart Profile of Hay MSL Ltd.

The Guide Chart Profile Method was developed by management consultants Hay MSL Limited, as a variant of the points rating technique. The scheme provides a total wage/salary package, and the widespread use of the scheme permits direct comparisons with other organisations to establish the market rate for particular jobs. The scheme is copyright, but a summary of some of its main aspects shows the *modus operandi*.

Following the scheme's extensive use, the consultants have

identified three generic factors, and further subdivisions into subfactors. No doubt there may be further adaptations to the scheme as it evolves. The generic factors, and sub-factors are defined in Table 8.

Accountability and 'know how' are evaluated on a points scale with varying degrees and 'problem-solving' is shown as a percentage of the 'know how' required for each job, the final results being converted into a geometric scale of scores under the three generic factors.

Job profiles are produced to show the different aspects of each job, under each of the factors, and helps to reveal the relationship between the required performance and the organisation's objectives, and show where the main job demands are, whether in acting or advising.

One of the benefits of this scheme is its recognition of the variable nature of managerial jobs which cannot be classified without taking the person specification into account in an individual way. However, although the concept of accountability could have a wide application in practice, the method seems to be favoured in tackling the problems of white collar and executive remunerations.

Table 6. Guide chart profile factors

Accountability (i) Freedom to act (ii) Magnitude of accountability	Dependent on the job's purpose, which should be related to the organisation's goals.
'Know how' (i) Skill, education, training (ii) Breadth of knowledge, including planning, organising, etc.	
Problem-solving (i) The 'thinking environment' (constraints) (ii) The 'thinking challenge' (how creative, routine, etc.)	Dependent on frequency and importance of problems.

THE INTRODUCTION OF JOB EVALUATION SCHEMES

We have devoted a proportionately large amount of space to the description of various forms of job evaluation because it is an essential first step towards the creation of a salary/wage structure which has a rational basis in the eyes of both management and work people. However, the way job evaluation is applied will be of fundamental importance in the acceptance of a scheme as a rational instrument.

Job evaluation committees have already been mentioned. Employee involvement is a part of the overall sharing of power. How management ensure the representation of the different interest groups is dependent on organisation structure, size, the current state of union/management relationships and existing relationships amongst the groups of employees affected by the evaluation.

As a general rule, small rather than large committees are recommended and they should reach decisions by consensus. 'Consensus' here means that each member of the committee should be allowed to express his opinion, and where there are genuine differences, the reasons for the differences of view should be argued out until a broad measure of agreement is found, even though there may be minor objections. The Chair's role is obviously important in directing these discussions. Whoever fulfils the role should be capable of balancing judgements and drawing together disparate outlooks, and should command respect from both employees and management. There are strong arguments for ensuring that senior line managers are represented, as well as the main body of employees.

It is essential that the type of scheme which is to be used should be agreed by employee representatives before the committee is instituted and that where unions are the recognised bargaining agents, they should agree the constitution and authority of the job evaluation committees. The watchword is to take pains at every step to involve and discuss any job evaluation proposals well in advance with unions and senior management, and only to proceed when there is agreement.

PAYMENT SYSTEMS ARISING FROM JOB EVALUATION

The outcome of a job evaluation scheme is an ordered and accepted pay structure, where there is a logical relationship between the amounts paid and the job factors and where the differentials between jobs fit into the structure and are approved. In practice, such a state of nirvana may not be reached. During the committee meetings, interest groups will achieve the redefinition of certain factors and will manage to push up or down the relative worth of some of the jobs, on the grounds of what is acceptable, comprehensible, and traditional. The fitting of the results of the evaluation to the 'market rate' prevailing may therefore be a result of negotiation.

The same job evaluation schemes are rarely used for both hourly rated and monthly paid employees. This imposes further constraints on each group, as the salary and wage structures which emerge are related in the minds of employees, but not through job evaluation, so that the final structures will have to be convincing.

The provisions of the Equal Value Amendment described in our

Employment Law chapter mean that employers should ensure that the factors used do not discriminate in favour of one sex. There is potential for an equal value claim if there is a special scheme for lower level employees if they are mostly female, while more senior employees covered by a different scheme are mostly male, for example.

We have already mentioned some of the techniques of putting a money value on a job. In the factor comparison example, this is intrinsic to the technique. From the points system, a salary band can be defined by plotting the values on a scattergraph. From such a scatter, a line of best fit can be drawn through the mid points to help create the grades. The cut off for each grade will always be a matter of judgement. To fit market rates to jobs requires a survey of the comparative data, including employee benefits. Job evaluation provides the data base on which judgements can be made, but we must turn to the problem of devising salary/wage scales for the important stage of setting up and administering scales.

QUESTIONS

1. What are the advantages of job evaluation in establishing a reward structure?

2. Describe the methods adopted in an *analytical* job evaluation scheme.

3. What have the ideas of Elliot Jaques contributed to the principles of job evaluation?

4. How would you set about introducing a job evaluation scheme in a company employing 500 people, the majority of whom are monthly paid, semi-skilled and are represented by two trade unions which have bargaining rights in respect of their members (300 workers being in one union, 50 in another, there being 80 non-union members, and 70 monthly paid non-unionised employees)?

16

Pay and Benefits

WAGES AND SALARIES

In most organisations, the approach towards pay and benefits still differentiates between staff occupying posts at different levels of the hierarchy. The main difference is that those in 'blue collar' jobs, at the lower end, are usually hourly rated, their wages being paid weekly or monthly, whereas 'salary earners' are employed in middle to senior posts with 'salaries' quoted as an annual amount, which is paid monthly in equal instalments.

The connotation of salaried staff as professionals is still with us. These differences in approach are not just based on the way pay is calculated, therefore, but extend to the whole range of employee benefits and to the way the two groups are treated by management. The representation of employees by different trade unions according to their occupational status may have helped to preserve the tradition, and opposition to monthly pay from employees is not without justification since it means waiting for payment although expenditure is often weekly, or sometimes required in advance. However, the distinctions are no longer so clear, there being a movement towards monthly pay for white and blue collar jobs.

POLICY

The objectives of a policy towards payment could be best described as 'to remain competitive for labour whilst rewarding good performance and adopting a position on pay which is felt to be fair by all employees'.

Issues such as whether or not to make distinctions between groups of employees in the method of payment and the benefits they receive are matters of company policy. They reflect the company's personnel philosophy. Some of the other issues which are also questions of policy, and which should be decided by the company's executive board, with the advice of the personnel manager, are:

1. Where the company wishes and can afford to be in the labour markets. For example, whether or not to follow a 'high wage' policy, demanding sustained effort of a high standard for large rewards.

2. What kind of total remuneration package it wishes to offer—for example, whether or not to give a range of 'perks', such as cars, inflation-proof pensions, etc. or whether to let the employee make the choice of what he spends his salary on.

3. A further question is whether or not to trade off benefits against wages. Consideration will have to be given to the consequences, for the retention of employees, for the kinds of people who work for the company and for their motivation to work.

4. Profit share bonus schemes also have to be thought through, to see whether they reflect an incentive element in the employee's wage, and whether there will be any real feeling of participation.

5. The policy on variation of pay has to be resolved. The questions here are: whether or not pay is to be regarded as the main incentive to good performance, what kind of job evaluation scheme to adopt, and how to run it.

6. To what extent will company policy on pay be delegated to local managers, and how does the degree of autonomy fit in with policies on profit centres and management accounting?

7. The frequency of pay reviews, who is to be consulted, what kinds of evidence will be sought, and the negotiation posture of the company have to be decided.

These are some of the policy options available, the choice of what is suitable being dependent on individual company circumstances, and the philosophy of management espoused.

WAGE STRUCTURES

Wage rates for hourly rated personnel sometimes include a proportion which is calculated on the individual's output. The various terms used are described below:

1. **The 'basic' or 'flat' rate:** This is the amount of money paid for an hour's work. It is also sometimes called the 'hourly rate'. Time rates are predetermined rates per hour paid at the end of the week. The flat rate is often used where the work does not lend itself to any kind of measurement.

Sometimes in addition, or instead of, the basic rate an individual bonus payment may be made.

2. Payment by results systems are either:

(*i*)   **Straight piecework.** This is the system whereby the employee is paid according to his output. The method is either to agree a fixed amount of money for the production of each item, or a time is allowed for the completion of the item which is being made. In the latter scheme, sometimes called the 'time allowed' system, if the employee completes the work in less time than planned, he is still paid for the original time, and thus is able to increase his earnings by completing more of the pieces, the calculation of his bonus being based on the difference between the time allowed and the actual time expressed as a percentage of his wage.

(*ii*) **Differential piecework.** This is similar to the 'time allowed' system of piecework, except that the amount of the bonus earned (which stems from the time saved) is shared between the company and the individual, the wage cost being adjusted with output, so that the company takes a proportion of the bonus as production increases. Schemes of this sort may be known under various names, such as 'premium bonus schemes'.

The employee has a choice with piecework of the level of output he wishes to gain.

3. **Measured Day Work.** The pay of the employee is fixed on the understanding that he will maintain a specified level of performance. This level of performance, known as the 'incentive level', is calculated in advance and the employee is put under an obligation to try to achieve the level specified, as his pay does not vary in the short term.

There are individual rates and bonus systems. In addition, there are bonus schemes which aim at providing a group incentive, either to a work group, or factory-wide.

4. **Small Group Incentive Schemes.** Typically, a bonus is given to group members when their output targets are achieved or exceeded. There are numerous schemes, which vary according to the time-scale adopted for measuring output, the size of the group, and the intergroup competitiveness which they encourage. Payment of the bonus may be equal amongst the group's members, or proportionate to an individual's earnings or status.

Advantages of group schemes:

 (*i*) They have the advantage that they draw on the natural tendencies of working people to develop norms based on what the group believes is an acceptable and 'comfortable' level of production, thereby harnessing the team spirit.

 (*ii*) They are administratively simpler than individual schemes; the cost savings come from less clerical, inspection work, and savings on time study.

(*iii*) 'Indirect' production workers, such as cleaners, stores assistants, who also contribute to the production process can be included.

(*iv*) Flexibility amongst the group is encouraged, and one might anticipate that workers would be anxious to help remove production bottlenecks and to encourage training.

Disadvantages of group schemes:

 (*i*) The impact of group pressures on the less efficient individual may not be beneficial where he needs advice and help in order to work up to the target.

(*ii*) Holidays and sickness may upset the working of the scheme. Special arrangements may have to be made to stagger holidays carefully, and shut down may result in lower pay for the holiday weeks.

(*iii*) Variations in production targets due to problems of supply, or a sudden fall in demand can be a cause of complaint, and disillusionment with the scheme could set in.

(*iv*) Large or scattered groups may not respond to the implicit appeal to group cohesiveness which is at the heart of these schemes.

(*v*) Group norms of production may not be adequate, and if translated into official 'targets' will then not create any real increase in production. If a level is set which is too high, the group scheme will be a non-starter. It is therefore very dependent for its success on the targets being achievable, but being really worthwhile for the company.

Bonus schemes stand in different ratios to the base rate, and a guaranteed or 'fall back' rate is frequently part of the wage for pieceworkers. There are agreements and legal requirements concerning payments during lay off and short-time working in the UK (see Chapter 23).

5. **Long-term, large group schemes.** The main difference between these schemes and those outlined above is that they apply on a long time-scale, usually across the whole factory, and are often seen as an attempt to involve the workpeople in the organisation of production. The bonus calculation would typically be made monthly, and would be based on changes in the value of goods produced, or improvements in the actual output per man hour against the standard.

There are many variants of these schemes. For example, the Scanlon plan (1947) was both a suggestion plan and a collective incentive scheme. The suggestion scheme was part of a system for drawing on ideas from the workforce about improvements which could be achieved jointly by management and union. It operated a bonus depending on reductions achieved by the workforce in labour costs compared with the sales revenue. Reductions in sales revenue could result in no bonus, however, although employees worked as hard.

The Rucker plan (1955) used 'production value' (or added value) as a basis for a collective bonus scheme. This value is defined as the difference between the sales revenue and the cost of the raw materials and supplies (i.e. the inputs to the production process). From Rucker's USA studies, labour there consistently received around 40% of added value, and in 1961 Marriott estimated that in the UK the ratio ranged from 18% to 57% of added value.

'Added value' bonus schemes make use of the idea that if the ratio of total employment costs to sales revenue falls below the level it has been, then the improvements in productivity this represents should be shared by granting a bonus to the people who have produced the change. A scale of bonus payments (as a percentage of basic pay) may be calculated. This approach is less susceptible to market forces and ICI are amongst a number of companies adopting a similar scheme.

Advantages of long-term, large group schemes:

(i) The long-term aspect should provide steady earnings.

(ii) Employee participation through production committees helps to overcome the 'them and us' attitudes which can be destructive, and helps to build trust.

(iii) There is a wide range of applications to different businesses.

(iv) Value-added schemes can be adjusted more readily to the company's trading position than those which use simple numbers of items produced.

Disadvantages:

(i) If applied across a whole factory there may not be a sufficient sense of identity from the scheme to help create teamwork.

(ii) For the schemes to have any incentive value a bonus of at least 10% would be expected by employees to make it worthwhile. The larger the numbers covered, the less the percentage to each employee, hence reducing its usefulness.

(iii) It is questionable whether individuals see how their own particular effort will contribute to the achievement of the target over a long time-scale. Here it is worth remembering the many variables which can intervene (changes in personnel, super-vision, customer requirements, machinery, etc.)—a list which increases as time passes.

SALARY STRUCTURES

Salary structures range in flexibility from the most rigid rate for age or service scales, to those which are so malleable that they can accommodate most individual increments. The salary administrator's objective is to retain consistency in approach, to keep the 'purity' of his scales whilst keeping sufficient scope to be able to reward outstanding performance.

Most scales relate salary to the grade of the job. Following a job evaluation a series of job grades may be constructed, using any of the methods we discussed in the previous chapters (not only as an outcome of the classification method of job evaluation). If the scales are drawn on a diagram, with grades lettered A–E (A being the lowest), a salary scale could be as Fig. 16.

Clearly, one of the questions to be decided is, should the scales for each grade overlap (as in the example above) and if so, by how much? Related to this is the question of what should be the range for the scales?

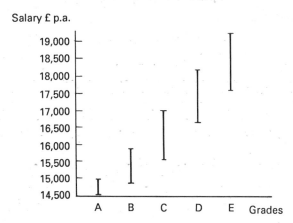

Fig. 16. Salary scales by grade.

The overlap needs careful thought because of the implications for transfers between grades and promotions. To determine the range of the salary, as a rough guide, an overlap of 10–20% is usual between associated grades, the salary level at the top of the range being 20% to 50% higher than at the bottom of the range. Higher percentage spreads for higher grade jobs are normal, so that in the example shown the range for A is £500, whereas for E it is about £1800.

CREATING SCALES FROM JOB EVALUATION RESULTS

In our discussion of job evaluation, the various techniques were all seen to have as their outcome an ordered positioning of jobs relative to each other. The results will be a list of job titles placed in order, and they will still need to be placed into specific grades (unless a classification scheme has been used).

1. **Creating a scale**

(a) The list of jobs is placed in order, together with the associated salary, and if a points scale has been used, the points value. We will then have to decide the number of grades required. This will be dictated by the size of the organisation, and in the percentage salary difference between the mid-points of the grades. If we take the average salary for those ranked lowest, and the average for the highest, we can get some idea of the spread of salaries, and the step intervals will then have to be decided taking the job evaluation results into account, using the principles on overlap between rates we outlined above. It would be as well to aim for only as many levels as is consistent with the evaluation results.

(b)   As a matter of policy, it may be that more than one set of grades is thought necessary. In this case, the top group of grades will have different criteria applied from those at lower levels.

(c)   When there is a points scheme we can allocate an equal span of points to each grade. The 'classification' techniques of job evaluation will provide a predetermined list of grades, but in the ranking methods some kind of arbitrary cut-off point for each grade will be needed. Jobs which fall on the boundary of two grades will have to be looked at carefully, to ensure that a correct decision on the grading has been made, looking for example at the salary progression implications of the grading decision.

(d)   Finally, show the relationship between the jobs on the new scale, by plotting the relative position of jobs which can be listed along the horizontal axis with their grades, whilst salary per annum is shown on the vertical axis, as in Fig. 17. From this the mid-points of the new scales can be calculated, and the range of the scale then decided.

Assuming that a salary survey has been undertaken, or that information is available to deal with the question of what is the new market rate for jobs of each category, existing scales will have to be up-dated. The design and interpretation of salary survey information is rather a specialised task, and details of how to tackle that problem are given on page 225. A new line will have to be drawn on a graph similar to Fig. 17 which will be the new mid-point for the up-dated scale. Such an important policy step has enormous policy implications for costs, recruitment and existing relationships, since it will form the basis for the new scales.

Scales may have to be adjusted and any anomalies identified. There will almost invariably be a few people who do not fit easily into the salary bands, and, once identified, plans for the individual's increments to bring him into the scale will be required.

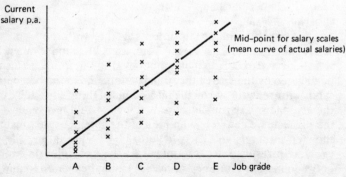

Fig. 17. Mid-point for salary scales.

SALARY ADMINISTRATION

How the policy is operated within the agreed structures is a matter of salary administration. Large companies will usually have a specialist salary administrator, and in the small- to medium-size organisation the task will probably fall on the personnel manager, or could be performed by the chief executive, company secretary or chief accountant.

There are two types of scale to administer. There are those which have scope within each range for rewarding varying levels of performance differently, and there are those which grant automatic increments based on age and/or length of service. There are sometimes scales which give a mixture of the two. A typical rate for age scale is shown in Fig. 18.

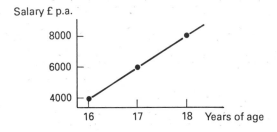

Fig. 18. Rate for age scales.

The problem then arises of where is the person placed on the scale of a graded structure when he passes 18 years of age? This is again a matter of policy depending on the incremental system.

The type of scale which provides for varying levels of performance over time can be shown as a 'box' on the graph, with overlaps between the grades (Fig. 19).

The problems of administration are how to move individuals through these scales, and how to shift the scales themselves.

WAGE/SALARY REVIEWS

The impact of inflation and the annual cycle of wage negotiation have made an annual review of salaries and wages normal practice. The distinction between the hourly rated and monthly paid is often made with different review dates. This can lead to serious problems when trying to maintain a rational basis for salary/wage differentials—evidenced when hourly rated employees transfer onto the monthly payroll, and when increases for monthly paid supervisors or indirect workers such as storemen are considered in isolation from their hourly

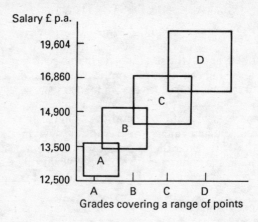

Fig. 19. Overlap between grades. All those in A grade are in the range £12,500–£13,500 p.a., etc.

rated fellow workers. It is strongly recommended, therefore, that the same review dates for both groups are used.

Preparatory work on the reviews should be started well in advance, we would suggest from three to six months, depending on the size and complexity of the organisation. Wage and salary increases can be for one or more of the following reasons: (*i*) cost of living; (*ii*) merit; (*iii*) service; (*iv*) age; (*v*) market shortages (in skills, for certain groups); (*vi*) the correction of anomalies; (*vii*) consolidating bonus or other restructuring.

Managers ought to be involved at various stages in the reviews. If the increases are to be negotiated, the preparatory work will include the development of a negotiating strategy and much supporting evidence will be required, together with the financial consequences of various prospective agreements (see Chapters 19 and 20).

Assuming that either the negotiations agree the new scales and the criteria for merit increases, or that there are no union negotiations for the salary review, the following procedure is consistent with good practice:

(*i*) Personnel department initiates and pilots through a job evaluation (may take some months to complete).
(*ii*) The personnel department undertakes salary surveys of local companies.
(*iii*) Estimates of costs are prepared from new scales which are constructed using the data of the survey. These are submitted to the Board for approval.

(*iv*) Once approved, senior line managers are given guidelines for recommending increases for merit, and an indication of the cost of living increase which has been incorporated in the new scales.

(*v*) Line manager recommendations, confidential at this stage, are vetted by the personnel manager.

(*vi*) The personnel manager refers back any problem cases, taking particular note of the costs and trends, notably the effect on relativities, progression policies and recruitment.

(*vii*) Personnel manager summarises costs and presents consolidated list to the Board (this may not include details of individual cases, but should be a breakdown of the costs into different groups). The report should include an outline of any trends, and the likely effects of the increases.

(*viii*) Notifications are sent to individuals through their managers, and to payroll. The information is entered on personnel records. The new scales are then published.

The same procedures can be followed for hourly rated or monthly paid staff.

COST OF LIVING INCREASES

Inflation ran at double figures in the UK for most of the 1970s although it fell in the 1980s. Other Western European countries were similarly afflicted, as were the USA, Canada, and many third world countries. Real wages (the amount of goods and services that money wages will buy) therefore fall unless maintained by cost of living increases. It is argued that this in turn fuels inflation producing a cost push for prices to rise, rather than a demand pull. The pressure for groups of employees to gain cost of living increases, and the practice of incomes policy norms in the UK which set out expected percentage rises, have resulted in all wages being under upward pressure on an annual cycle. Some organisations have linked their pay to a cost of living index. Taking the retail prices index over the period January 1968–January 1974, the index has risen from 121.6 to 191.8 (all items, 1962 = 100), and from January 1975 to January 1987 from 119.9 to 394.5 (all items, taking 1974 = 100).

One of the consequences of inflation has therefore been that salary scales are increased overall by an amount which is usually between what is demanded and what the company can afford, this being based on the effect on revenue to the company from price increases. Given the threat to living standards which is posed by inflation, employees often anticipate cost of living increases in their demands. Index linking is to be avoided if possible, because it gives a hostage to fortune and takes no account of the company's ability to pay.

When a scale is revised upwards, employees will expect to rise to at least the same position relatively on the new scale. However, it is possible, with the employee's agreement, to use the increase as a means of lowering the relative position in the grade, where an employee is being down graded: for example, where he has transferred at his own request to a new area, accepting a lower grade job as the only one available, or where on health grounds he wants a less arduous job. In these circumstances rather than lower the pay, the employee is best kept on a 'standstill' rate until the increases in his new grade affect his salary. This reflects a convention that wages are rigid downwards (see also, the section on constructive dismissal p. 305).

When an employee is promoted, he will expect to receive more than the cost of living increase so he will anticipate a move to a higher position on the new scale. Exceptionally, it may be agreed that there is a period before he receives an increase; for example an interim review at six months after his appointment.

MERIT INCREASES

One of the tests of a salary scale's adequacy is its efficiency in matching ability, potential and current performance with satisfactory rewards. To retain employees, the recognition of their performance must occur on time and equate with their own sense of what is fair. Following Elliott Jaques we might expect individuals to have a preconceived notion of what is a 'correct' salary for the work they perform.

Merit increases are therefore given to show recognition and to imply the kinds of actions and attitudes which the company wishes to reward. This has a bearing on how other employees define success in that organisational context, and thus merit increases are an essential element in the drive towards the company's objectives.

There is increasing interest in performance related pay, through merit increases tied closely to objectives. This places greater emphasis on appraisal schemes.

STARTING RATES

Where discretion is given on the rate at which a new employee is to start, some guidance is necessary from the scales, to avoid anomalies. Normally, new starts should enter the scale at the minimum for their grade, unless age and experience would indicate a slightly higher point. Under no circumstances should the new employee start at higher than the mid-point for the grade, although there is often pressure to do so when a particularly good applicant is earning a high salary in his previous job. However, the risks to good relationships

with the other members of the staff and the consequences for the salary
progression of the newcomer are such that it is unwise.

FIXED INCREMENTAL SCALES

Some organisations have fixed scales. A regular increment is given on
completion of each year's service. This is similar to rate for age
increases (see Fig. 18), but continues to the maximum for the scale. To
retain some elements of discretion, double or triple increments can be
provided for within a scheme, or indeed, no increment.

DISCRETIONAL INCREMENTS

A further method is to make judgements at the stage of starting (or
being promoted) of how long it will take for an individual to perform
the full range of duties satisfactorily. If this is, for example, four years,
then the difference between his starting rate and the top of the grade is
divided by four years to give an even rate of increases. Should
performance change during the four years, then the remaining
difference between his current salary and the top of the scale can be
made divisible by a smaller or larger number.

THE DIVIDED BOX

The salary box (i.e. the range over time) can be broken down into
sub-ranges which show appropriate rates for performance predictions
on a basis of previous experience and evidence of 'track records'.
Again, an individual can be switched from one salary progression line
to another if his performance warrants it. An example of the divided
box is shown in Fig 20.

This shows three performance levels, outstanding, good and
adequate, with three different progression curves through the range.

GRADE FUNNELS

This is a way of describing minima and maxima of a range which can
change with the length of service or with the age of those in the grade.
The placing of the individual's salary between these parameters would
therefore give room for high levels of performance at any age, reduce
the uncertainty on where to place the new starter or those who were
promoted, whilst giving room for changing the line of the salary
progression if performance changes.

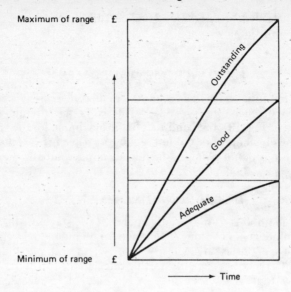

Fig. 20. The divided box.

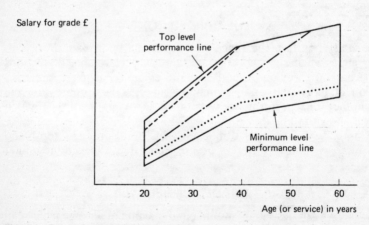

Fig. 21. Grade funnel. The figure shows three rates of progression:
- - - - -   High rate at start which is maintained, and improves, peaking at 38.
— · — · — ·   Good performance anticipated which is kept steadily, peaking at 50.
· · · · · ·   Good performance anticipated which slows down and is just adequate at the end.

MARKET PRESSURES

The reaction of managers to market rates and pressures is partly a problem of how to cope with short-term changes in market rates due, for example, to a temporary skills shortage, without upsetting an agreed grading scheme which has arisen from job evaluation. If the change is not temporary (for example, a shortage of various kinds of computer specialists) the benchmark jobs will reflect the importance and rarity of the skills when the next job evaluation takes place, and a negotiation for a new pecking order will occur when the job evaluation committee meets. In practice, in the example cited, it means the organisation has to place a higher value on computing skills because of their scarcity.

Short-term (say up to two years) fluctuations may be met by considering a market supplement which gives the shortage jobs a temporarily higher rate, which is recorded separately on their documents and records. It should be explained to the people concerned that such high percentage increases will not always be given. When market pressures abate, the salary will be brought back to the place on the salary curve which has been projected. Special bonus payments and other premia are sometimes used to retain staff, but the use of special payments outside the scales is to be avoided, as these anomalies create precedents for other groups, distort existing relativities and, if allowed to persist, make a total nonsense of the scales.

OVERTIME PAYMENTS

Overtime is most frequently paid to hourly rated employees; the premium may be full time and a quarter, time and a half, or double time. Overtime is yet another 'plussing-up' tendency which needs careful control. The concept of overtime is usually seen as a means of overcoming a short-term requirement for longer hours. Where companies have started to rely on overtime, either because of labour shortages, or because it is a way of increasing earnings without revising scales officially, there is every likelihood of serious problems in the offing. A time will surely come when an employee does not wish to work 'compulsory overtime', or there will be a lull in orders, or a new manager will be appointed who does not agree to the 'blind eye' overtime, which is not really overtime at all, but just an excuse to increase earnings. As expectations are not met, there is the making in all those situations of a classic industrial dispute.

A few simple rules for the control of overtime may help:

1. Overtime should always be authorised in advance by a senior manager (not the immediate supervisor).

2. A return showing the number of hours worked, and the reasons, should be made, and statistics of overtime by department kept.

3. Some allowance should be made in the wage/salary budget for overtime when it can be projected (e.g. during holidays or at peak periods).

SALARY PLANNING

We have already pointed out the importance of a policy on salaries and wages. To carry through a policy necessitates planning for both the individual's salary and for the groups of people under review. Piecemeal salary decisions are likely to result in distortion to the overall policy unless careful planning takes place. For example, there is a steady attrition of salaries when a high labour turnover brings in new employees at lower rates than existing staff to the extent that the salary mean for the grade is reduced. Although this does afford opportunities within the overall salary budget for adjustments to other salaries, the global effect is to distort differentials and to make reviews more crucial. Salary administration can turn to a number of devices for planning salaries.

Maturity Curves

Projections of salary curves for groups of staff can be plotted to establish future trends. This is simply achieved by recording the salaries of people within the group on a graph, showing salary against time or age. The median salary of the group is usually taken to be a good enough measure for planning purposes. Future trends can be plotted using regression techniques. The benefits of planning a group of salaries, as distinct from individual salaries, are in the build-up of data concerning performance by the group—how long do they typically take to reach maximum for their grade, and at what stage in their careers would you expect the increases in salary to level off, are some of the questions this approach helps to answer. The more stable and career-minded the group is, the greater the benefit from this kind of planning. As far as actual salaries are concerned, one can either make allowances for inflation, or predict salaries at present levels, assuming constant price/wage levels, and adjust later.

Compa Ratio

The compa ratio is a measure of the general level of salaries in a grade compared with the mid-point. It is calculated by applying the following formula:

$$\frac{\text{Average of all salaries in the grade}}{\text{Mid-point of the salary range}} \times 100$$

This can reveal that the salaries in the grade are unusually high if the ratio is over 100, for example, or that attrition in the salaries for the grade has taken place when it is low. It is sometimes useful to calculate the compa ratio for each of the grades in a department at the time of the salary/wage review so that in discussions between the department manager and the personnel manager an overall view of the salaries for the department can be taken into account. The personnel manager, or salary administrator, may also wish to use the compa ratio in comparing the recommendations for merit increases between department/line managers by calculating compa ratios for the different departments. Further useful comparisons can be made across the whole company to see how the salaries for each grade stand in the structure, and thus what actions are needed to correct anomalies.

WAGE/SALARY SURVEYS

Where the company stands in relation to the wage/salary rates being paid in the labour markets is a question which exercises all those concerned with recruitment and with pay negotiations.

There are many published sources that one can draw on. In the UK, the Department of Employment Gazette contains regular tables of current earnings and comments generally on the prices index as well as on wage rates, overtime and hours worked. The Institute of Administrative Management publishes a biannual survey of clerical and administrative salaries using their own grading scheme which has a wide general usage. Another useful source is the information supplied by Incomes Data Services which disseminates details of wage settlements, surveys, trends and also comments on a wide range of matters related to employment.

In spite of all these secondary sources, up-to-date information is often needed quickly, and the personnel manager frequently has occasion to conduct his own survey. Details of local rates and salaries for specialist groups may not be available from anywhere else.

If the company is well known in the locality, or if there are good personal contacts with colleagues at other companies, a quick telephone survey will give a general indication on salaries. However, to establish accurate comparisons, something of a more formal nature has to be done.

A postal survey will require careful preparation, and will also require much effort in the analysis of results. A quick guide on conducting a survey is given below, but it should be emphasised that experience is necessary to carry out this rather difficult exercise without problems, and that time spent in piloting questionnaires and in reading on survey design will pay dividends.

1. The scope of the survey must first be decided—who is covered, and the amount of information which is to be sought.

2. In order to make accurate comparisons, detailed descriptions of the jobs to be covered must be included. (You should avoid using company jargon.)

3. Make clear what you are looking for: basic wages, total earnings, the hours these represent, overtime rates and bonus earnings, need to be separately recorded.

4. If the salary information given is in the form of scales, responding companies should be asked to indicate where new starters enter, and where most of their current staff are in the scales.

5. Information on other benefits, for example, company cars, pension schemes, and holidays, is also a useful guide to the total package. Some of this may be quite sensitive—for example, where senior staff are concerned, or where sales commission earnings are involved. A guarantee of confidentiality, by avoiding naming individual companies when publishing results and ensuring that there is no way that a particular company could be identified, should be a part of your arrangements with the responding companies.

6. It is only to be expected that participating companies will require some feedback, and a copy of your analysis of results should be sent to them.

7. The results should be collated in graph form, with each graph clearly labelled, and each axis marked. A short narrative report summarising the findings will be helpful. To facilitate the analysis of the results it is often useful to consider the kinds of graphs you will find beneficial when designing the questionnaire so that the questions can be phrased to produce results in a convenient form.

8. A high non-response rate to a postal survey would not be unusual, but can be minimised by including a personal letter with the questionnaire and a pre-paid reply envelope, by keeping the format of the questionnaire short and simple, giving adequate time for completion, and by telephoning those people whose reply is still outstanding after the due date.

INTERNATIONAL COMPARISONS OF SALARIES

A personnel director once illustrated his problems in trying to harmonise pay and benefits throughout his European companies, by referring to the occasion when the manager of the Greek company pointed out that the annual bonus was given in kind to his employees in the islands and that they expected to receive one or more goats each year, depending on the level of profits achieved.

Although there is now freedom of movement for labour amongst the

Common Market countries in Europe, in practice there are wide variations in conditions, hours, holidays and state regulations, so that comparison is difficult. One of the biggest problems in comparing pay internationally is the variability of exchange rates, where, for example, a rate change of only 0.5 DM to the £ Sterling would lead to a large increase or decrease in pay per annum at the higher salary levels.

Since the value of money is dependent on the goods and services it can buy, comparisons of earnings must also include some kind of weighting according to the level of prices in each country. However, this, in itself, is not enough, since there will be different patterns of purchasing between countries. Assuming that a representative range of goods and services can be found in each country, the ratios of the costs of these between countries can be determined. These ratios are referred to as 'purchasing power parities'. Although, if exchange rates and purchasing power parities are taken into account, the results of a comparison of salaries between countries will be more accurate, there is bound to be a margin of error because of the non-salary elements in the total remunerations, because exchange rates are volatile, and because patterns of consumption in such matters as transport and housing may not be comparable at all.

PAY-RELATED BENEFITS

Profit Share

We have already described some of the schemes operated for hourly rated employees. These are typically related to output. There are other types of schemes which are more often applied to monthly paid staff where the level of net profit determines the bonus. The intention behind profit share schemes is to make the employee feel involved and to give him a sense of participating in the company's future growth.

A number of schemes exist. To give one example, the employees may receive a number of ordinary shares each year after the annual dividend has been calculated. The number of shares can be determined by translating the money set aside for the bonus into shares purchased at the current rate, and then issuing these to employees. The number of shares, and the cut-off point of the scheme, may include qualifications of service, grade level, etc., and a clause stipulating that the shares should not be sold for a fixed period after the bonus. Some companies retain the shares for a term after the bonus, only issuing them to employees after a year, or if the employee leaves, the bonus may be paid out in cash.

One of the difficulties of giving shares to employees is that there is a risk that the share value will fall and the employee then receives less than if he had taken cash. If the option to take cash is part of the scheme, since the number of shares granted is likely to be small, and the dividends of only a token amount, there may be less inclination for the employee to build up a sufficiently large portfolio of shares to make it worthwhile.

The motivational force of a profit share scheme is open to doubt. Long-serving, stable groups of employees are most likely to benefit, and these are the more likely to be loyal and interested in the company than the short-serving employee. The amount of money represented by the profit share is unlikely to be sufficient, by itself, to make employees wish to stay. It is as part of a total remuneration package that profit shares may have most importance.

Sales Commissions

There are some groups of employees for whom commission payments represent their main earnings, such as sales staff, sales managers and various kinds of representatives.

Questions about the usefulness of self-employed agents are beyond the scope of this book. However, it is worth considering the impact on relationships of a high percentage of commission earnings. If a small basic salary is supplemented by high commission, or bonus earnings, the sales staff become almost self-employed agents. Commission earnings not only provide an incentive, but also give the employee a choice on the work he does, where he concentrates his efforts and how he plans his time. Whilst this is necessary for the typical sales job, it does entail a loss of control and a lack of stability in earnings. Some kind of balance is necessary. To provide an incentive, at least 10% of earnings should be in commission, but more than 30% of earnings as commission provokes a heavy reliance on immediate performance which is inimical to training and development, and which gives an instability to earnings. This might encourage the employee to supplement his income by working for other companies at the same time, or to regard himself as self-employed.

Company Cars

Policy on company cars will need to be laid down at the same time as the salary scales. Here the choice is whether or not company cars should be given for use by employees privately as well as on company business, and at what level this extra benefit is to be granted. For some companies, a car goes automatically with the level of the job, and in some cases two cars are now given, one for the manager, the other for the manager's spouse.

The main consideration here is to ensure that there are rules which govern the award of a company car, and that these rules should refer to the job content. If a car is essential for the job, then it is easy to justify, both to the rest of the employees, and to the Inland Revenue.

Alternatives to this approach include company car purchase schemes which allow the employee to own the car by granting him a loan which he repays over a period. The choice of the type of car is left to him, and as it is his own vehicle, he might be expected to take care of its condition. Maintenance, petrol and running costs are borne by the company.

TOTAL BENEFIT PACKAGES

When planning salaries, an approach which takes account of all the benefits and their inter-relations is to be preferred. Salaries and wages should, therefore, not be examined without considering the other personnel policies on holidays, sickness, pensions, hours, etc., and also the differential effect of taxation on the take-home pay of employees.

The tax effectiveness of benefits, such as company cars, and the increasing range of benefits such as private health insurance and stock option schemes has led some companies to offer a flexible benefits package from which employees may select the mix appropriate to their needs.

QUESTIONS

1. Describe the hourly rated payment methods which are variable with performance.

2. What are the advantages of long-term group bonus schemes? Illustrate your answer by reference to an added value scheme.

3. What should be the main objectives of a modern salary/wage policy? How can we ensure it is being applied equally?

4. How can we reward individual merit without upsetting the salary scales?

5. What are the steps to take in conducting a salary survey?

6. What place should profit share schemes have in a total reward package?

17

Conditions of Service

We outlined earlier the significance of those personnel policies which provide a framework of conditions influential in creating the quality of work life. Conditions of service governing such issues as hours of work, holidays and pensions are fundamental to the contract of employment which exists between the employer and the employee.

Companies face a number of options when constructing their personnel policies. The decisions made will reflect their philosophy of personnel work. A number of factors will have to be taken into account by managers who confront the range of options available.

1. **Financial considerations.** The direct and indirect returns on investment have to be investigated, which entails a cost/benefit analysis of each policy.

2. **The stability of the labour force.** Here, the impact of the proposed policy on those groups who seek organisational careers should be examined.

3. **The age and sex distribution of the labour force.** This raises the question of what influence these measures have on the operation of the policy.

4. **The administrative costs involved in servicing the policy.** (For example, the costs of running a pensions scheme.)

5. **State welfare benefits.** How do these affect the policy?

6. **Industrial relations implications** which may derive from the policy—such as the sort of groupings which are created, and the interests which are reinforced or weakened by the policy chosen. What are the consequences for the company's industrial relations strategy?

In this chapter we will look at hours of work, holidays, sick pay, pensions, and welfare policies.

HOURS OF WORK

The hours of work for any job are a result of tradition, collective bargaining, technical necessity, convenience for management control and for communication needs. There are some people, such as salesmen, for whom there are no normal hours of work.

The distinction should be drawn between 'basic hours' and the normal hours worked, which may include overtime. For most of the major industries, the basic hours are subject to negotiation between employees and trade unions at a national level. When thinking of basic hours, we have to be sure of what is included: for example, does the time include tea breaks, lunch breaks, time for starting machinery, for cleaning up, etc? Such legislation as exists in the UK on hours, defines basic hours exclusive of meal breaks and other intervals.

The UK and Denmark are the only two EEC countries not to have general legislation on hours of work. Irrespective of the legal maximum basic hours, most European countries have collective agreements which stipulate a lower basic of 40 hours per week. The average number of hours worked, including overtime, is around 43 per week. There is legislation in the UK covering the permitted hours of work for women and young people, and for occupational groups such as drivers for health and safety reasons.

There are many variations in hours, according to industry, occupation, and, of course, where there is shift working, or where flexible hours are used. These two aspects of hours are worthy of special attention.

Shift Working

Shift working is introduced to make more efficient use of machinery, to increase production, or because the market or the technology requires continuous staffing. There are five main types of shift working as shown in Table 7.

In addition to these shift patterns, there are different forms of part-time working used, and mixtures of the systems outlined in Table 7, e.g. one part of a factory may be working say permanent nights, whilst another part operates a 'twilight shift' from 16.00 to 22.00.

Shift working leads to problems with domestic and social life for many employees, and may give rise to health worries. Most of our lives seem to be structured to a working existence where 8.00 to 17.30 is the norm. In the provision of children's schooling, shopping, and services, the assumption of daytime working is made. Although there may be compensation in being at home when others are at work, marriage partners and children can be upset by the irregularity of hours and absences in the evening. The change of the shift cycle from days to nights and then back disturbs the bodily functions—the circadian rhythms of heart, respiration, body temperatures, blood pressure and digestion. 'Stress' manifested in sleeplessness, digestive disorders, and even depression may be felt by some shift workers therefore.

The research on the effects of shift work on health is inconclusive so far, but it is possible that some people are more able to accept the

disturbance of different shift cycles than others. The extent to which
the shift worker's family accept the pattern of the hours, and whether
or not the worker is psychologically prepared to accept the changes
may be the key factors.

There are also managerial problems with shift work. Communications between the members of each shift are often inaccurate, the night
shift personnel may feel left out or come to regard themselves as a
separate unit. Friction between the shifts can arise from apparently
trivial incidents, such as the cleaning up of machinery, or failure to
report a new technical problem. It follows, therefore, that management must make a special effort in:

1. Training managers in the special problems of shift work.
2. Attending to shift workers' communication problems, for
example, by working along with shift supervisors and using written
communications.
3. The provision of welfare and catering facilities, such as canteens,
social clubs, etc., which cater for the needs of the shift worker.

Clock Time and Task Time

Hours of work are not important to those whose activities are
directed towards the accomplishment of tasks irrespective of when
they occur. To use Berne's phrase, we can distinguish between 'clock
time' and 'task time'. Attendance at work for particular times may be
essential for jobs which give a service to others, but for other posts
where there is an amount of work which has to be completed quite
apart from the time, attendance can be more flexible. The
development of a more flexible approach to working hours stems from
the desire of employees to avoid rigid time keeping, and from the
difficulties which employers have in recruiting and retaining staff in
some areas.

Flexible Working Hours

The basic principles of flexible working hours have been described
by Baum and Young (1973, p.19) as follows:

'The essential aim of the flexible working day is to replace the
traditional fixed times at which an employee starts and finishes work by
allowing him a limited choice in deciding his starting and finishing time
each day.'

A 'core time' is established by the employer when attendance is
required—usually the middle period of the day, excluding the meal
break. The start and finish times are variables on either side of this.
The contract between the employer and the employee fixes the
number of daily contracted hours which are assessed over periods of
from one week to a month. The employee thus starts and leaves work

Table 7. Examples of shift work patterns

Shift type	Hours	Typical start and finish times	Cycle
Double day	16 h per day	06.00–14.00 14.00–22.00	2 groups of workers rotate each week, early: late shift.
Day and night alternating	16 or 24 h	08.00–18.00 22.00–08.00	2 groups of workers alternating weekly or fortnightly, with rest days in between.
Permanent nights	9 or 12 h	18.30–05.30	2 groups of workers, 2 week cycle, with rest days: 3 rest days after 1st week, 2 rest days after 2nd week.
3-Shift discontinuous	24 h per day for 5 days	06.00–14.00 14.00-22.00 22.00–06.00 Monday to Friday inclusive	Weekly or fortnightly for the 3 groups of employees.
3-Shift continuous	24 h per day for 7 days	As above but for 7 days Monday to Sunday inclusive	4 groups of employees' cycle for 3–24 weeks. (*i*) Traditional pattern: one week of each type for each man, with rest days (*ii*) 'Continental' pattern: 2 or 3 shifts of the same kind with rest days between.

at times which are convenient for him, times which can vary day by day
to suit his own circumstances. When an employee works longer than
the contracted daily hours a credit is carried forward, or if he works
less, a debit. The period over which the employee is expected to
balance debits and credits is known as the 'accounting period', and can
be a week, two weeks, four weeks, or a calendar month. The idea was
pioneered in Germany, but has now spread to the UK where there are
a number of different types of flexible working hour schemes (FWH) in
operation. Electronic recording equipment is used because of the
necessity for large numbers of accurate records to be processed.

As an illustration of the variety of schemes we can note that there are
those which have flexibility over the lunch break, and there are
different approaches to the amount of core time, the total debits and
credits allowed to accumulate, the length of the accounting period, and
the methods of calculating holidays and overtime.

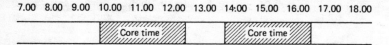

7.00 8.00 9.00 10.00 11.00 12.00 13.00 14:00 15.00 16.00 17.00 18.00

Fig. 22. An example of a FWH scheme. Core times 10.00–12.00, and
14.00–16.00. Lunch: a minimum mandatory lunch break of half an hour to be
taken between 12.00–14.00. Contracted hours = 7 per day, 35 per 5-day
week, 4 weekly accounting period.

In this case, the employee may start any time between 7.00 and 10.00
and the time of leaving is flexible from 16.00 to 18.00. He must take at
least half an hour for lunch between 12.00 and 14.00.

Let us take the case of an employee who works under these
arrangements. He starts work at 8.00 on Monday morning, takes lunch
12.30 to 13.30, and leaves at 17.30. He has thus obtained a credit of 1½
hours, having worked 8½ hours against the contracted 7 hours. On
Tuesday he starts work at 9.00 and takes the same lunch as the previous
day, and leaves at 17.00, which means he has worked 7 hours. He
continues Tuesday's pattern until Friday when he starts at 9.00, leaves
at 16.30 and takes an extra half an hour for lunch, thus working 6
hours, producing a debit for the day of one hour. At the end of the
week he therefore has a balance of a half hour credit. This is carried
over to the following week, although it must ultimately be settled by
the end of the four week accounting period.

A further refinement is used where the employee can carry credits
over to the following accounting period, and these can be put towards
the entitlement to holidays. The company would need to have agreed a
formula for credit leave units, which could be half or whole days based
on the number of contracted hours per day. For example, a credit over

the accounting period of 3½ hours in the above example would entitle the employee to a half day's holiday (being half the contracted hours).

The introduction of a FHW scheme requires care and preparation. Care is needed in the early stages of the negotiations with employee representatives to make clear the opportunities for personal choice and the attendant responsibilities which such a scheme offers. Consultation with employees over a number of months before the scheme is to come into operation may help to raise to the surface hidden doubts and misconceptions, and give time to explain what it is about. A company policy on the 'core time', the accounting period, and how credits and debits will be dealt with should be thought out well in advance. Questions about how overtime is to be calculated, what to do about domestic crises, the problem of part-time staff, and explanations about the equipment on which records will be kept must be dealt with early on in the planning. Communication about the scheme needs expert handling, and the role of the first line supervisor is crucial in this process.

The over-riding constraint on FWH schemes is the needs of the business and there will be many occupations where it is not practical. FWH seems to be most used where there are large numbers of administrative staff, such as in national and local government departments, and large insurance companies, and the benefits of the scheme for recruitment in tight labour markets are clear.

Annualised hours

Flexible working hours should be distinguished from agreements made between employers and trade unions, to work a total number of hours per year, the precise start and finish times to be decided by management. Such annualised hours contracts allow organisations to match closely the amount of labour to market demands. This is helpful, for example so that there is sufficient labour to meet the peaks in a seasonal demand. Annual hours agreements give control to management over working time, the flexibility is at their discretion, whereas flexible working hours are (within limits) under the control of the employee.

HOLIDAYS

In addition to the 7 public holidays per annum, the norm in the UK is for around 3–4 weeks paid holiday per year. This is still parsimonious by comparison with the rest of Europe both in the case of individual and public holidays.

The holiday 'bonus' is unusual in the UK, although as can be seen from Table 8, in many countries it is normal to pay a bonus, sometimes in the form of a '13th' month, at the end of the year.

Holiday Entitlement

Most companies will have rules about the length of service which is necessary before an employee is eligible for holidays with pay. The main difference is between rules under which the employee has to build up his entitlement first, by working for the full 'holiday' year, and schemes where the employee can anticipate his completion of a year's service.

The holiday entitlement year is the year during which entitlement is built up. This may be the same as the calendar year, or based on 'financial', 'accounting' or other 'years'. The following two cases help to explain the differences in entitlement provisions.

Table 8. Holiday comparison between EEC countries, in number of days

Country	Legal Minimum	Min. under collective agreements	Public holidays	Additional holiday allowance
Belgium	18	21—23	10	18 days' wages
Denmark	24	24	9½	0.9% of annual salary
France	24	24	8–10	25–30% of weekly wage
Germany	15–18	20–26	10–13	30–50% of weekly wage
Ireland	10–12	15–18	7–8	
Italy	12	18–24	17–18	
Luxembourg	18–24	18–24	10	
Netherlands	15–18	19–21	7–8	7%–8% of annual salary

Table represents 1974 EEC report results and is quoted in Stewart (1976, p.26)

Assuming a case where the entitlement year is January to December, there are 4 weeks' paid holiday, and only complete calendar months of service count towards the entitlement. If a new employee joins on 1st February, and has arranged 2 weeks' holiday in August, after 6 months' service, if the policy is to pay holidays in the year they are earned, the employee in this case would be paid 6/12, i.e. half the four weeks, that is two weeks, which would cover his holiday in August. If he is expected to work to the end of the holiday entitlement year before taking a paid holiday, he will have to wait for a period of possibly more than a year from his starting date. The company may allow the new starter to take his holiday without payment. A further two alternatives (where the new starter is taking his holiday soon after joining) are either to anticipate that he will work the full year and pay him, or pay him at the end of the year when his service is completed.

What these different approaches demonstrate is the degree of trust which the management has in its employees. There may be occasions when payment is made in advance when the employee leaves owing money to the company. This would seem a reasonable risk to take, given the necessity to trust employees anyway with goods, cash and machinery.

Close-Downs for the Whole Holiday Period

Factory shut-downs are common in some industries. For example, the wake's week in Northern England, and there are localised traditional days such as the 'Glasgow Fair'.

There are often good technical reasons for a total shut-down, which provides time for essential overhauls, and maintenance on the factory buildings. Shut-downs also avoid difficulties where the work is so interlinked that staggered holiday arrangements would not be practical. Where families are working in different companies in the same locality, a local shut-down helps cases where husband and wife want to go together. If the couple work for different employers, however, and they have different shut-downs, then this can result in an employee leaving, or wanting holiday without pay.

Joint Careers

With the advent of both members of the household pursuing careers, domestic problems can arise where there is insufficient flexibility by either the husband's or the wife's employer to make joint holidays possible.

Other than a general commitment to be sympathetic to this problem, a policy response is not really required, difficulties being better dealt with on an individual basis. Department managers can help to relieve the problems of joint careers and clashes in holiday dates by initiating a holiday roster early in the year, giving priorities where there are severe family problems and ensuring that people with firm dates record them on the roster as quickly as possible.

SICK PAY

The fear of losing earnings through sickness absence haunted workers until social security and sickness schemes were introduced.

To operate any sick pay scheme necessitates the creation of a set of rules which, as in the case of holiday pay, may entail rough justice in the attempt to provide consistency, and to avoid complexity.

Payment for absence during periods of sickness is often related to length of service and to formal status. Although there is no real justification for the perpetuation of these distinctions, it is perhaps too much to expect senior staff to abandon their preferential treatment willingly, and there are good arguments for not extending improved benefits to everyone in the organisation on the grounds of cost.

Absenteeism

Unscheduled absences from work give rise to serious management problems. Planning is brought to nothing by the absence of a significant number of the workforce.

Sick pay schemes are sometimes blamed for influencing those who are not genuinely ill to stay at home, because the threat of loss of earnings has been removed. However, the subject is more complicated than it may appear. There may be more illness amongst certain groups of workers because of the nature of their work. Hourly rated personnel may have to take days off for spurious illnesses, since unlike their monthly paid counterparts, they are more stringently supervised, and can only attend to personal problems in this way. Although it is easy to accuse someone of malingering if he takes a number of single days off, for rather unconvincing reasons, the person concerned may be under some form of stress, or just have a general feeling of unease, tiredness and fatigue. Absenteeism may also be a safety valve preventing serious industrial unrest, as it allows individuals a way of expressing a token protest.

There are some more clearly identified trends in absenteeism. Alcoholism is a significant cause of absences on Mondays. There are occupational reasons for illnesses—drivers often suffer from ulcers and digestive complaints, and 'jet lag' has come to be accepted as a reason for absence for globe-trotting executives, for example. The stress of each job is not obvious to outside observers.

If managers are fretting about malingering, they must separate out the genuinely sick from those who are not genuinely ill. Illness has no precise definition; it is therefore best left for managers and supervisors to deal with individual cases. Perhaps the most useful approach is to try to create conditions under which employees want to go to work, and look forward to the experience rather than fear it.

PENSION SCHEMES

Since April 1978 pensions in the UK have been on a two-tier basis. The two parts of the State scheme are:

(*i*)   The basic level which for those with a full contribution record is equal to their average earnings up to the basic amount set.

(*ii*)   An additional pension which is equal to a quarter of the earnings between the basic level and an upper limit, taking the employee's best previous twenty years as a basis for the calculation.

The scheme was outlined in the 1975 Social Security Pensions Act, which tried to improve the pension to the levels which were becoming common throughout Europe.

The Government has introduced a measure which allows employees to opt out of an occupational scheme, provided they enter a private scheme of their own choosing, which is as good. 'Portable pensions' should encourage labour mobility.

Redundancy/Early Retirement

The general trade recession, and the structural changes in the older industries of Western Europe, such as steel, mining and transport, have led managers to look at how they can reduce their labour force in a 'painless' way. Early retirement is one approach used to overcome the trauma of dismissal.

The benefits can be summarised as follows:

1. The support given by a retirement pension takes away some of the financial anxiety, giving time for the employee to look for other employment.

2. Older employees may have fewer financial responsibilities (children left home, mortgage paid for, etc.) whereas redundancy for a younger man may have a more harmful effect on his family.

3. Early retirements can 'unblock' promotion opportunities in the future, and create a more dynamic organisation.

4. It may be less psychologically damaging to be 'early retired', given that a person who is going to retire in a year or two will be preparing already for his retirement. The term 'redundancy' is also rather unpleasant to some, implying uselessness, and reflecting on the job holder rather than the job.

5. Early retirement gives some financial advantage to the person who can find other employment, as he may still draw his pension.

The disadvantages of using 'early retirement' to slim down a labour force are:

1. Early retirement is costly to the company. The costs of paying both the employee's and the employer's contribution to the pension scheme will obviously be higher the longer the employee would have served. Ten years is the maximum most employers would expect to buy for all practical purposes. A straight redundancy payment (even including a 'golden handshake') is likely to be cheaper.

2. The option of early retirement is only open when there is a pension scheme of which the employee has been a member for some years. The loss of increments up to the normal retirement date, although mitigated by extra allowance by the company in its pension calculations, will be felt as a serious blow if settlements in wage rates are higher than the allowance made to compensate for inflation.

3. The early retirements that are voluntary may be in groups from which losses are not required, whilst others hang on to their jobs when they ought to go for the sake of economic efficiency.

4. The company loses its most experienced workers. The loss of skills is potentially damaging to the training of younger employees.

WELFARE POLICIES

Personnel management originated in part from the early welfare workers of the 1890s to 1918. With the growth of employment management from the 1930s, specialist welfare departments have become only adjuncts to the main personnel department. The welfare role has moved into specialist services, and has also become more diffuse in its general applicability to all managerial jobs.

The Welfare Role of the Manager

All managers have a welfare role to perform for their staff. The immediate line manager or supervisor will be first to notice the signs that an individual has a problem—poor performance, absence, sickness, difficulties in relationships, will be seen by the perceptive manager who should be conscious of the importance of a sense of well being for the achievement of results.

Such an approach by managers does mean that they see themselves as helpers to their staff. Helping in this sense is being supportive, problem-solving with subordinates and constantly seeking ways to make the employee successful. Given such a manager/subordinate relationship, personal problems and sickness, for example, will be problems the subordinate will want to share, and, if it is feasible, to look to the company for help in solving.

There will be occasions when expert assistance is required. The skill for the manager in his welfare role has two aspects, therefore. He must be able to diagnose with the employee what the problem is, and if possible, help him to solve it, and he must be able to persuade the employee that expert help is required, where necessary.

Counselling at Work

In both cases, the first stage is the 'counselling interview'. This kind of interview requires a problem-solving approach. To apply this technique experience and training are needed, but the following outline gives an impression:

1. The identification of the problem. This requires a non-directive approach, using open-ended questions which allow the problem holder to explain his problem, listening, and *not* offering advice or evaluative comments. The manager or welfare officer must remain

neutral at this stage. To allow the employee to talk about topics which are highly sensitive, it is important that he be given time to think and express himself—thus silences should be allowed, and techniques for opening up the problem should be used: for example, 'reflecting back' key phrases to elicit some further expansion of the issues raised. The imaginary dialogue which follows may help to explain:

Subordinate: '...you see, I've not been getting on well with the wife ... (pause), she doesn't understand ...' (silence)
Manager: 'Doesn't understand?'
Subordinate: 'What I mean, she doesn't think my work should take priority over the family.'
Manager: 'What do you feel about that?'

It was vital in the dialogue outlined above that the problem holder should come to formulate for himself what he meant by 'doesn't understand', a phrase which if left on its own would gloss so many different meanings, and would be a convenient cover for the subordinate to avoid coming to terms with his problem. In the last question, we have reached the nub of the problem definition; it must be defined by the problem holder and it is in his definition of the situation that the starting point for the resolution of the problem resides.

2. The conditions under which the problem occurs. By exploring the conditions under which the person experiences the problem, the 'boundaries' of the problem can be found. If the conditions changed, would the problem change? The 'conditions' include the feelings of the person whose problem it is. These 'feelings' are 'facts'. By allowing the problem holder to reveal to himself what his own feelings are, he will come to accept his own part in the problem. Active help which a supervisor might contemplate to alleviate problems could include changes within the job, relieving pressures for a temporary period, getting the subordinate to use his workmates in helping to resolve a problem.

3. Solutions to problems will only be real solutions if the person who believes he has a problem also believes in the solution. It is most likely that he will believe in the solution if he puts it forward himself. He should be encouraged, therefore, by the manager to do so, and a useful role for the manager is to get the subordinate to evaluate his own solutions rationally.

4. If a problem is identified which requires expert help, it switches its focus to the problem of how to achieve a fruitful conjunction between the problem holder and the expert agency (e.g. drug addiction centres, marriage guidance, etc.). Various kinds of supportive behaviour will assist—for example, giving time off, respecting confidentiality, accompanying a nervous person on his first visit, etc.

It is clear from the above rather brief account of counselling that there is a difference between 'counselling' and 'discipline'. The distinction is in the concept of discipline which the manager possesses. If he believes the employee can change himself then the counselling role is appropriate. Only when this has been tried and failed should he move into the discipline procedure (see p. 287).

Specialist Welfare Roles

Specialist welfare officers can offer a unique role. Where they are neither part of senior management, nor within the employee groups, they can portray a kind of neutrality which makes them valuable as helpers in the wider social problems which society faces. The personal problems experienced are sometimes so serious that they need to be discussed with someone outside the chain of command. For the person with problems of alcoholism, or whose children are in trouble, for example, the neutral welfare officer may also have useful contacts with outside help. Their specialised experience will also enable them to recognise problems more readily. The most productive arrangement is where there are both well-trained, sympathetic line supervisors, and experienced welfare officers. Given a mutual desire to help employees, much can be accomplished by these two working together.

Typical Welfare Problems

Young Employees. Line managers and welfare officers should take a particular interest in young people. Line managers are giving a lead to youngsters by their example, and are building up the new entrants' supervisory skills when they inculcate a helping, caring attitude. Welfare officers should make themselves known to new employees and should be active in bringing sports and social activities to their attention. It is particularly valuable for the welfare officer to bring together young people who can then share common problems in a mutually supportive relationship. Accommodation is often a problem for new employees in large cities, and one might expect a register of accommodation to be kept within the personnel or welfare department which should be vetted for standards and the list kept up to date.

Sickness. Long-term sickness produces problems of coping with a lower income and extra costs for hospitalisation, as well as a variety of other difficulties, such as finding help to look after the children and emotional upsets. Here, expert help from a welfare officer, plus assistance from the personnel department with sick pay, time off problems, is necessary. Sick visiting has long been a function of welfare and line management and shows that a real interest is being kept up in the employee's welfare.

Retirement. Retirement comes as a shock to many people. The whole of a family's domestic and social existence is predicated on the assumption of a regular income and the security provided by employment. Patterns of behaviour which have come to be regarded as normal for forty years are suddenly changed on the 60th or 65th birthday. There is a need to prepare people for retirement, therefore, by pre-retirement courses and discussion groups. The preparation will cover the practical questions about pension and social security benefits, taxation problems, how to keep fit, how to develop new interests, and will give employees a chance to become acquainted with the idea of retirement. Welfare officers and senior line managers should continue meeting ex-employees after retirement and be on the lookout for hardship.

Canteen Facilities. Welfare policies are not only concerned with individuals. Canteen facilities, sports and social clubs, company outings, long service awards and preferential purchase schemes are just some of the areas which welfare policies cover. Of these, canteen facilities tend to be most contentious. Amongst these general welfare policies, the quality of the canteen facility and the amount of subsidy are most likely to affect relationships. This is quite disproportionate to the costs, but it reflects the concern of people who will take even minor failures in catering very personally. Matters such as the cleanliness, the quality of the cooking, and the prices are amongst the most crucial. To help diminish the contention, many companies have put the control of the canteen in the hands of a committee representing employee interests.

CONCLUSION

In the broadest sense, welfare is what personnel management is about. To grant employees a sense of well being requires more than just a felt fair pay and benefits policy; it needs a positive approach to the welfare of people at work, by managers and specialist welfare staff alike.

QUESTIONS

1. What are the problems of shift working?

2. What are the benefits of FWH schemes?

3. Discuss the impact of personnel policies on the level of 'trust' in a company.

4. What factors would you have to weigh when considering an early retirement option in order to reduce the organisation's labour force?

5. What approaches can be used in the early identification of welfare problems?

FURTHER READING: PART 5

Baum, S. J. and Young, W. E., *A Practical Guide to Flexible Working Hours*, Kogan Page, London, 1973.

Bowey, A. M., *Handbook of Salary and Wage Systems*, Gower Press, Epping, 1976.

Egan, G., *The Skilled Helper*, Cole Publishing, Monterey, California, 1976.

Jaques, E., *Time Span Handbook*, Heinemann, London, 1964.

Livy, B., *Job Evaluation: A critical review*, Allen & Unwin, London, 1975.

Lupton, T. and Gowler, D., *Selecting a Wage Payment System*, Kogan Page, London, 1969.

McBeath, G. and Rands, D. N., *Salary Administration*, Business Books, London, 1969.

Marriott, R., *Incentive Payment Schemes*, Staples Press, London, 1961.

Paterson, T. T., *Job Evaluation*, Business Books, London, 1972.

Stewart, M., *Employment Conditions in Europe*, Gower Press, Epping, 1976.

PART 6

Industrial Relations

The term 'industrial relations' is used in a general sense to describe the formal relationships between employers and trade unions or other collective groupings of employees together with the institutional arrangements which arise from these relationships.

In only granting one section of our book to this subject, we are aware that it is impossible to cover the whole range of topics which could be included, but it is our intention to provide a general introduction to the subject of industrial relations in the United Kingdom. We hope that in doing so we will give managers with personnel responsibilities some practical insight into industrial relations problems, and that our discussion of techniques and approaches to solving these problems will prove helpful.

UNITARY AND PLURALISTIC 'FRAMES OF REFERENCE'

The approach managers take to formal relationships at work is crucial because their success in this field depends upon their own values, their deep-set beliefs about the legitimacy of managerial authority, and the distribution of power in organisations. Fox has suggested that the 'frame of reference' which managers adopt conditions their response to the problems they face. The 'frame of reference' is a term coined to describe the typifications and tacit understandings people use to make sense of their everyday world.

We argued in Part 1 that each individual is socialised by experiences which result in his possessing values and attitudes which he comes to regard as conventional wisdom. The possession of these values is reinforced by the groups within which the individual moves (management colleagues, or workmates). Thus 'frames of reference' become touchstones for making judgements and the filter through which evidence is passed.

The 'unitary' frame of reference is common amongst managers.

According to this unitary perspective, all people in the organisation are working towards one goal, where there is one sense of authority, and where conflict is anathema. Managers often see themselves and other managers in the company as part of a 'managerial team', and they expect their subordinates to subscribe to the same point of view.

An alternative way of looking at organisations is to see them as pluralities of interest groups, each with differing and sometimes competing interests, which may come together in alliances, although these alliances shift and change as circumstances dictate. Whatever the long-term interdependence of interest groups, in their day-to-day struggle for resources, and in their operational activities, they assert sectional interests. The manager's role from a pluralist frame of reference is to balance the various interests in order to achieve objectives, including those of shareholders, customers, the government and employees, allowing as much freedom of expression and action as possible. Each group, in addition to having markedly different interests, is also subject to schisms and will become part of various cross-cutting alliances. The management process thus becomes one of creating an open climate of relationships in which these varying competing interests can be expressed.

THE BRITISH SYSTEM OF INDUSTRIAL RELATIONS

The idea of a 'system' is used in this context in an abstract manner. The notion is helpful when analysing and describing an inter-related set of activities. The most famous formulation of industrial relations as a 'system' is by Dunlop:

'Every industrial relations system involves three groups of actors: (1) Workers and their organisations, (2) Managers and their organisations, and (3) Government agencies concerned with the workplace and the work community. Every industrial relations system creates a complex of rules to govern the workplace and work community. These rules may take a variety of forms in different systems—agreements, statutes, orders, decrees, policies, practices, customs. The form of the rule does not alter its essential character: to define the status of the actors and to govern the conduct of all the actors at the workplace and work community.

(J.T. Dunlop, 1970, p. VIII)

Given the significance of income and status deriving from the occupational position taken in society, it is inevitable that broad political questions arise when we consider the institutionalisation of the relative power positions of management and unions.

This 'institutionalisation' has taken the form of the large-scale organisation of working people into trade unions to protect their economic interests, and the development of employers' associations which seek to protect and further the interests of employers. The internal structure of the unions, and their relationships with each other derive from their history, the industries where they operate and the work situation of their members. Employers' Associations are groups of employers who combine to form a 'club' which negotiates wages, and other conditions of service, and for mutual support and advice, in such areas as training, and to operate with the unions a common disputes procedure.

The main tradition of the British system of industrial relations has been the tradition of voluntarism, where employers and trade unions have negotiated and agreed terms at the national level, without recourse to legal backing for the agreements.

The growth of committees of shop stewards at the local level and trends towards productivity bargaining have led to more local negotiations in the private sector of the economy. A counter-trend has been the increasing involvement of the State, and increasing militancy in the public sector where bargaining is at national level. During both World Wars, and from 1945 at times of periodic crises, the State has become concerned with the regulation of labour. The need to manage a mixed economy and the control of inflation specifically have brought the government directly into the industrial relations arena.

Political ideologies are, of course, linked to management ideologies, since both are concerned with the use of power. The Labour Party gains its main financial support from the trade unions, a movement in which the Party had its early roots. The Conservative Party has long been associated with the City of London, and with professional and upper middle class beliefs.

A simplistic view would see the two main political parties as representatives of polar differences in society between the interests of labour and capital. However, another interpretation of recent events would see the State interventions through employment law, incomes policy and trade union law by Governments of both political persuasions, as a sign of a new trend. In this, the State may be seen as acting on behalf of a 'third party' interest, separate from capital and labour. This could be construed as a stance where the State takes to itself the pluralist role of maintaining the balance between different interest groups so that essential freedoms in our society are maintained, and so that the individual's rights (as consumer or worker) are protected. The role of the State in industrial relations over the 1960-80 period could be said to have intensified. The State's adoption of a pluralist mantle (a role which it has traditionally fulfilled in other areas of social life) is a sign of management's failure to create and sustain trust with work people, and of the unions' failure to reform their procedures.

It is the function of this part to go into the practical problems that are encountered in the management of industrial relations. The history of trade unionism helps us to understand the traditions and conventions of industrial relations which are influences on current actions. The arrangements which exist for collective bargaining and the industrial relations policies which are available will be considered, together with techniques for negotiation, and procedures for the resolution of disputes. Finally, we will examine the law relating both to individuals and to collectivities in employment.

18

The History and Development
of Trade Unions

This chapter is a very short summary of the development of trade unions in Britain. Our intention here is to set out the history of trade unions only in relation to three main areas: trade unions and the law; the political consciousness of trade unions in the United Kingdom; and the main changes in unionisation which have occurred. Although this is a limited account of union development, a knowledge of these areas will inform our discussions in succeeding chapters.

THE EARLY HISTORY OF TRADE UNIONISM UP TO 1914

In the early history of trade unionism we should distinguish between unskilled unions and the craft societies. The craft societies were unions of workers who had served an apprenticeship, which was seen by the craftsman to give him a right to a customary wage, control of entry, the maintenance of standards, and the general regulation of the craft. Craft societies set down rates, and offered their members friendly society benefits, notably benefits in cases of sickness, accidents and retirements.

Local control of rates was soon augmented by national organisation in the mid-nineteenth century, so that the Engineers, Ironfounders, Boilermakers, Carpenters and Joiners, each formed amalgamated societies out of local or regional societies, which gave sufficient local autonomy in custom and practice whilst providing standard minimum rates, hours, and benefits to members. Trades councils also developed in the towns from the mid-1850s, representing all trades in one district, and were a forum for ideas on unionism to spread.

The political ideology of the craft societies was based on an individualistic doctrine represented by the Liberal cause. In the beliefs of the artisans, self help and the freedom to associate with their colleagues to further the aims of the craft were not incompatible objectives, since it was through hard work and sacrifice that the tradesman learned his craft, and the benefits granted by the union were based on the insurance principle through contributions.

The industrial revolution changed employment conditions fundamentally. Some of the newer industries adopted apprenticeship schemes, others relied on training through experience.

One of the features of early trade unions was the discontinuity of their organisation. They rose and fell in strength and influence with the trade cycle; growing in booms and failing in the slumps. Cuts in wages were not unusual since employers regarded labour as a variable cost which should be subject to the same principle of price determination as other 'commodities'. The casual nature of the employment contract, together with the large pool of unskilled, poor people anxious for work, made the organisation of unions difficult. Unions possessed little in the way of financial reserves. Until the 1880s, there were many small unions with localised membership.

There are few statistics but, by about 1890, membership is thought to have covered approximately 5% of the working population, 10% of adult male workers. Half the membership was in the North of England, and the density of membership (the proportion of actual to potential members) was variable across industries, the largest numbers being in metals, engineering, ship building, mining, quarrying, the building trades, printing, textiles, and woodworking.

The mid-Victorian period of unionism was characterised by a rather pragmatic non-militant approach, deriving from the policy of a 'Junta' of union Secretaries based in the London Trades Council. The opposition to the Junta's domination of policy, and emerging working class radicalism, led to a counter movement. A Trade Union Congress was organised in Manchester in 1868, and Birmingham in 1869, by the provincial trades councils. After 1871, there were annual TUCs which conferred on questions which were of importance to unions and working people. The TUC has never sought either to control individual unions or to be a federation of unions. One of the main information-gathering arms of the TUC was its Parliamentary Committee which also sought to influence Ministers and MPs.

In the late 1880s a new unionism emerged. This was the start of large-scale organisation of the unskilled and semi-skilled on a national basis, pursuing claims for better wages by hard-fought strikes as exemplified by the famous London Dock Strike of 1889, the seamen's strike in the same year, and the improvements gained by the gasworkers. These 'general' unions owed their stability and growth to their success in a few large industries, and the larger works where the strengths of the leadership could exert an influence. These general unions had a more militant outlook on collective bargaining, and put forward a broad socialist doctrine on the redistribution of ownership, and the removal of the worst abuses of capitalism.

The legal status of trade unions has always been uncertain. The law has frequently been involved to repress groups of workers. In the early nineteenth century there were the Combination Acts, and it was not until 1871 that the position of the unions was clarified by the Act which established that members were not liable to prosecution as criminal conspiracies because they were in 'restraint of trade'. The Act also sought to make unions responsible for their own internal organisation, whilst granting them protection for their funds and allowing them to register as Friendly Societies. Unfortunately, the contemporaneous Criminal Law Amendment Act made most of the actions of a union in dispute subject to severe penalties, and it was not until 1875 that a new law, the Conspiracy and Protection of Property Act, permitted peaceful picketing and strike action. Similarly, the 1875 Employers and Workman's Act made breach of contract a purely civil matter.

The union cause received a further set-back from the Taff Vale Judgement 1901, when the House of Lords on appeal held that employers have a right in law to sue trade unions in the Courts and to obtain damages from their funds for the actions of their officials during disputes. The judges found that, although trade unions were not corporations, the rights granted to them in the earlier legislation gave them a corporate character so that they could be sued for damages. In 1906, the new Liberal Government reversed the effects of this judgement by passing the Trade Disputes Act which again made peaceful picketing legal, and gave trade unions and their officials immunity from any claim for damages caused by actions in furtherance of a trade dispute.

The rising cost of living and declining real wages in the period 1896 to 1914 resulted in a strengthening of the newly emerged Labour Party, and more people joined the trade unions. There was a further legal tussle in 1909 about the political levy, which trade unions paid to the Labour Party. The House of Lords on appeal decided that payments of money from union funds to the Labour Party were *ultra vires*. The 1913 Trade Union Act again reversed the decision, although the Act required union members to ballot for a political contribution. It is not difficult to see the origins of trade unionists' suspicion of the law in these cases.

1914–18

We have already commented on the development of welfare work during the First World War.

The war had a significant effect on industrial relations for a number of reasons:

1. The involvement of Government in directing employment and the regulation of wages moved thinking to the position where the cost of living was seen as a basis for wage determination.

2. For the first time, a Government had to develop a dialogue with the unions over such issues as 'dilution', and the planning of manpower encouraged bargaining at a national level.

3. With the advent of large-scale production, employers sought the help of local union representatives in exercising control over labour.

4. The war was important in the political experience of the Labour Party and trade union members. They saw what the State could do to organise production on a large scale.

At the end of the war society had changed from pre-war times. There was a feeling expressed in the slogan that 'homes fit for heroes' should be built, that life should be better, and that we should not return to the old class conflicts. The revolution in Russia gave encouragement to the belief that some form of world-wide social change was possible.

1919–39

Unions were more militant, and sought long-term benefits in negotiation immediately after the war, when labour was scarce. This was a period of amalgamations between unions, which resulted in the formation for example of the Amalgamated Engineering Union, the Transport and General Workers Union, and the Amalgamated Union of Building Trade Workers. Financial problems were one reason for amalgamations. The small local unions could not compete, and were soon to disappear. The combinations of employers who faced the unions were another major reason for seeking to present a united front.

Towards the end of the 1920s, unemployment rose and trade unions went on the defensive, aiming to protect jobs rather than to increase wages. Employers sought to restore wages to a supply and demand basis. This was a time of the famous 'triple alliance' between the miners, transport workers and the railwaymen—an alliance in areas of policy and for mutual support at time of difficulty and confrontation. The attempts by the unions to maintain their socialist gains from the wartime economy were opposed by the employers and the government, which sought to decontrol the mines and the railways.

The General Strike of 1926 lasted nine days and was a result of a breakdown in the negotiations between the Miners' Federation, the coal owners, and the government over the employers' demand that the miners should work longer hours for less pay. The TUC was not a 'revolutionary body'. It would appear that all the TUC wished to do was to put pressure on the government by the threat of a General Strike, and they were quick to call off the strike when it was pronounced illegal.

Up to 1926 the unions had retained their political objectives. They sought a different kind of society, although not outside the concept of Parliamentary democracy. After 1926, until the war in 1939, the unions were more concerned with local industrial matters.

The result of the General Strike was the Trade Union Act of 1927. This made all sympathetic strikes illegal, and State employees were prohibited from joining any union whose membership was open to workers in other occupations and 'contracting in' to the political levy was made necessary. Large-scale unemployment together with the draconian approach of the 1927 Act resulted in less militancy by the unions in the end of this period.

The General Council of the TUC was concerned to reduce the problems of inter-union clashes over recruitment of members, and in 1924 the Congress approved an inter-union Code of Conduct. More precise and binding rules were laid down by the TUC in 1939, when meeting at Bridlington. The 'Bridlington Agreement' stipulated that where a union already represented and negotiated on behalf of a group of workers, at an establishment, no other union should attempt to recruit members there. Although restricting choice, this agreement helped to introduce order into collective bargaining.

1939–51

The Second World War was again the occasion for co-operation between unions and government. This 'total' war involved everybody, and from the perspective of trade union development was significant for two reasons. Firstly, the need for local control and co-operation in production assisted the growth of the shop steward movement. Managements needed stewards as much as the union as a vital communication channel with working people. The large scale and increased pace of work made communications even more important. Secondly, with the changed role of the State and a Labour Government, initially as part of a coalition during the war, and at the end, elected with a large majority to carry through reforms, union leaders felt that the tide of history was with them. The welfare state and the nationalisation of basic industries brought socialist aims nearer. Indeed one of the first steps of the new Labour Government was the repeal of the 1927 Act, making sympathetic strikes legal and returning the position on the political levy to 'contracting out', where it remains.

However, even during the war, in spite of compulsory arbitration, a number of strikes did occur, and after the war there was an 'outbreak' of unofficial strikes. It could be argued that as unions become more associated with the centre of power so their role as advocates of the non-managerial cause is weakened. The large-scale organisation of unions made members remote and their involvement in union affairs sporadic and problem-centred. The rifts between rank and file and the leadership are a feature of the large-scale organisation of people. Since unions are supposed to be operated democratically, this can result in the leadership having to take a less moderate view than they would wish.

1951–1970s

The membership of trade unions has grown mostly in the white collar area, although the density of white collar membership did not increase dramatically until the 1970s.

Table 9. Increase in trade unionism from 1948 to 1974

	Membership %	Density %
White Collar	+117.1	+9.2
Manual	+ 0.1	+7.2

The reasons for the growth in white collar union membership are as follows:

1. There are more white collar jobs due to changes in the occupational structure. The growth areas in the British economy are the service areas, and process industries. More women have joined unions as a result.

2. White collar unions achieved a higher density possibly due to incomes policies and a need felt by their members for professional negotiation on their behalf.

3. White collar jobs have emerged in large concentrations—the 'clerical' factories especially in the public sector. The standardisation of functions helps to create a common identity.

4. The duty imposed by governments that nationalised industry should bargain with the unions also encouraged white collar union growth.

5. Most of the growth was in the public sector, and it was in this area that employment expanded sharply; so that local and central government became largely unionised.

6. Associated with the last point, the impersonal relations and standardisation of conditions of service stimulate the representation of interests through union officials.

Having achieved a good penetration of most sectors (including junior and middle managers) and increased the density, white collar unions were more militant in pursuit of wage claims as was seen during the winter of 1978/9.

One of the major areas for confrontation between unions and government was over the issue of pay controls. Since 1945 there have been numerous attempts to control inflation by some form of prices and incomes policy. There have been two main effects of incomes policy and price rises.

1. A 'threat effect' caused employees to join unions to protect themselves against falling living standards.

2. There was also conflict over pressure for local level bargaining against incomes policies which are more readily applied at national level.

The 1960s were years of low unemployment and union militancy. There were large numbers of unofficial strikes and it became common for Britain's economic problems to be blamed on the union movement. A Royal Commission under Lord Donovan investigated some of these issues, and its report was published in 1968. It concluded that management should assume a more direct responsibility for industrial relations, and that, amongst other improvements, bargaining should be at a local level.

This in fact has been the trend. We will discuss the emerging role of the shop steward more fully in the next chapter. Here, it may be noted that shop stewards, encouraged by the size of companies and their independence from employers' associations, have come to fill a vital place, both for management and workpeople.

The advent of incomes policies and the 'social contract' slowed down the movement towards local autonomy in bargaining. It was clear, however, that the greatest difficulty with incomes policy was for the union leaders to obtain the agreement of the members.

The growth of employment legislation since the 1960s will be commented on in the chapters that follow. Both Labour and Conservative Governments have sought to introduce some kind of legal framework within which trade unions should operate. The Labour Government's White Paper 'In Place of Strife' was never translated into legislation, but the Industrial Relations Act of 1971 under the Conservative Government provoked an enormous wave of protest, over its attempt to make collective agreements legally binding on the parties, and the extension of controls over union affairs. With the defeat of the government following its confrontation with the miners over pay, the new Labour Government repealed the 1971 Act.

INDUSTRIAL RELATIONS IN THE 1980s

The industrial relations scene has changed in the last decade. Some previous trends, such as the move to company level bargaining, have continued, and the individualistic ideology of the 1970s has grown in the 1980s, finding political expression through government policies. There is now a new climate for relationships at work. What has caused these changes?

1. High levels of unemployment have reduced trade union militancy.

2. The move from 'smoke-stack' industries to a service-based economy means unions have lost support in their traditional areas, especially in the nationalised industries.

3. The changes to the occupational structure, blue collar to white collar jobs, has affected the number of trade union members.

4. New technology has changed job and working practices. There is now more competition between unions for members (as for example in the printing industry, and in the active recruitment by the EETPU).

5. There are more women in the workforce. Approximately 5 million people (mostly women) now work part time. It is always difficult for trade unions to organise part-time employees.

6. Government legislation has removed the possibility of secondary action, and has forced unions to ballot before strikes. The whole aim of government policy has been to reduce trade union power. Managements have shown themselves ready to obtain court injunctions against unions.

7. New approaches to industrial relations have been brought to the United Kingdom from Japan. There are now over 70 Japanese companies operating here. Their preferred approach is one union, single status employees and emphasis on employee involvement.

8. The recession has caused managers to act more strategically in the way they handle industrial relations. This has entailed managers opening up parallel communication channels to the unions, seeking longer term agreements, bargaining for gains in productivity and looking for quality improvements.

These trends have had an effect, therefore. Trade union membership has fallen by around 3 million people. The number of days lost through strikes has fallen from a high of 29.4 million working days in 1979 to 1.9 million in 1986. Some trade unions, notably the AUEW and the EETPU, are seeking ways of modernising the movement with new approaches. 'No strike' deals with employers, single union agreements, and strong local involvement of union and employees in the company are some of the threads which are emerging as a basis for the new approach.

However, during the recession, productivity has improved. Output increased, 1983 to 1986, by 12%. Inflation at that time was running at around 3.9% per annum, whereas wage settlements were on average 7% per annum, showing that some of the productivity gains have been shared by the workpeople. In spite of the loss in membership, the number of trade union members has held up in the proportion of full-time employees represented, given that almost half the working population in the UK is either employed part-time, self-employed, unemployed or on various training schemes.

CONCLUSION

The ebb and flow of power in industrial relations over the centuries has pushed the frontiers of control back and forth between management and workpeople. From this abbreviated history of trade unions in the United Kingdom, we can see how they play a part in the political processes of the nation. Conflicts with the law have been a feature of their relationship with the State. Unions are democratic movements and their power is dependent upon the support of ordinary working people. The emergence of shop stewards, and the move to local level bargaining leads to the conclusion that it is at the company level where industrial relations policies and strategies can forge productive relationships.

QUESTIONS

1. What differences in their history and development exist between craft and skilled unions and unions of unskilled people?

2. To what extent has state policy and the law influenced the development of trade unions?

3. What reasons are there for recent changes in trade union growth?

4. Do trade unions play a part in the political life of the nation? Give examples from the history of trade unionism to support your argument.

19

Collective Bargaining

The conduct of British industrial relations must primarily be the concern of those working at the plant or office level. We have seen from our discussion of the history of industrial relations, however, that there are a number of national institutions which impinge on relationships, and therefore actions and reactions at the local level have industry-wide and national dimensions. The relative power positions of the participants are crucial determinants of the outcomes in collective bargaining.

In this chapter we will describe the roles of shop stewards, union officials, employers' associations and managers so that we can identify the parts they play in collective bargaining. We will go on to set out the different forms of bargaining, and to suggest a model industrial relations policy which could be applied at the local or 'plant' level.

TRADE UNIONS AND EMPLOYERS

The Trade Unions

A rough classification of trade unions into the categories of 'craft', 'general', 'industrial' and 'occupational' is sometimes made. In practice, trade unions are not organised on these principles, as there are so many exceptions, often derived from historical precedents, that such generalisations are inaccurate. There are approximately 348 trade unions, with a total membership of around 10.5 million members. The largest single union is the Transport and General Workers Union with about 1.3 million members, closely followed by the Amalgamated Union of Engineering Workers (800,000), and the General and Municipal Workers Union (800,000). In the public sector, the National and Local Government Officers' Association (750,000) and the National Union of Public Employees (650,000) are the largest, with other unions such as the Civil and Public Services Association also growing in size. The nearest approach to an 'industrial union' is probably the National Union of Mineworkers (211,000 members) and there are unions which have expanded through amalgamations which now include a variety of trades and industries such as the Electrical,

Electronic, Telecommunication and Plumbing Trade Union which has around 370,000 members.

Shop Stewards   Shop stewards have been simply described as 'trade union lay representatives at the place of work' by Lord McCarthy in his research for the Donovan Commission. The title of worker representatives varies according to the industry and trade: for example, from the quaint 'Father' or 'Mother' of a 'Chapel' in printing, to 'works representatives', or 'staff representatives' in small factories and offices. There are also many variations in the size and nature of the constituency the steward represents. The duties a steward would be expected to perform are:

1. Recruitment of new membership, seeing new starters and explaining the union's activities to them.
2. Maintaining membership, through the inspection of union membership cards, and by keeping the interest in the union alive.
3. Collecting subscriptions. This is now often arranged through the company, who collect for the union (a 'check off' system), but stewards do still collect in some establishments.
4. Operating at the heart of the communication network between management, union and members, collecting views, passing on information, and sometimes determining the position which the members he represents are to take up. The steward represents this to management, union officials, and passes back to members the management response.

There is a difference between the '*de jure*' and the '*de facto*' rights and duties of shop stewards. Although few union rule books contain specific references to shop stewards, their performance of the duties summarised under (4) above have granted them a vital place at the centre of British industrial relations. Their functions have extended to the negotiation of terms and conditions, pay, piecework rates, overtime and hours of work, the regulation of work rules and manning levels, and together with stewards from other unions they influence inter-union relationships.

The practice has emerged therefore for shop stewards to occupy positions of power at the focal point of collective action in the daily interface with first line supervisors.

Shop stewards are usually elected by a show of hands, and their representative functions are conducted in informal meetings with members, and in meetings with management, arranged through local procedures. In multi-union environments, their meetings will probably be between the management and a joint shop steward committee. This latter body may be elected or appointed by the shop stewards, and where there is a large number of stewards, there is likely to be some form of seniority granted to facilitate organisation. Shop stewards may represent workers from other unions where it is impractical for a separate steward to be appointed. The extent of management recognition of stewards varies according to whether or not the company or an employers' association negotiates pay and all the terms with the unions at national level, and also on the extent to which there are local negotiating procedures even where national agreements exist.

The Official Organisation of Trade Unions There are many variations in the structure of trade union organisation. This is because of the origins of their constitutions, which have often emerged from amalgamations, and because of the structure of the industry in which they bargain (for example, one could compare miners with one national authority in the Coal Board, and computer operators working for a small employer). The organisation of people into unions follows the distribution of the labour force—geographically, and in accordance with the type of work and the size of the employer's unit. Generalisations about union organisation are hardly possible therefore, but for the sake of simplicity we will outline the usual union organisation.

Many unions have local branches which are organised into Districts and/or Regions. The members of the union elect the executive committee or council which is responsible for administering the union's activities, and for conducting agreed policy. All unions have General Secretaries, who are full-time officers, and who are responsible to the executive committee. The larger unions also have Presidents. The General Secretary and, where applicable, the President share responsibility for the day-to-day business and are responsible for the work of the other full-time officers. The policy of the union is decided by a representative conference, the delegates to which are elected by the membership, voting in their branches. In many of the white collar unions, this conference elects the executive.

The question of how democratic the trade unions are is often raised. The argument that unions are now large bureaucracies, as impervious to worker demands as the most remote employer, gains ground from the evidence that most union meetings are poorly attended and that disputes and grievances against union officials are only slowly investigated. Typically, the craft unions required periodic election of officials, but so too did the Mineworkers and the Railwaymen. There seems to be no connection between any lack of democracy and militancy.

There are a number of checks on the power of the leadership which prevents an autocracy developing: for example, the local autonomy of district committees, the trade group structure of some unions, and the balances within the unions' constitutions. In addition to checking power, such constraints also make for less decisive leadership, and restrict the freedom of the union leaders to act quickly in the settlement of disputes.

Shop stewards are not only representatives of the working groups, but also are frequently active in the local union administration, as one might expect. In some cases, the branch and district committee representatives are shop stewards, strengthening the steward's role in grass roots administration. McCarthy's research found that there was a marked variation in the degree of assistance that union officials gave to their stewards. Since then a good deal of effort has gone into the training of stewards by their unions. The use of workplace branches seemed to McCarthy to be the most efficient form of organisation, although the solution to problems arising at multi-union sites still seems dependent on informal *ad hoc* arrangements made amongst the shop stewards.

Trade Union Membership   From our survey of the history of trade unions we can say that union members possess different characteristics according to whether they are skilled or unskilled, blue or white collar union members, and that there are regional, occupational and industrial variations. Different kinds of behaviour therefore might be anticipated from these different groupings.

Briefly, members of the skilled sections of the unions tend to be more conservative than the unskilled. Skilled tradesmen have more at stake very often in the organisations where they work and probably have more stable working careers. Unskilled workers are more likely to be laid off or to be made redundant. Skilled blue collar members are concerned to protect their skill through maintaining apprenticeship schemes, and may be able to control entry to the occupation. Occupational differences in outlook are exemplified by electricians, whose job opportunities, rewards and conditions of working are different according to whether they are on construction contracts or maintenance work. As there are wide variations in levels of unemployment regionally, union members' reactions will depend on their local context.

This was shown by union members in the steel industry, where the reactions to closures in South Wales reflected the despair of men faced with no job prospects elsewhere. The growth of white collar unionism and the increasing density reflect a changed status and work situation for white collar workers. We mentioned in the last chapter that white collar employees were becoming more 'unionate'. Perhaps as significant as this attitude is the unionisation in the public and service sectors, attracting more women into union membership.

There are a number of general trends which have an influence on members' actions.

1. Improved education has made members more demanding and less easy to lead. They have high expectations but are interested in their union 'delivering the goods', in the form of shorter hours, more pay and job security. Paradoxically, they are not active in union affairs.

2. Inflation and stronger industrial relations policies have resulted in demands for professional bargainers.

3. The activities of successive governments through public policies and employment legislation have made trade union members more aware of the law and industrial relations.

4. The evidence suggests that for most union members attachment to work is instrumental. They work in order to obtain for their family and home the consumer goods, holidays, etc., and opportunities for satisfaction outside work which better living standards offer. This gives a centrality to the home and family so that work fulfils a secondary role.

5. We can no longer make the assumption that union members automatically support the Labour Party. The spread of unionism into white collar areas and the absence of any real political objectives means that union members have more volatile political affiliations. For example, it is estimated that around half the membership of unions voted Conservative in the 1979 General Election.

6. Trade union members want to be involved in the decisions which are taken at a local level. They do not accept managerial beliefs in authority or unwieldy union bureaucracies, and are much more inclined to seek their own, local remedies to problems rather than go through a lengthy disputes procedure.

The Closed Shop and Union Membership Agreements   A closed shop is an arrangement whereby employees come to regard membership of a particular union as a condition of employment in the unit to which the arrangement applies. Managements often see advantages in the control of labour through closed shops and sign union membership agreements (UMAs).

There are closed shops which do not have 100% membership, but where the substantial majority are in the union, and where membership of a particular union is recognised (sometimes only tacitly by management) as a condition of employment. The non-union members in a closed shop may object on religious grounds to membership, or as is often the case with UMAs, the closed shop arrangements may have only applied to new employees, existing employees being left as either non-union members, or as members of a different union.

We should distinguish between a pre-entry closed shop and a post-entry closed shop. In the case of the pre-entry closed shop the union seeks to control the supply of labour to occupations and to companies, by stipulating that job applicants should be members of a trade union, and also by restricting entry to the union. This can be achieved by the union selecting the person for the job or providing a pool of members from which the employer can select, or by determining promotions (usually applying a seniority criterion), or by restricting membership to those who have served apprenticeships and by limiting the numbers of apprentices at any one time through an agreed ratio of apprentices to other workers.

Post-entry closed shops are the more common. The situation here is that an employee is recruited on the understanding that he will join the union after taking up his appointment.

Until recently, there was an increase in the number of post-entry closed shop arrangements which have tended to be formalised into written union membership agreements. UMAs are widespread amongst a number of industries, including mining, transport, communications, food, drinks and tobacco and in distribution.

Recent legislation on the closed shop may influence the trends but closed shop provisions now cover at least 5.2 million employees in the UK (23% of the working population) which include 1.1 million white collar workers. More than 80% of employees in closed shops are in the post-entry type. In general, closed shops exist where there is a high union density (with the exception of some public sectors, civil service employment), and where union organisation is strong. Closed shop provisions have spread into white collar as well as blue collar areas, and the tendency of managements to encourage closed shops through UMAs with check-off, and union screening facilities, suggests that management see advantages in closed shops which give them a more disciplined workforce with whom to negotiate. Research has shown, for example, that, even in 'green fields' operations where a new factory or office is to be built, managements have encouraged UMAs.

The Working Group   In Chapter 2 we outlined the features of working groups. In an understanding of the institutions and procedures which are involved in collective bargaining we should not forget the influences of work groups on the process of collective action. We have described already how groups develop norms which are maintained by sanctions on group members. These norms govern output as well as behaviour.

The famous Hawthorne experiments documented the sanctions imposed on those in the 'Bank Wiring Room' of Western Electric's works in Chicago in the 1930s, and the restrictions on output which resulted. Then, the group being studied said there should be 'no rate busters' (no one should produce more than the norm), and 'no chisellers' (no one should produce less than the norm), and 'no squealers' (no one should pass information about the group to management). Studies by Roy, Lupton and others show that work groups are interest groups, which seek to promote and maintain their interests through the manipulation of incentive schemes, and the control of work rules. Face-to-face relationships between members of the group are more important to workers than relationships with management.

Group loyalties may bring working people into conflict with shop stewards or union officers, as much as with management. Sayles points to the importance of technology when he suggests that it is possible to distinguish four types of work group, according to their level of skill and the amount of interaction between group members. Thus, where there is a high degree of interaction between unskilled group members, the group will be 'erratic', and where there is less interaction, the group will be 'apathetic'. On the other hand, skilled workers with high interaction form 'strategic groups'. If skilled workers do not normally interact much at work, they will form 'conservative groups'.

These conclusions about working groups are of importance to managers in the assessment of the bargaining strength of the groups they negotiate with. For example, erratic groups without good formal representation produce difficulties in the negotiation of change, as exemplified in the docks. Groups which occupy strategic positions such as maintenance workers are often able to use these positions in wage bargaining. The strategic use of power by work groups is also found in the continuous bargaining process which occurs over piecework and bonus rates, sometimes with informal work-sharing to ensure job security.

Managements must accept a degree of independence by work groups as a fact of life, and the controls they seek to exercise over the work need to take account of the workpeople's orientation. One approach by management is to encourage participation at the local level or through the foreman or supervisor's leadership qualities to create interesting, rewarding work. Another approach is to establish honest relationships with worker representatives, and to be prepared to exercise patience and sensitivity in bargaining around an increasing range of issues whilst maintaining management's decision-making function. These questions we will explore in our chapter on participation.

EMPLOYERS' ASSOCIATIONS AND MANAGEMENT

Employers' Associations

Employers' associations consist of large and small organisations ranging from self-employed members, master craftsmen and the like to public companies and large conglomerates which may be members of several associations covering different industries. They seek to further the interests of a group of employers within an industry or section of the economy. There are around 1300 Associations in the UK covering about 40% of the working population.

The structure of employers' associations is extremely variable. The national federations are made up of a number of local associations who elect a committee or council. This national committee usually appoints other committees (for example, executive, finance, and negotiating committees) the members of which would normally be drawn from senior executives of the constituent companies. These committees are supported by full-time officers, who service the committees with policy documents, give advice, and help with research rather in the mode of a civil servant's relationship to a Minister.

The major functions of employers' associations have changed in emphasis from the days before the Second World War. Nowadays, they are less concerned with the control of members' activities, and are much more interested in providing advice and support.

The present functions of the larger associations are to:

1. Act as trade associations, offering commercial advice to members.
2. Act as pressure groups on Government, public authorities, etc.
3. Provide uniformity of collective action with trade unions.
4. Negotiate at a national level with trade unions.
5. Operate a disputes procedure with trade unions.
6. Disseminate information and advice about industrial relations to members.

The advent of productivity bargaining and the refusal by large employers to adhere to a uniform line with smaller companies or their competitors on wages issues have resulted in pay structures being determined at the local, plant level. According to Clegg, industry-wide negotiations add to the amount rather than alter the pay structure. Local agreements usually take industry settlements into account, but add or vary them according to local conditions. Conditions of service, such as hours, holidays, etc., are more likely to be the same across an industry and here the bargaining is more effective at national level. This does enable some order and rationality to be achieved, since the unions have usually had to come together in order that negotiations could take place—for example, between the Confederation of Shipbuilding and Engineering Unions and the Engineering and Allied Employers' National Federation.

Another useful function of employers' associations is in dealing with disputes. The aim of these procedures is to prevent stoppages occurring which could be resolved by meetings between employers and unions, taken through a series of stages to national level if necessary. The disputes procedures offer a means of conciliation on domestic disputes and if the procedure is exhausted the employer can expect moral support from the remainder of the employers in the event of a strike. There seems much less possibility of employers taking concerted action themselves, however, and the uniformity of action which can be anticipated is more a means of preventing trade unions from succeeding with leap frog claims, or in establishing precedents which they can use to the employer's disadvantage.

Management

Industrial relations is an integral part of the management of any business. Throughout this book we have stressed the importance that managers must place on relationships if they are to be successful, and of the need for consultation and good communication. Increasingly, larger companies are appointing industrial relations or personnel directors to company boards, and the spate of employment legislation as well as the difficulties which have emerged through inflation and incomes policies over recent years have given an impetus to this move. In smaller companies, the managing director or chairman may take responsibility, but in all companies these senior managers should be involved in the establishment of a sound industrial relations policy.

Management's role in industrial relations begins, therefore, with a recognition of the implications for relationships of the decisions that are taken. For example, when deciding corporate strategy on the acquisition or disposal of assets, when planning new products, investment in new machinery or increases in the size of the workforce, there are implications which must be picked up at an early stage so that they can be weighed in the decision-making process.

The responsibilities for the implementation of policies should be spelt out at an early stage also. The Board, having determined policy, will no doubt look to its functional heads—in production, sales, finance and personnel—to put the policy into practice. Responsibility for industrial relations is thus made diffuse, and because the most probable areas for conflict are in production, it is the production and works managers who have been in the forefront of negotiations with the unions.

The trend towards 'professional' personnel management has provided a counter-weight to professional union negotiators. So much seems to depend on personality and negotiating skills that it is not possible to generalise about who should take the lead in negotiations. The model of a senior personnel manager as the responsible person with perhaps a line manager supporting has certain advantages if the personnel manager reports to the Board.

1. The 'distance' between the Board and the negotiator can be used during the negotiations and subsequently, as the negotiator is not expected to be privy to all management's future plans, and if negotiations break down, there is room for further action in compromises from the Board.

2. A senior and well-briefed personnel manager should have a wide knowledge of the existing agreements, and may be familiar with the union officials through other negotiations. A line manager may tend to act in a sectional interest, or look for a short-term expedient which may have unfortunate long-term consequences.

3. Personnel managers should be able to offer continuity since it is their specialism, whereas line managers may anticipate promotion or movement to another production job.

4. Given a personnel manager as lead in the negotiating team, a knowledgeable line manager is invaluable as a member of the team, because of his awareness of the technical processes and the job content of the unit.

5. If a senior line manager is accountable for the whole group on whose behalf negotiations are being conducted, he should be a member of the team also. Alternatively, he could be involved in briefing sessions before, during and after the negotiations (debriefing). He is more likely to accept that the best deal was gained, however, if he has been concerned in the negotiations themselves.

If the policy on industrial relations has been carefully thought out before hand, the implementation is less difficult. Where companies are proposing the rather dangerous step of determining their industrial relations strategy in the negotiations themselves, clearly the more senior the negotiator, the better, as he will have to sell not only the terms of the deal to the Board, but also the direction this takes the company into.

THE INTERNAL BARGAINING PROCESS

Too little attention has been paid to the internal bargaining process within companies, and the assumption of two power groups, employers and unions, facing each other across the bargaining table to set the seal on the company's future industrial relations is an overstatement. Just as in trade unions, there are different groups—stewards, officials and militant or non-militant members, forming a loose coalition, so, on management's side, there are interest groups. Local-level managements, for example, may not agree with a group policy, or foremen and supervisors may see an identity of interests with shop stewards and seek to frustrate any deals which produce extra work.

Management organisation is, therefore, not a monolith and the informal processes which occur include attempts by Boards to control their negotiators and the organisation of workshop pressure against the unions. The real control of what happens is on the shop floor itself. This is where the internal bargaining process is utilised to maintain order and to control the rules of work, the participants in this process being the foremen, supervisors, the shop stewards, the department managers and the workpeople themselves. No doubt this is the source of inertia in British industrial relations, but it is also a force preventing the more radical or zealous amongst senior management and union officers and stewards from forcing changes on to a traditionally minded, conservative workforce.

DIFFERENT APPROACHES TO BARGAINING

Collective bargaining comprises the settlement of wages, conditions and procedures by bargains expressed in the form of an agreement made between employers' associations or single employers and trade unions. The objective of all bargaining is to find an agreement. Agreements may be divided conveniently into procedural and substantive agreements.

Procedural agreements set out the rules by which the formal relationships between the company and the union will be regulated. These could include disputes procedures and procedures by which substantive agreements are to be interpreted.

Substantive agreements are agreements about the terms, conditions and pay of a group of workers. These would include hours of work, holidays and the rules governing how the work is to be done. A further subdivision is into bargaining at the industry and at the domestic level. At the industry level, bargaining between employers' associations and a confederation of trade unions settles both broad procedural and substantive areas. In the domestic bargaining of particular companies with the unions representing their workforce, the rates paid for specific jobs, and the regulation of the work as well as local procedures for dealing with discipline and grievances are negotiated. Examples of this fourfold classification are given in Table 10.

Industry-wide bargaining usually has to take into consideration sectional or occupational interest. For example, craftsmen in the steel industry and on the railways negotiate separately.

PRODUCTIVITY BARGAINING

A productivity agreement is arranged where an employer agrees to higher pay and/or to improvements in benefits in return for an

Table 10. Substantive and procedural agreements

Agreement	Domestic	Industrial
Substantive:	Wage agreements, Productivity agreements	Hours of work. Apprenticeship schemes, Holidays
Procedural:	Local disputes, Discipline and grievance procedures.	Industrial dispute procedures (applied through various joint councils, for example)

agreement from the union to changes in working practices or numbers employed which will result in an improvement in productivity, measured by unit costs, total output, or by some other sign.

A new era in productivity bargaining was started at the ESSO refinery at Fawley in 1960 where, for the first time, workshop representatives of all the unions were brought into an agreement with the management in which the company agreed to increases in pay in return for changes in working practices.

Productivity bargaining has since proved to be an approach which other companies have adopted as a means of removing demarcation lines between jobs, and problems caused by different union membership. These changes in bargaining have helped to move the main arena for negotiating down to the 'domestic' or plant level. Some employers' associations have left the settlement of pay rates to individual plants so that local productivity agreements could be concluded. Domestic bargaining has also been encouraged by the spread of measured day work, and by the need to rationalise payment schemes.

Productivity schemes focus attention on the role of the foreman, and by making him responsible for the achievement of improved performance there is the opportunity to build up his role. But for the agreement to be effective, he has to have powers of control which make his already difficult 'man in the middle' position even more stressful. For schemes to be implemented satisfactorily, therefore, the supervisors down to the shop floor must be given training and support in what is probably a new role for them. The introduction of quality circles where employees work with their supervisor on ideas to improve the quality of their work has also given greater emphasis to the supervisor. Productivity agreements result in managements looking for more information on output and may put the spotlight on performance standards. Clearly, in negotiating new schemes, companies should be aware of the likely effect these schemes will have on worker/supervisor relationships, formal control systems, and on the pay relativities with other groups in the organisation not covered by the scheme.

INDUSTRIAL RELATIONS POLICY

The management's industrial relations policy increasingly will be based on local circumstances. Most industry-wide agreements, apart from those in the nationalised industries, and the public services, are largely used for guidance, with the emphasis on day-to-day affairs on the domestic level, so that a policy on industrial relations is essential.

From the perspective of the company, there are a number of areas of major concern when framing an industrial relations policy.

1. The preservation of harmony in relationships, or the creation of harmony where none exists. This does not imply that management should avoid disruption of the business at all costs, but it does mean that a main objective of an industrial relations policy will be to keep the respective groups of workpeople contributing to the organisation's success.

2. The orderly introduction of change. No industry can avoid technological change and there are implications for the customs and practices which have grown up over decades with management's tacit agreement. To gain the advantage of improvements in productivity, the changes need to be introduced in a way which is acceptable to the workforce.

3. The costs of employment must be controlled and have to be compatible with the company's pricing policy. The pricing policy will have been set with the market place in mind.

Labour costs are an important element in total costs, so any change in the proportion of costs attributable to labour results in a reduction in the company's profit margins and there are implications, therefore, for the corporate plan.

4. Industrial relations policies should influence the productivity of the organisation. In many recent instances, this has been achieved by introducing greater flexibility in contracts, in working time, and in jobs; and by pushing through a greater concern for quality.

The company should express its industrial relations policy in writing, which may then be communicated to all levels of staff and to the unions. Ideally union officials should be involved in consultation before the policy is finalised.

The statement should cover the following:

1. The company's attitude/philosophy towards trade unions. The circumstances under which the company will recognise unions for bargaining purposes, and any agreement on membership.

2. The negotiating procedure and the people with whom negotiations will take place (junior shop stewards, district officials, etc.), the frequency of negotiations and procedures for resolving disagreements and for interpreting provisions of agreements.

3. The scope of the negotiating bodies, and the numbers and positions of the members. For example, if the company has a number of sub-units (a group or divisional structure) the arrangements for collective bargaining should be set out. Sometimes joint negotiating committees are formed, or a senior committee may be established with responsibility for several bargaining 'units'. The scope of each committee's negotiations should also be stipulated together with the mechanism for referring problems to the appropriate committees.

4. The facilities and information to be given to the union representatives. These topics are covered broadly by the legislation (see Chapter 23) and by Codes of Practice, but particular headings of information and the practical facilities will have to be decided. Procedures for determining the number of union representatives granted facilities will be one of the procedural issues which must be negotiated.

5. The relationship of any plant or company agreement to the industry agreement must be established. This is a statement of what will be followed automatically from the industry level agreements (for example, on hours, overtime rates, etc.) and what will be the subject of further negotiation at domestic level. The policy should state how the arbitration and conciliation arrangements will be put into force at the local level.

To be successful, a statement which covers the areas above should involve all (from senior management to worker representatives) in consultation.

The next stage is the negotiation of the substantive and procedural issues which are in the scope of the policy through the bodies which have been established:

1. The substantive areas for negotiation include the wage and salary systems, incentive schemes, grading and job evaluation schemes, recruitment, training, promotion and redundancy policies.

2. The procedural and consultative arrangements on discipline, grievance procedures and the procedures for redundancy and dismissal.

In most cases, management do not have the chance to set up a policy from scratch. Only in a 'green fields' situation will that be possible, but the model above is still valid as a framework, which can be adapted to circumstances. Typically, the area over which negotiations can take place has extended, and recognition of this fact within the policy is within management's control. The objective is to keep bargaining orderly and in many companies it is now necessary to recognise that there is joint regulation of the rules governing work.

Where it is possible to negotiate a plant/company agreement, it is advisable to start from those matters over which there is already agreement. First, a tentative agreement on each area in turn should be sought, before moving on to the next. Nothing is finally settled, however, until both parties have agreed the whole range of issues, so alterations are still possible (see Chapter 20 on negotiation techniques).

A further complication can arise when there is no obvious single union or group of unions with whom to bargain. Inter-union rivalry is still a fact of life in spite of the Bridlington agreement. Joint committees of all the unions involved may be one way around the difficulty.

Where management is faced with competing claims by different unions, management must make a judgement as to which union has the power to do the most damage and then should settle with that union first. Management should then seek to promote a more rational basis for future dealings.

Given that a principal objective for any industrial relations policy is to obtain harmony, management should not seek to play off one union against another. A better approach is to work with the unions concerned to try to bring some order into the bargaining arrangements.

Bargaining with a single union brings many benefits. It has been possible for some companies to achieve recognition with a single union in return for no strike deals, pendulum arbitration (where the arbitrator decides on the merits of either the claim or the offer, not on an average between the two), and agreement over pay lasting two years or more.

These agreements are not easy to secure. This is illustrated by the case of the Ford Motor Company. After a two week strike, Ford was able to obtain a two year pay agreement in 1988, for its factories in the UK, but without all the productivity gains desired. The US parent later refused to invest in a new plant in Scotland because the unions could not agree which trade union would represent the workforce (the investment being contingent upon a single union at the proposed new plant).

CONCLUSION

In this chapter we have outlined the part played by the protagonists in collective bargaining: trade unions, their officials, shop stewards and members, employers' associations and management at different levels. The plurality of interests these actors represent is reconciled at the industry and at the domestic level through bargaining processes.

To bring order to the process of joint regulation of work, industrial relations policies need to be devised at the company or plant level which cover both substantive and procedural issues. These agreements should provide the opportunity for maintaining harmony in relationships, rewarding effort, and promoting high levels of productivity.

QUESTIONS

1. What part do shop stewards play in the process of collective bargaining?

2. Comment on the benefits of the closed shop for an employer. What are the current trends in UMAs?

3. What benefits derive from national agreements between employers' associations and trade unions?

4. What is productivity bargaining? What are the difficulties in making a success of agreements on productivity?

5. What principles should a good industrial relations policy follow?

20

Negotiation Techniques

In the last chapter we outlined the institutional arrangements for collective bargaining between workpeople and employers. Although the power bases of these groupings will help to determine the outcome of the bargaining, their power is expressed through negotiations.

When the two groups meet, whether in national, company or local bodies, the negotiating strategy that each side has prepared, and the way the strategy is acted out will affect the result. Negotiations are not usually about winning or losing everything, but rather are concerned with small shifts and marginal gains or losses in pay, changes in rules, working methods, terms of employment and so on. Matters of principle may often be felt to be involved, notably where redundancy schemes, managerial prerogatives, or disputes over disciplinary measures are concerned, but agreements are achieved through compromises which avoid a total capitulation by either party.

There are two different approaches to negotiation:

1. **Distributive Bargaining.** Where the negotiation is about the distribution of resources, which are always finite, where a gain for one party is a loss for another. Distributive bargaining is sometimes called zero sum bargaining. For example, if an increase in pay of 15% is gained against a management budget of 10%, the 5% extra achieved by the union has to be funded either from profits or investment, or from other groups in the company, or by increasing productivity (producing more for the same cost) or by increasing prices (increasing the proportion of wage costs: total costs). If productivity can be improved then the bargaining need not be distributive.

2. **Integrative Bargaining.** This is where the negotiations are about how to resolve a problem to the mutual satisfaction of all parties. The approach entails 'problem-solving' by management and unions looking for the best solution to grievances about management actions, discipline problems and matters which lend themselves to joint management/union co-operation. This is especially appropriate in real productivity deals.

In this chapter we will concentrate on distributive bargaining, leaving the integrative approach to our chapter on consultation and participation.

Negotiation is not always a formal affair. Managers and shop stewards may find themselves taking a continuous negotiating stance. Pressure from management or pressure from the unions for changes are part of the everyday interaction in which either side may be engaged in persuasion. Our description of negotiation techniques will assume that the negotiation is sufficiently formal for a number of stages to be followed. However formal the arrangements, the principles remain the same, and it is the responsibility of management to ensure that they are not rushed into agreements, or give way to pressures, but that they have prepared a strategy that they can follow. The chapter is divided into two parts: preparing the case and conducting the case.

PREPARING THE CASE

The Aim   The first task is for an overall aim to be set. This should be consistent with the industrial relations policy, and should be achievable. For example, one aim could be to change the production system in order to improve productivity, or another to achieve an agreement with the unions in line with the corporate plan on wages/salaries. From the aim, objectives which are not so rigid that they are unalterable in negotiation should be thought through. In the first instance, these may be to do with the types of machines, numbers employed, etc., or in the second example, amounts to be paid to the various groups.

Research   The issues over which negotiation is to take place should be researched. A good understanding of the history and background to date is invaluable. The researcher will be looking for trends; signs of the way the union is going on particular issues. It is as well to use more than one source for the accounts you gather or to check minutes of previous meetings. Where the negotiation is over pay, recruitment or similar substantive matters, management should be armed with a survey of pay rates or of labour market information.

Bargaining Power   The strategy to be followed will be dependent on the bargaining strength of the union. This will be a variable, according to the issue on which it represents the workpeople.

One way of analysing power is to list the issues over which the negotiation will take place and then to note the costs and benefits to each party of the different outcomes. Where the negotiation is over substantive issues most of the costs are likely to be to the company, although as inflation rises a pay increase of less than the inflation rate is a reduction in real wages which is a cost to union membership. Similarly, in productivity bargaining, overtime or bonus earnings may be traded for other benefits, which can be costed.

Chamberlain used the following model to define the relative costs of agreement or disagreement between two parties, A and B:

$$\text{Bargaining power of } A = \frac{\text{The costs to } B \text{ of disagreement with } A\text{'s terms}}{\text{The costs to } B \text{ of agreement with } A\text{'s terms}}$$

$$\text{Bargaining power of } B = \frac{\text{The costs to } A \text{ of disagreement with } B\text{'s terms}}{\text{The costs to } A \text{ of agreement with } B\text{'s terms}}$$

Thus, if A is the union, B management, the greater the cost of disagreeing in relation to the cost of agreeing to a union's demands, the more power the union possesses. If, for either party, the ratio is less than 1, there will be disagreement. Concessions or strikes can lower the cost of disagreement to the point where a settlement is possible.

The Strategy

Given an understanding of what the union is likely to raise, and an assessment of their power on these issues, management should be in a position to predict the demand the union will make, or what kind of offer they should attempt. There is an opportunity now to work out the argument for and against each proposal, notably the benefits/disbenefits to each party of agreeing/disagreeing. In particular, managers should look for the weakness in their own case and try to find counter-arguments.

The position of each side on the issues can be determined under the three possible situations which may emerge, which Atkinson has labelled:

1. If management achieves its objectives entirely, what would be the ideal settlement?

2. If management makes some progress, but with power from the union realistically assessed, what would be a realistic settlement?

3. If management is forced to concede or to make no progress, what is its fall-back position?

As an example, if the union is demanding an increase of £10 per week, the three positions for the two parties could be as in Table 11.

Table 11. Example of union and management positions

Positions	Ideal	Realistic	Fall-Back
Management	£4	7	8
Union	£10	8.50	7

There is clearly room for agreement since the union's fall-back position and the management's idea of a realistic settlement coincide. If the union is able to discover that management's fall-back position is higher than their fall-back demand, they would no doubt revise their fall-back demand upwards, and the final settlement would be nearer the £8 mark.

Management should now be able to work out what its own demand would be or its response to the union's demand. If management intends to make an opening statement containing a first offer, the amount of movement this will allow should be considered. Any possible concessions should be thought through, and to gain maximum response from the other side their timing has to be calculated.

Management's strategy is established therefore from the range of issues to be covered, the strength of the parties on each issue, management's position on each issue and where the union is anticipated to stand, and the arguments which can be marshalled for and against the management's case. There is the tactical question of whether or not to open with a bid, and how high this should be, which has to be resolved in the light of how much movement is possible, and how much power each side has. It is also useful if managers can agree in advance what reaction they will have to any threat of sanctions that the union might propose.

The Agenda

This raises tactical and practical questions. It is valuable to have items on the agenda which can be linked so that there is the prospect of gaining movement on problems which otherwise might remain unresolved. The agenda should not be cryptic, however, and must be acceptable to both sides, so that both have time to prepare. The ordering of the items on the agenda can be used to put time pressures on the last items, but it must be remembered that the other side may not accept the order.

Pre-Conditioning

The history of the dispute will already have pre-conditioned the participants. Active attempts are sometimes made to formulate a climate of opinion in which the outcome of the negotiations is made more acceptable. For example, advance publicity of poor trading results, statements in newspapers and company journals which reflect the strength of the competition and the company's problems, all influence attitudes. On the union sides, large pay settlements in other parts of industry, results of comparability studies, the inflation rate, etc. may be used in a propaganda war before negotiations commence.

Providing Unions with Information

There is now a general duty on employers to disclose information at all stages of collective bargaining to representatives of independent trade unions, and a code of practice for this has been produced by ACAS (see p. 302). The code gives examples of the kinds of information covered—which includes cost structures, gross and net profit figures, sources of revenue, as well as data related to performance and details of pay, benefits and manning levels, including the bases on which these matters are decided.

The Management Team and the Setting

Whoever is selected to conduct management's case must be articulate, persuasive, and carry sufficient authority to make decisions. He should be acceptable at a personal level, to the other side. His intellectual abilities should be sufficient to enable him to translate the possible effects of proposals on company policy. As we have argued, it is a useful ploy to retain some distance between the negotiators and the ultimate authority (say the Board of Directors), although the negotiators should always remain in their confidence. Whilst the chief negotiator is conducting the case for his side, other members of his team should be keeping a record of what is happening, and listening to the interplay of the argument, looking for strategic developments and able therefore in an adjournment to give an analysis of the negotiations. There should be sufficient rapport between members of the negotiating team for the members to pick up non-verbal as well as verbal clues that they are needed to intervene. The setting for the negotiations ought to be comfortable, free from interruptions, with the chief negotiators facing each other in central positions.

CONDUCTING THE CASE

The Opening Statement

This is a broad statement of the position as you see it. It should leave enough room for further negotiation. No detail or contentious counter-demands should be attempted at this early stage. It is sometimes quite effective to give parts of the opening statement to other members of the team to make. In listening to the opening statement from the other side, try to find clues on the strategy they are adopting, and be prepared to revise your strategy accordingly. Look also for areas of agreement. Both sides will derive a sense of achievement from early agreement on part of the negotiations.

The Argument

A number of techniques are common in the art of persuasion.

1. Gaining commitments from the other side which can then be used to further you own case. For example, an agreement by the union that its members should not suffer any job loss can lead on to a

conclusion that increases in pay would result in a reduction in employment, and then be used to reduce the union's demand.

2. The argument should dwell on the benefits to the other side of acceptance. Opportunities for the other side to agree without losing face should be provided.

3. Appeals to emotional issues as well as to reason may be effective. There is sometimes a sense of relief from all sides when the problems are expressed in human terms, instead of concentrating always on the financial or business implications.

4. State the case with conviction, and if necessary, forcefully, but without shouting or using abusive language. You must convey your own belief in your arguments.

5. Information should only be released during negotiations for a reason, and this should have been decided in the planning phase. The timing and method of releasing it (verbal, written) may be important and the negotiators will have to decide during the negotiations when the moment is right.

6. If no progress is being made on one point, having clarified the problem which is holding up agreement, it is probably as well to set it aside and return to it later.

7. Linking issues together may help over a stumbling block. Conversely, if there is a halt on all fronts because of a sticking point on one of the items, the technique of isolating the issue as in (6) above can be used.

There are interpersonal skills in negotiation which help.

1. Listen carefully to what is said.

2. Ask questions rather than make statements all the time.

3. Do not try to score personal points. If the opposition descend to personal vituperation, either ignore it, or make your stance clear by stating that you will not continue if abuse is used.

4. Avoid taking advantage of any division in the opposing team. It will result either in unifying them against you or in the break up of the negotiations.

5. Do not use long convoluted sentences; use instead simple language and a tone of voice which treats your opposite number as your equal.

Concessions

The timing of concessions can be crucial to the outcome. Concede too early and the opponent may accept the concession as of right, and then move on to his main argument. If a concession is to be made, it will probably yield most value if it is granted in response to the opponent's main argument, and if it is attached to a push for a reciprocal action on his part, it may result in a modification of his demand.

In negotiations, one sometimes encounters the 'phoney concession', which is a gesture which appears to be a concession, but on reflection it is seen to be an inevitable or worthless concession. It is a trick, rather like selling a pass in rugby football, and as such may not work. Where it does, and can be carried off convincingly, your opponent will believe he has scored a victory, and may be prepared to make a real concession in return.

If it appears you are being forced into concessions, the best plan is to try and slow the pace, either by creating a diversion, taking up another point with a suggestion that you will return to the problem later, or by adjourning the proceedings for a short time.

Adjournment

There are a number of reasons for wanting to adjourn. The most important occasion is when the negotiating team need to consider the other side's proposals. The time should be fully utilised by analysing what has happened, and going back through the record of what has been said and agreed. This kind of adjournment allows the team to consult with senior management or to seek advice from experts on a topic (for example, if changes in the pension scheme rules are being discussed, actuarial advice may be necessary).

As we indicated above, adjournments can also be used judiciously as a break point to prevent oneself from being swamped. The time can still be used to advantage so that the team is able to formulate a reply.

Finally, adjournments at natural breaks are sensible, for lunch, tea or in the evening. Fatigue in negotiations can be as dangerous as time pressures, since there is a temptation to speak without thinking or to give away an important point merely out of tiredness.

SETTLEMENTS

The objective of negotiation is to obtain agreement. Before the negotiation teams break up it is as well to agree how the settlement is to be communicated to the work force. If a new agreement has been negotiated, the length of time the agreement will run will have been part of the negotiations. Stability is achieved by longer term rather than short agreements, but if the agreement is for a long time it ought to contain provisions for interpretation and the disputes procedure ought to be sufficient to cope with any disagreement which may result from the long period the agreement is in operation.

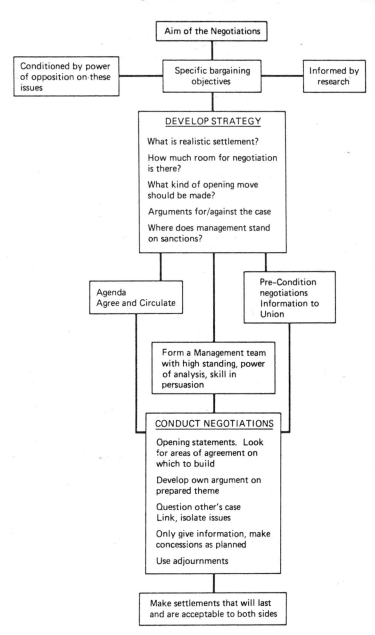

Fig. 23. Flow chart summary of negotiation techniques.

CONCLUSION

Good negotiating styles only come from practice. Preparation, and care in the negotiating arena, will help, however, and the summary in Fig. 23 shows in the form of a flow chart the important steps in the negotiation process.

QUESTIONS

1. What preparations should you make before any negotiation?
2. How does the 'power' of the contending parties influence negotiations?
3. Describe the key issue you should think through when developing your negotiating strategy.
4. Under what circumstances should you make concessions?

21

Disputes and Ways of Resolving Conflict

We suggested at the beginning of Part 6 that a pluralist stance towards industrial relations is necessary. What we come to regard as 'conflict' in an organisation depends on our interpretation of events.

The reality of most organisations is that people hold a multiplicity of personal objectives. There would seem to be some truth in the claim that really employees work for the material and psychological satisfaction they can achieve, and that their work is therefore an instrument used towards their own ends. In addition to this instrumental attachment to work, interest groups form in organisations, where individual interests coalesce. These groups seek to achieve their ends through alliances and by following group strategies.

A number of sociologists have suggested that our attention should be addressed to the explanation of 'order', or lack of 'conflict', which is perceived by some to be unnatural, the normal pattern being one of disagreement, conflict and often violence. One outcome of such a view is that 'political activity' is necessary to avoid a state of anarchy. This political activity includes the formation of alliances, the representation of interest groups in consensus decision-making and mechanisms for containing and canalising opposition.

The values of managers govern their attitudes towards workers taking action in pursuit of claims, and condition the manager's response to 'industrial action'. Whether such action is regarded as a legitimate part of the bargaining process will depend on a manager's view of conflict in organisations as a whole. Questions we must face are: can we expect to have the total commitment of people to their tasks, do groups of workers have the right to express their disagreement, and to use their power in confrontation?

In this chapter we will examine the nature of industrial conflict and its resolution.

THE CONFLICT CYCLE

There are a number of distinct phases in a conflict 'cycle'. The cycle begins with substantive or emotional issues being triggered by an event, which seems to focus attention on what are regarded as the underlying issues. Tension escalates to the point where sides are drawn, and the two sides make judgements of the opposition's power and goals. Those involved in the situation experience fear at the confrontation according to the risks they are taking with family, income, job, prestige, etc. There is a negotiation or a series of meetings where both sides work through their disagreement, and the outcome will either be a resolution by compromise or the conflict cycle will start again.

Conflict takes place at different levels. There may be a 'running fight' between a foreman and a group of workers over a period of years, with occasional outbreaks of overt conflict in the form of 'wild cat' strikes, or the conflict could be at a national level, where for example an event such as the pay offer by British Steel in 1979 sparked off feelings of insecurity, fear of job loss as well as a prospective loss of income and status (these being some of the problems union members felt were important during the 1980 strike).

DIFFERENT TYPES OF DISPUTE

There are signs of disaffection with the organisation which are explicit, such as strikes, confrontation leading to lockouts, and various forms of withdrawal of co-operation by workers in furtherance of their claims. High labour turnover, absenteeism, high accident rates due to inattention, poor training, and customer complaints could also be regarded as implicit conflict in the sense that they are indicative of at least a lack of interest or motivation to work, and at worst animosity towards the company and what it represents. Strikes are therefore not of themselves an indicator of low productivity (except, of course, for the period of the strike itself). A study of coal mining for example revealed that the pits with few strikes were not outstandingly productive. Apathy and a low level of energy at work are probably more damaging than outright confrontation over differences.

Industrial conflict takes a variety of forms. Overtime bans, working to rule, refusal to use new machinery have all been seen in different industries over the past two decades. The draughtsmen's union invented an ingenious form of pressure on management: 'working without enthusiasm'. White collar workers and managers who are unionised have considerable scope for this type of action since their work frequently requires them to use their initiative and creativity.

Apart from sanctions against management, workers sometimes take action against those of another union, or employer, by 'blacking' the goods they produce, that is refusing to use them, or to handle them. For example, dock workers have 'blacked' goods manufactured by employees who did not obey a strike call by the union, and have refused to unload imported cargoes of coal when the miners were on strike, out of sympathy for their cause. Sanctions against individual workers who do not obey the majority decision also occur. Unofficially, these may include 'sending to Coventry' (i.e. not communicating with the offender at work), and physical sanctions have been known, although never approved by unions officially. We may recall here the way offenders who broke group norms were struck on the upper arm as recounted in the Hawthorne research (see p. 9). Perhaps the most powerful official sanction against an individual is the withdrawal of his 'union card'—his membership of the union, particularly where there is a closed shop operating.

STRIKES

The strike is therefore not the only type of sanction workers can apply. It is, however, one of the most effective. Withdrawal of labour puts pressure on an employer immediately, and although there are costs to employees through the loss of pay, the employer faces an immediate need to negotiate so that he can ensure a return to work and a resumption of his business. Other forms of industrial action can become a running sore, and may cause as much difficulty for employees as for management. Overtime bans are only effective when overtime is regularly expected, and working to rule can be inconvenient for the workers. The 'lockout' by an employer is not so frequent nowadays, this being the situation where the employer refuses to allow a group of employees to return to work unless they accept management's terms.

Recently, strike action on a selective basis has been used to minimise the cost to the union, and to maximise the effect on the employer. This is exemplified by the withdrawal of a small number of key workers such as those operating a computer installation. For a strike to be effective, the employer's business has to be stopped, and thus strikers place great emphasis on solidarity, and regard picketing as an essential element in their tactics. The use of pickets on the premises of employers not directly related to the dispute, but who can bring pressure onto the employer who is engaged in a dispute ('secondary picketing'), has recently been the subject of legislation (see Chapter 23).

Strikes and other forms of industrial action are not always sanctioned by the union. We can therefore differentiate between 'official' and 'unofficial' strikes, the former providing the benefit of strike pay to those on strike, and the use of the union organisation. Matters are not always so clear-cut. Strikes which start as unofficial are often made official as they progress.

The classification of strikes for comparative purposes is therefore problematic because each strike is a complex phenomenon in which people with different and changing motives are acting out the various stages in the conflict cycle. As there are many other forms of industrial action, statistics on strikes cannot be taken as a definitive measure of industrial unrest. There are also serious difficulties in collecting strike statistics. It is probable that many small strikes are unrecorded and the different methods of recording in each country make international comparisons imprecise.

Strike statistics are usually kept in the total number of stoppages beginning in a year, and in the aggregate number of working days lost due to stoppages in progress during a year. The caveats extended above counsel caution when interpreting these statistics. The benefit gained from studying the statistics is to derive a general impression of signs of militancy, and to see which industries are strike-prone.

Up to 1926, the pattern was for large numbers of working days to be lost from a relatively small number of strikes. After the general strike in 1926 until 1956, the number of days lost was not typically so high, but the number of strikes increased. The late 1960s saw an increase in militancy; from 1968 to 1977 the average number of working days lost per 1000 workers was 452, which is nevertheless better than the record of Italy, Australia, Canada and the United States. The number of strikes starting per year has been around the 2000 mark since 1957, except for 1970 when almost twice that number started. In 1957, the engineering strike pushed the number of days lost up to 8.4 million, and there have been three particularly bad years since then: in 1972, 24 million working days were lost, in 1974, 15 million and in 1979, 28 million.

Economic reasons account for 80% of stoppages and 90% of man days lost. Piecework and wage payment systems used to give rise to many disputes, but in recent years there has been a trend towards measured daywork and incentive schemes are less of a factor. However, the threat of inflation and the urge to protect living standards are more important now. The growth of the public sector where incomes policy and cash limits have been most felt has resulted in a number of confrontations there, where white collar unions have grown sharply. There are also strikes over dismissals, trade union recognition and manning levels.

Most stoppages are unofficial, but the majority of working days lost has been through official action. This is because most strikes are short, sharp affairs, where the employees walk out when an event triggers the examination of a number of underlying problems, over which there has been frustration and annoyance, for example, over grading decisions, or work rosters. The set piece, long-drawn-out battles in steel, transport and the mines for example have come at a stage when negotiation has broken down. Thus, the 1980 steel strike counts as only one stoppage, although there will have been a large number of man days lost. The trend will probably be towards more official disputes since in the growth area of unionism, the white collar area, the members are more prone to strike on union instructions.

From research completed by the Department of Employment, we can see a profile of strike-prone industry:

1. Labour-intensive.
2. High union density.
3. The average size of the units managed is large.
4. High paid, skilled labour force.
5. Majority of labour force is male.
6. Industry is subject to fluctuating market pressures.

PROCEDURES FOR CONFLICT RESOLUTION

Discipline Procedures

There are many disputes each year due to management's disciplinary actions. Dismissal and suspensions occur for breaches of rules (such as sleeping on the job, negligence, breach of safety regulations) and for more general problems of conduct including absenteeism, and bad timekeeping.

Discipline procedures are local procedures devised by management, sometimes negotiated and agreed with the unions concerned. Shop stewards and/or local union officials may take part by representing their members at any hearings or appeals against management's decision. The advent of unfair dismissal legislation (see Chapter 23) and the ACAS Code of Practice on disciplinary practice and procedures in employment has led to more formalisation of procedures. Under the 1972 Contracts of Employment Act, employers were obliged to provide written information for their employees about disciplinary rules which are applicable to them, and details of the person to whom they should apply if not satisfied.

The following prescription for a discipline procedure is drawn from the Code. Discipline procedures should:

1. Be in writing.
2. Specify to whom they should apply.
3. Be quick in operation.
4. State the disciplinary actions which may be taken.
5. Specify the levels of management with the authority to dismiss (usually those at senior manager or director status).
6. Give the individual details of complaints against him.
7. Give individuals a right to be accompanied by a trade union

representative, or by a fellow employee of their choice at any disciplinary hearing or interview.

8. Unless it is a case of gross misconduct, no employee should be dismissed for a first offence.

9. Disciplinary action should not be taken until a case has been carefully investigated.

10. Give individuals an explanation of any penalty imposed.

11. Provide a right of appeal with an established procedure.

This leaves a number of questions to be resolved. How should a manager decide whether or not a subordinate's action is misconduct? What is serious misconduct? How and when should action be taken on cumulative problems such as lateness or inefficiency? How many warnings should be given, and who is to be involved in the discipline process?

Let us start to deal with these questions by saying that the purpose of discipline at work is to change behaviour. If an employee behaves in such a way that he shows he has no intention of being bound by his contract of employment, then the employer can regard the contract as broken. There should be no moral purpose behind disciplinary action, and it is not the responsibility or the right of the manager to impose his own moral code. If it is possible for the employee to change his behaviour or performance then the manager has the responsibility to offer an opportunity for improvement and to help the employee to progress.

We can distinguish between four different sorts of problems which result in disciplinary action of some sort, sometimes resulting in the termination of employment.

1. Inefficiency (failure to perform up to the required standard).

2. Sickness and unavoidable personal problems (for example, the serious illness of a child).

3. Cumulative discipline problems (for example, absenteeism, bad timekeeping).

4. Immediate discipline problems (for example, theft, fighting).

Inefficiency   The incapacity of a subordinate is initially a problem for the immediate supervisor, and before any disciplinary action is taken the procedures which we outlined in our sections on appraisal, induction and training should be followed. Only when these have failed to improve the performance of the individual, and the possibilities of transferring the person to a more suitable job have been exhausted should a discipline procedure be instituted. Having tried all these possibilities, managers should move to stage one of the discipline procedure outlined below, and give the employee a formal warning.

Sickness/Unavoidable Personal Problems   The first step is to spend time on investigation of the problem through sick visiting, or a counselling interview as we explained in Chapter 17. It is important to ask the employee whether or not he is able to return. The decision on termination of employment will depend on the length of the absence, and the needs of the work. It may be necessary to terminate the employment if a long absence is likely and there is urgent work to be done. This decision must be taken only as a last step, of course, and employers should show compassion in dealing with all sickness.

Cumulative Discipline Problems   The stages in the discipline process are:

1. Immediate supervisor should interview the employee to discover the cause. The union representative should be advised, and asked if he would like to be present, or a friend/colleague of the employee may come with him to the discussion.

2. The supervisor issues a verbal warning, recorded on the file by Personnel, and the employee must be told in what ways he can improve and what help is available, and over what time period the improvement is expected.

3. If there is no improvement, a further interview is necessary, and a written final warning should be given (either by senior management or by the personnel department). The steps that are to take place if he fails to improve should be explained and the employee should be given every assistance to improve and extra efforts should be made to help him, with a time limit by which an improvement should be made. The union representative should be informed.

4. If the final warning is not heeded, the employee should be told he will be dismissed, with a provision for an appeal to the personnel director, or managing director, if the employee has reason to believe there has been any unfairness. Whilst such an appeal is taking place, the employee should be suspended from duty on full pay. The appropriate union official should be informed.

Immediate Discipline Problems

1. An interview should be held to establish the cause of the problem. By the nature of these problems it may be necessary to institute an enquiry with other employees called in to give their accounts of the incident. When the 'offender' against the rules is asked for his version, he should be allowed to call other witnesses and to be accompanied by his trade union representative or a friend.

2. If the investigation is likely to take days to complete, it may be wise to suspend the employee on full pay during this time. Suspension under these circumstances should be distinguished from suspension as a penalty imposed as a consequence of a hearing.

3. When the investigation is complete, the employee should be interviewed again, and advised of any action which is taken. Should a penalty be proposed, written particulars ought to be handed to the employee concerned, and a copy given to the union representative. If a warning is proposed, then the manager should continue from Stage 3 of the procedure for cumulative problems as outlined above. There should be provision for appeals against any penalty in the way already suggested.

Provided management follow an appropriate procedure, and the grounds for dismissal are fair, mistakes which could result in an unfair dismissal, with the attendant tribunal problems, can be avoided. We set out reasons for dismissal which are fair in our chapter on Employment Law.

Grievance Procedures

Grievance procedures are necessary to ensure that employees have a recognised channel through which they can bring their grievances to the attention of management. The objective of grievance procedures is thus to grant employees the right to have their grievances heard, investigated and, if proved justified, remedied. No matter how good the procedure is, the maintenance of good communications is only possible where the climate of relationships favours open criticism, honesty and fairness in dealings between people. A grievance procedure which is simple, and is respected by management, should help to continue such a climate.

We can draw a distinction between individual grievances, which should be handled by the grievance procedure, and group grievances which would normally be the subject of negotiation, joint consultation, or to a formal disputes procedure.

The stages of a grievance procedure are represented by Fig. 24.

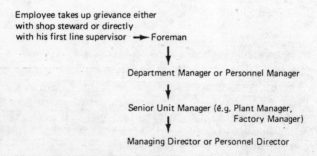

Fig. 24. Grievance procedure.

There are variations in the role that the personnel manager can play in grievance procedures. The personnel specialist should not be called in at once, however, and there are advantages in personnel managers being at the end of the procedure, to avoid clashes over authority among line and 'staff' functions, and to help preserve the status of personnel as the last 'court of appeal'.

The time that must elapse before an employee can move on to the next stage of the procedure should be stated. Grievances should be dealt with quickly. If a delay is unavoidable before a manager can get the answer, he should make sure that the employee knows why and what the time scale is for a resolution of any difficulties.

The clear-cut distinction between individual and group grievances becomes blurred in some circumstances. Although applying to one person, grievances may be seen as representative of the actions by management, such as changes in work rules which a group of people oppose.

Dispute Procedures

There are dispute procedures which operate at a local domestic level and procedures at an industry-wide level. In some industries, the industry-wide procedure will only deal with disputes about the interpretation of national agreements, whereas, in others, any type of dispute, substantive or interpretative, can be put through the recognised industry procedures. Where industry procedures will only accept interpretative disputes, any other form of disagreement has to be handled at the local or domestic level.

At the domestic level, procedures work through local committees. Shop stewards (where there is unionisation) take part in the procedures in Joint Consultative and Works Committees and in combined committees with management. Local disputes are usually taken up by the local employee representatives with management as part of their normal bargaining. Long-term questions may overcome the more immediate disputes, and the immediate issue is incorporated into a longer term strategy sometimes by the union.

Large organisations have formal procedures at the local level. There are different levels of conflict settlement offered by a series of committees in tiers. A failure to agree at a local level results in the dispute being passed to district or company level, and so on upwards to national or industry level.

Engineering Industry Procedure

Works committees with a maximum of seven representatives of the management and up to seven shop stewards meet regularly and will consider complaints from individuals or groups of workers. If no settlement is reached, a further meeting of the Works Committee may be held with the Union District Officer and the employers' federation representative present. If there is still failure to agree, the disagreement may be referred through the procedure's 'Provisions for Avoiding Disputes'. The objective is to avoid either a partial or a full stoppage of work until the procedure has been exhausted.

The stages are:

1. Either party may bring a problem before the local conference held between the local employers' association and local union officials.

2. If no settlement is reached at the local conference, either party may refer the disagreement to a central conference (held monthly), with a panel of employers and national officers. The central conference tries to reach an agreement.

If it is not possible to arrive at a mutual recommendation, then the whole matter will go back to the shop floor for settlement by the normal means of collective bargaining.

There are a number of different procedures operated by different joint industrial councils, such as those in Gas and Electricity, and in Chemical and Allied Products. In the Building Industry, there are four stages:

1. A site meeting with union and association officers.
2. A local joint committee meeting.
3. Regional conciliation panels are held.
4. National conciliation panels are the final stage with the provision that further disagreement can be referred to arbitration, and there is an emergency procedure which is used for urgent problems when, for example, a stoppage is imminent. Under this, the national officers can refer the dispute directly to a regional joint emergency disputes commission, and finally to a national emergency body.

Arbitration

There is nothing to stop either or both sides in a dispute seeking arbitration. Some procedures for settling disputes have clauses concerning arbitration built in. These are mostly in the public sector, including the Civil Service and Local Authorities. Arbitration is also provided for in disputes on the railways, although the awards are not binding on the parties, and in coal mining, arbitration is at three stages—at the pit, district and industry levels.

Public enquiries have been used to settle disputes where a long strike is thought to be damaging to the public interest. The Advisory, Conciliation and Arbitration Service (ACAS) is an independent, State-backed body which seeks to conciliate and to offer advice to either or both parties whenever requested to do so. When it is impossible for employers and unions to agree through collective bargaining, ACAS may appoint a mediator from outside or a board of arbitration if both parties request this. Any attempts by ACAS at arbitration do not have any binding force on the parties.

In addition to ACAS, there is a Central Arbitration Committee, which can hear claims for improvements in terms and conditions of employment where the union is not recognised by the employer. However, there is no legal way of enforcing recognition in Britain, this being a major difference between the British and European approaches to trade unionism.

Inter-Union Disputes

Within the union movement, arbitration in the settlement of disputes between unions can be provided by the TUC, which has the power to suspend a union and to recommend its expulsion from Congress. In recent times this has only occurred for a short period with the Electricians' Union in 1961.

The TUC has an Independent Review Committee, the jurisdiction of which is confined to the operation of the post-entry closed shop, where a member has been expelled from his union and will, therefore, lose his job. The 'IRC' is independent of the unions and was set up to solve the problem of whether or not an individual can be readmitted to the union. It operates informally, without legal powers, and tries to conciliate between the parties in the resolution of any 'Bridlington' type problems which emerge over conflicts of interest.

Interpersonal Resolution of Conflict

Conflict and problems in relationships are sometimes more susceptible to less procedural solutions and may not be due to claims by employee representatives.

1. Conflict as a consequence of organisation structure. For example, structures which inhibit communication, cause separate feuding groups to develop or place impossible demands on the people who are expected to work within the 'structure'. Various changes in the formal reporting relationships can be contemplated:

(i) Multiple overlapping groups can be created, with a common membership, so that a carefully structured integrative role can be planned.

(ii) Structures which are task-oriented can be developed. For example, various kinds of matrix organisation structures, which attempt to make the best use of the organisation's resources, and to preserve a balance between workflow requirements and functional management. A matrix organisation (Fig. 25) is one which operates both on a project and on a functional basis, e.g., the employee works on projects, but retains his accountability to his functional manager.

(*iii*) We have already discussed participation, and there are lessons to be learned from research with small autonomous work groups, which can be utilised to overcome a lack of commitment from the work force. Measures which change structures are often effective when combined with a reform of payment systems, improved management training and greater union involvement in decision making.

2. There are conflicts which are a consequence of interpersonal relationships. For example, when an individual has problems in integrating into a larger unit. Managers in these circumstances need to adopt a style which keeps communication flowing. This may entail:

(*i*) Supportive behaviour on the manager's part. Supporting and counselling the individual with the problem. 'Difficult' behaviour by subordinates may be a cry for help rather than a challenge to managerial authority.

(*ii*) Work group problem solving. Using the resources of the group to resolve the problem. This means opening up a dialogue between members of the group and persuading them to be open about any problems that they experience. This is a strategy which requires a high trust relationship, and the manager must be prepared to take criticism of his own performance.

(*iii*) Job design techniques. The objective is to design jobs which both give satisfaction for individuals and opportunities for improving performance.

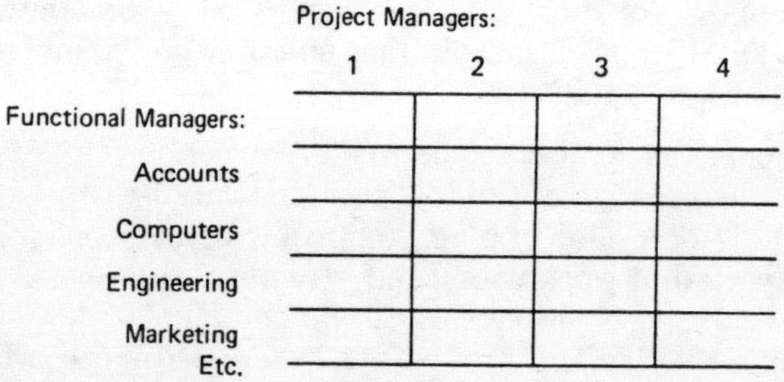

Fig. 25. Matrix organisation.

CONCLUSION

Conflict resolution starts with a careful diagnosis of the causes of the problem. It is then the responsibility of the manager to apply an appropriate procedural, structural or personal solution or some combination of all three. The manager's greatest assets in resolving conflicts will be his own preparedness to adopt a pluralist stance, and the interpersonal skills he can bring to bear—supplemented by perseverance, honesty and pragmatism.

QUESTIONS

1. What is the difference between a unitary and a pluralist 'frame of reference'?

2. Describe the main sanctions workers can apply. Why are some sanctions more effective than others in producing an ultimate resolution of the conflict?

3. What are the main reasons for strikes?

4. Set out the main steps in a discipline procedure. What are the different approaches towards cumulative and immediate discipline problems?

5. What are the stages in a grievance procedure?

6. What are the benefits of a formal disputes procedure? At what stage would you expect there to be arbitration?

7. When conflict is a consequence of interpersonal relationships what sorts of solutions are available?

8. What are the main sources of conflict—summarise each type and note the possible solutions.

22

Consultation and Participation

The width of interpretation we can give to the idea of participation is reflected in the many levels at which we can see employees participating in a modern democracy. There is participation through national institutions, through industry-wide bodies, and at company and sometimes department or section level. Collective bargaining in its many forms could be said to be employee participation in the distribution of wealth in society.

DESCENDING AND ASCENDING PARTICIPATION

One way of distinguishing between different forms of participation was described by Walker in 1977, when he differentiated between 'Descending Participation' and 'Ascending Participation'.

Descending participation includes schemes for enlarging and enriching the employee's job, so that some of the functions of the next level of supervision become part of his work, and this approach to participation can also be found in forms of supervision where decisions are made by the work group acting with the manager by problem-solving as a group. In this latter case, the manager becomes very much the spokesman or representative of the group which operates its own control and discipline functions. In the former instance, job enlargement schemes seem to some supervisors to be threatening because they tend to squeeze the middle and junior levels of management. To be successful, therefore, they have to be applied from the top of the organisation so that power and responsibility are devolved downwards.

Ascending participation is characterised by joint consultative committees and arrangements which recognise the employee's demand for more information from management and for involvement in decision making.

There has been a tradition of joint consultation in the United Kingdom since the end of the First World War. The advent of both World Wars reinforced the need for co-operation between employers and their workforce to achieve the production targets essential for victory. The early experiments in joint industrial councils, which the

Whitley Committee advocated in 1919, eventually faltered in most industries, except in the public sector. Nevertheless, the idea has blossomed at a local level in industry and a number of organisations have maintained joint consultative committees through the years. The principles behind joint consultation have also been influential in the training of Personnel Managers.

JOINT CONSULTATIVE COMMITTEES

Joint Consultative Committees usually operate at company level. They are committees of managers and workpeople, with a formal constitution, which meet regularly to discuss problems of mutual interest which are outside the normal area of negotiations. Employee members of such committees are elected and serve for a fixed term. The arrangements can apply to any form of organisation structure, irrespective of whether or not the employees are members of a trade union.

The principles on which joint consultation is based are those we have outlined in our comments on problem-solving. The approach to employee relations is integrative rather than distributive and could be summarised as follows:

1. For employees to be concerned about the achievement of the organisation's objectives, they must be made aware of the objectives and understand the reasons for the policies that are followed.

2. Good communications between management and the workforce are vital. Employees should be advised in advance of areas under discussion so that they can express their views and can contribute to the thinking that goes into the decision.

3. Problems which stem from the application of rules to local situations, and matters which are of direct concern to the employees in their working lives such as working methods, attendance at work, and canteen arrangements, are best dealt with by management and staff representatives meeting regularly to talk and put forward solutions.

4. A reservoir of goodwill and interest should be built up which can be drawn on when unpopular decisions have to be accepted by the workforce. One of the benefits of the JCC meetings is that employee representatives receive training and experience in how to present cases at meetings, to report to their constituents and to research into problems.

The constitution of a Joint Consultative Committee should specify:

1. The scope of the JCC. The areas which fall within its scope, such as working arrangements, information about products/services, the organisation's financial position, security, suggestion schemes,

physical working conditions, catering etc., should be set out in general terms.

2. The relationship between the JCC and other bodies—notably any committees which are concerned with negotiation, or with the flow of information from management to workpeople, ought to be agreed and stated. If there is more than one JCC, the areas each is to cover should be set out and the procedure for referring matters to the next level up (e.g. from company to division to group level) specified.

3. The intervals at which the JCC meets. Monthly or bi-monthly would probably be sufficiently frequent to prevent the JCC from being by-passed with urgent problems and its consequent relegation to a 'talking shop'.

4. A list of the officers of the committee, such as Chairman, Secretary and their deputies, together with their functions. At least one of these officers should be representative of the workforce. The method of electing the officers should be set out.

5. The arrangements for the election of representatives to the committee. This would normally be achieved by obtaining nominations and then holding a ballot, jointly supervised by management and by the unions or other worker representatives. In some companies, the shop stewards may automatically serve on the JCC, or representatives of the stewards may be voted on to the JCC by the stewards voting as a whole.

6. The length of time members should serve on the committee, and what to do if members leave in mid-term (e.g. through illness, resignation, etc.). Management members may be co-opted onto the committee.

7. The agenda should be prepared in advance by the JCC secretary with the items submitted by any member of the committee. The Secretary should be responsible for the minutes and their circulation to senior management and noticeboards. Minutes should be brief and be quickly produced.

Some critics of joint consultation see it as merely a device for preventing militancy by union representatives, as a trick to gain consent. Another criticism is that JCCs become bogged down in trivia. It is sometimes suggested that the meetings are rituals and that no real change occurs as a consequence of them. When JCCs *do* become influential, the argument runs, then they become negotiating bodies.

As a counter to these points, we may say that if a JCC is operated as intended, as a forum for a discussion of the matters which are of importance to the workpeople, then there is no reason why a JCC should not be an extremely effective way of aiming at consensus decisions which resolve problems for the organisation as a whole. Much will depend on the qualities of the Chairman and the impartiality and real interest in joint consultation he brings to the role. Trade union criticism of joint consultation is often motivated by the vision of one communication channel between management and workers which the union controls, and which is primarily a channel for negotiation.

THE RECENT DEBATE ON PARTICIPATION

During the 1970s, the debate on participation was heightened by the combination of economic circumstances and the mutual dependence of a Labour Government and the trade unions. Hyper-inflation made an incomes policy essential, whilst a strong union movement was able to take advantage of a sympathetic Labour Government to bring the union leadership into economic policy-making, and to give the unions more say in the operation of statutory bodies. This push for 'industrial democracy' built on attempts by previous Governments to bring together the Government, the CBI and the TUC in long-term planning, through the National Economic Development Council and its offshoots. 'Tripartism' spread into the control of quasi-governmental organisations such as ACAS, the Manpower Services Commission, the Health and Safety Commission, etc., whilst the 'social contract' between the Labour Government and the unions in the mid-1970s allowed the unions to trade pay restraint in return for agreement by the Government to put some of their political objectives at the top of the policy agenda.

From 1976, the fourth medium-term economic programme of the EEC encouraged participation in management's decision-making, and sought greater capital accumulation by workers. This led to the Bullock Report in January 1977 which contained a number of recommendations on participation in decision-making.

THE SOCIAL DIMENSIONS OF THE EUROPEAN COMMUNITY

The programme to complete the European internal market aims to remove all the remaining barriers to trade between the members of the EC. Amongst the many proposals it is those which concern the participation of workers in decision-making which have caused greatest controversy.

The Single European Act, ratified in 1987, added three obligations to the Treaty of Rome. These covered the harmonisation of national provisions to improve the functioning of the labour market, improvements in health and safety of workers, and Article 118B which stipulates: 'the Commission shall endeavour to develop the dialogue between management and labour at European level'. The Social Dialogue was started in 1987 between 'UNICE' (the European

Employers' Organisation) and the ETUC (the European Trade Union Representatives).

The arguments which have been deployed have centred on the need for a 'level playing field' if competition is to be fair. There is a view that poorer member States might avoid improvements to working conditions, in order to take advantage of low wage costs, and that a plinth of social rights is necessary to avoid social dumping. A price competition spiral might ensue, when companies in the richer countries might be tempted to try and reduce costs by reducing pay and social benefits. From this destabilising price war there would be no winners.

The British Government has been vociferous in opposing the idea of a social charter largely, it seems, for ideological reasons. Having 'freed up' the UK labour market, there is a desire by the British to keep it free of restrictions imposed by what is seen as the Brussels bureaucracy.

The version of the Community Charter of Fundamental Social Rights published in September 1989, contained twelve sets of 'fundamental rights'. These included inter alia: to social protection, to freedom of association, to vocational education and training, to equality of treatment between men and women and to information, consultation and participation, as well as to health protection.

However, these proposals were not acceptable to the British, at the European Heads of State meeting in Strasbourg in December 1989, and the original ideas have now been 'watered down' to become more a matter for guidance than a mandate for action. In practice, many of the proposals (such as equality of treatment between men and women) were already enacted in British law. Any increase to employees' participation in decision-making is more likely to be brought about through the health and safety regulations, where the statutory rights for health and safety committees and the free flow of information to employees are likely to be strengthened, than through the enforced adoption of Germany style 'co-determination', which was once feared by employers. Whatever the objections to formal participation schemes, large modern companies accept the necessity to obtain the agreement of employees to change.

The increasing pace of change, and the importance of gaining commitment is essential. Many large companies have consciously adopted a more participative style, sometimes announced in a statement of the company's philosophy. For example, GEC, ICI, GKN and United Biscuits have developed their own way of dealing with the participation question, through such means as communications exercises, autonomous work groups, and committee structures. The public sector Whitley Committees have long been a way of consulting civil servants, although there are signs that the Whitley system is breaking up in the civil service because of its unresponsiveness to local problems, and because the individual unions in the public sector are much stronger than before and do not always perceive a commonalty of interests with their other union members.

Movements by workers themselves in response to threats of closure have become more common, sometimes getting Government help as in the case of the Meriden motor cycle co-operative. Direct action by workers, such as sit-ins, and attempts at the formation of producer co-operatives have tended to be unsuccessful, as the circumstances are usually the least favourable for any marketing initiative. In addition, there are a number of problems associated with producer co-operatives:

1. The difficulty of attracting capital for a new venture.
2. A lack of management skills.
3. The apathy of the trade union movement towards this form of participation.

CONCLUSION

Co-operation between management and workpeople is essential for success in business, and the way that this is achieved will vary according to the size, structure, the market share and financial support. There are signs that less formal methods of participation are effective, and the need to share information is increasingly accepted.

QUESTIONS

1. What is the difference between 'descending' and 'ascending' participation?

2. What does management seek to gain from formal methods of joint consultation? What are the benefits of a JCC for workpeople?

3. Taking the case of an organisation you know well, how would you introduce formal representation of employee interests to the main Board of Directors or other central decision-making body?

23

Employment Law

Changes in the law may be said to represent broader social change. In recent years the employment contract has increasingly become subject to regulation. Individual employees have developed 'property rights' within their jobs and have come to 'own' them. General duties towards workers have been laid on employers, and there is now a legal framework encompassing the collective action of workers in strikes, ballots and picketing, and laws to influence the way trade unions conduct their affairs.

The complexities of employment law grow daily, presenting a problem for a general text of this kind. To give a detailed description of each statute would take several volumes, yet in omitting 'detail' we could be accused of misleading readers. The best solution to the problem would seem to be to take the main areas where the law impinges on employment, and to describe in outline the current constraints and obligations without going into details on the specific statutes. The chapter will be divided into nine parts: contracts of employment, dismissal, redundancy, pay, maternity, discrimination in employment, data protection, collective bargaining, and health and safety.

A number of institutions have grown up to help the interpretation and to administer the law, and to give advice to management, workpeople, and trade unions.

ACAS

We have already outlined the advisory role of ACAS, and its function of promulgating codes of practice. The Advisory, Conciliation and Arbitration Service has a positive role to play in 'promoting the improvement of industrial relations' especially the machinery of collective bargaining, according to the 1975 Employment Protection Act. The possible forms of intervention by ACAS include:

1. Conciliation (attempts to get both parties together).
2. Mediation (offers grounds for settlement).
3. Arbitration (assists in appointment of one or more arbitrators).

Amongst its activities as an independent body, ACAS can be required under the Employment Protection Act to try to settle recognition issues by conducting an inquiry and publishing recommendations. ACAS is also involved in individual cases of conciliation, before complaints by individual employees are heard by a tribunal. These are mostly in the area of 'unfair dismissal', over half of which are settled with a formal hearing.

THE CENTRAL ARBITRATION COMMITTEE (CAC)

The CAC was established under the 1975 Employment Protection Act. It replaced the old Industrial Court, and is a permanent tribunal which deals with references: on arbitration, trade union recognition, the disclosure of information to trade unions for collective bargaining purposes; under the Equal Pay Act, and from the disputes procedures of a number of organisations.

INDUSTRIAL TRIBUNALS AND THE EAT

The Industrial Tribunals which have now been established throughout the UK deal with most of the cases which are brought under the statutes relating to employment. These tribunals are informal, consisting of a legally qualified chairperson and two members, one selected from an employers panel, one selected from a trade union panel. Evidence is given on oath, witnesses are called and legal representation of the contending parties is permitted. The decision by the tribunal is legally binding. Appeals against a Tribunal's decisions are only permissible on points of law to the Employment Appeal Tribunal (EAT) from which a considerable case law has flowed.

CONTRACTS OF EMPLOYMENT

A contract of employment exists when one person employs another to perform a particular task as part of his business, in a manner he dictates. The relationship will then imply certain duties on the part of the employer: for example, to pay National Insurance contributions, to deduct income tax, and to conform with the requirements laid down in employment legislation.

The contract may be formed by conduct or by a document or orally. All that is required to establish that a contract exists is agreement of the essential terms by the parties.

Written Particulars of a Contract

The Employment Protection (Consolidation) Act 1978 obliges the employer to give full-time employees certain written particulars of their contracts within 13 weeks of the start of the employment. Employees who work between 8 and 16 hours per week are entitled to this statement after 5 years service. The document may contain the particulars or may refer to the place where they can be inspected. However, the document should:

(*i*)   Identify the parties to the contract.
(*ii*) State the date on which employment began.
(*iii*) State whether or not previous employment is continuous with any previous period of employment.

Up-to-date information should be available in the contract, or for inspection on:

(*i*) The scale of pay and the method of calculating it.
(*ii*) The intervals at which paid.
(*iii*) Any terms relating to hours of work.
(*iv*) Any conditions on holidays (including public holidays).
(*v*) Terms relating to incapacity for work due to sickness.
(*vi*) Details of company pension schemes.
(*vii*) The length of notice which employer and employee are required to give.
(*viii*) The title of the job.
(*ix*) Disciplinary and grievance procedures, rules for settling grievances and the person to whom the employee may go with a grievance.

The employer may refer his employee in the written particulars to some document readily available to him in the course of his employment (e.g. a collective agreement, company rules, etc.), instead of setting out all the above details in full.

Express and Implied Terms of Contract

Express Terms are those which the parties specifically agree upon, and these will typically include some of the items mentioned above, such as rates of pay. The express terms may also include the nature of the work itself. An agreement between the employer and a trade union may be referred to as containing certain of the terms of the contract.

Implied Terms are those which are not stated, but which nevertheless impose obligations and duties on both parties. For examples of implied terms we may quote the employee's duty to give the employee reasonable notice in the event of the parties not having agreed the length of notice, e.g. where an employee has not yet served four weeks.

Unlawful Contracts and Restrictive Covenants

Any contract which is unlawful, or which is contrary to public policy, cannot be legally enforced.

Under circumstances where an employer is anxious that former employees might either set up in opposition to him, make use of his trade secrets or in some way damage his interests, recourse is frequently made to some form of restrictive covenant in the contract, forbidding the employee to engage in the same business within a specified period after leaving (sometimes this is coupled with a geographical limitation).

Restrictive covenants are unenforceable if they are considered to be in undue restraint of trade, i.e. unreasonable in the interests of the parties and of the public. Attempts at removing competition by preventing former employees from exercising their skills are considered to be against public policy. However, if the employer merely wishes to protect his business secrets he might be able to justify a restrictive covenant.

It is difficult to distinguish between the two purposes but the courts have decided in the past on a basis of whether or not the employer was trying to preserve 'objective knowledge', which is the master's property, or if it is the employee's skill and expertise or mental/manual ability which is the property of the individual, and should be transferable to other businesses without hindrance. Legal advice is necessary before drawing up a covenant of this kind, in order to ensure its validity. It may be enforced by the employer applying to the court for an injunction to restrain the employee's breach or proposed breach.

An unenforceable covenant does not invalidate the remainder of the contract, although if an employer himself breaks the contract, a restrictive covenant which would otherwise have been acceptable would not be enforceable.

Changes in a Contract's Terms

If the parties to the contract agree, the terms may be changed. Unilateral attempts to change the terms to the disadvantage of either party would result in the contract being broken. Changes to the terms must be communicated to the employee within one month after the change. This can be done by giving the employee written particulars of the change, or making the amendment available for inspection. The employee, exceptionally in a contract, has no right to prior consultation on a proposed change, even though it may be to his disadvantage. Such changes however, or behaviour by the employer may constitute 'constuctive' unfair dismissal if the employee leaves.

Fixed-term Contracts

It is advisable to give fixed-term contracts in writing, for even the shortest periods of time. All fixed-term contracts should be for specific duties and there should be a good reason for giving one. Fixed-term contracts for 12 weeks or less exclude holders from the rights to minimum periods of notice, and to guaranteed pay (see p. 313).

For fixed-term contracts, once the person has been employed for 104 weeks, unfair dismissal may be claimed (see p. 307). If short-term employment can be justified by the employer, the termination may not be unfair. For fixed-term contracts of two years or over, where an agreement has been signed beforehand waiving the employee's rights to claim unfair dismissal and/or redundancy when the contract is completed, the waiver is binding.

If the contract is renewed at the end of the fixed term, an agreement is required in writing, stating that the exclusion clause shall apply to the new contract also. It would be wise for an employer who is contemplating offering a fixed-term contract to seek legal advice beforehand.

The Termination of a Contract

The Employment Protection (Consolidation) Act 1978 lays down minimum periods of notice. For the employer this is one week's notice after 4 weeks' continuous employment, and then increases after 2 years' continuous employment by one week for each year of continuous employment between 2 and 12 years, and is at least 12 weeks notice if the period of continuous employment is 12 years or more. The employee must give at least one week's notice after 4 weeks' service. The employer's and employee's period of notice may be extended beyond that by agreement expressed in the contract. Payment in lieu of notice may be made by agreement (though this does not deny the employee the right to claim unfair dismissal or redundancy), and, unless stated to the contrary, notice may be given on any day of the week.

A full-time employee with 6 months service has a right to a written statement giving particulars of the reasons for dismissal. Employees who work between 8 and 16 hours per week are entitled to a statement after 5 years' service. These reasons must constitute a full explanation, not just 'misconduct' or other abbreviations. The employee's request, which can be oral or written, must be met by the employer within 14 days, or a claim to a tribunal may award up to 2 weeks' pay as compensation. Employees with over two years' service can claim unfair dismissal.

DISMISSAL

Wrongful Dismissal

We should distinguish between wrongful dismissal and unfair dismissal. It is still possible for an employee to claim that he has been wrongfully dismissed in an ordinary common law action for breach of contract in the civil courts. This applies where the employee claims that the employer did not dismiss him in accordance with his contract.

This might arise, for example, where the employer had failed to give proper notice as stated in the contract. The amount of the compensation or damages awarded would normally aim at placing the employee financially in the position in which he would have been had he not been wrongfully dismissed. The employee would not be entitled to re-instatement or re-engagement, however.

Unfair Dismissal

The Trade Union and Labour Relations Act of 1974 stipulated that employees have the right not to be unfairly dismissed. There are two aspects to 'unfair' dismissal.

1. The manner of the dismissal must be fair. That is, the tribunal must be satisfied that the employer has acted reasonably and fairly in all the circumstances, in the manner of the dismissal. The Tribunal will decide this 'in accordance with the equity and the substantial merits of the case'. In doing so, the Tribunal will take into account the size and administrative resources of the employer. The extent to which the employer has followed a discipline procedure which accords with the practice recommended in the ACAS code on discipline is taken by Tribunals as evidence that the employer has behaved reasonably.

2. The 1974 Act laid down a number of reasons for dismissal which might be considered sufficient if the manner of the dismissal is fair. These reasons are:

(*i*)   Redundancy.
(*ii*) Ill health or lack of capability or lack of qualifications for the job on which the employee was engaged.
(*iii*) Misconduct. This must be sufficiently serious to warrant dismissal.
(*iv*) Where the employee could not continue to work in the position without breaking the law (for example, driving whilst licence is suspended for a long period).
(*v*)   'Some other substantial reason of a kind such as to justify the dismissal of an employee holding the position which that employee held.'

In regard to this last point (v), a number of reasons have been used to justify dismissal under this heading, including an irreconcilable conflict of personalities, caused by the dismissed employee; and an ultimatum from an important customer which forced the employer to dismiss the employee. However, the manner of the dismissal must be shown to be fair, so the employer should make efforts to search for vacancies or try to transfer the employee to a job where he will be successful.

If the selection for redundancy is for some reason other than a diminution in the amount of work, or the circumstances applied equally to one or more other employees in the same undertaking in similar positions but who were not made redundant, or the selection for dismissal contravened a customary arrangement, then the employee may claim he was unfairly dismissed.

The Employment Acts of 1980 and 1982 introduced the right of individuals not to be dismissed because of a refusal to join any particular trade union. This also applies where a worker refuses to make a payment to charity as an alternative to paying union dues. Employees should also not be subject to any action short of dismissal taken in order to compel them to join a trade union and employers should not select people for redundancy because of their union membership, or because they are not members of a trade union. Commercial contracts which stipulate that contractors should employ union-only labour, or that require the contractor to consult with trade unions were outlawed.

Statements within the written particulars given to employees that they are encouraged to join a trade union are not of themselves unlawful, however, the legislation is clearly aimed to establish the absolute right of individuals not to belong to a trade union, and there is no length of service requirement in this case of unfair dismissal.

REDUNDANCY

Definition of Redundancy

An employee may be redundant if:

1. The company he worked for ceases or intends to cease trading for the purposes of which he was employed.

2. The employer ceases to carry on business altogether.

3. There is a diminution of the requirement for employees to carry out work of a particular kind, in the place where the person is employed.

In the case of (1) alone, the employer should terminate the contract with proper notice where there is a change in ownership. If the new owner wishes to take on the contract he may do so with the agreement of the employee and provided the contract is continuous, and the business is transferred to the new owner, so that the nature of the employee's work does not change, there will be continuity of employment and no redundancy will have taken place.

Where an employer wishes to offer alternative employment he should do so in writing, before a new contract is due to start. The written particulars of the agreement between the employer and the employee should state the terms and conditions of the new employment, rates of pay, location and duties, etc. If the employee does not believe this is a suitable alternative offer, he may apply to a tribunal for redundancy pay.

If there is to be a trial period in the new employment the trial period will begin with the ending of the previous employment, and should not last more than four weeks unless a longer period is mutually agreed for retraining purposes. Such an agreement must be in writing, and must state the date of the end of the trial period, and the terms and conditions of employment during the trial period.

A renewal of contract or of re-engagement should take effect within four weeks of the termination of the old contract. Where the employee accepts the suitable alternative offer his employment is deemed to be continuous.

Rights to a Redundancy Payment

Employees who are made redundant are entitled to a payment from their employer.

The right to receive a payment depends on a number of conditions:

1. Employees must have been dismissed because of redundancy.
2. Some employees may be entitled to a redundancy payment if they are laid-off or kept on short time.
3. The employee must have served for at least two years, be over the age of 18, and be aged under 60 years if female, or 65 if male. Companies which employ fewer than 10 people are entitled to a rebate from the State of a proportion of the payment.

Dismissal due to Redundancy

Irrespective of whether the employee is given notice, or in cases of constructive dismissal leaves, the termination may count as a redundancy if the definition outlined above is met. The date of the dismissal is the date on which the notice expires, or the termination takes effect. If the employer, after giving notice, substitutes a shorter or longer period of notice, the date will be the new substituted dismissal date. Employees who refuse to work to the later date may lose this entitlement to the full redundancy payment, depending on the circumstances of the case.

If the employee anticipates the expiry of the employer's notice by indicating his intention to leave earlier than was originally agreed, the employee will still be taken to have left due to redundancy, and the effective date will be the new date the employee gives. If the employer objects, he can write to the employee, requiring him to withdraw his notice, and to continue in employment until the original notice of the employer has been served, and stating that, unless he does so, the liability to a redundancy payment will be contested. The issue might have to be resolved by reference to a tribunal. This is true of dismissals due to misconduct during the notice period, when the employer may withhold redundancy pay, but may equally have to fight out the case at a tribunal hearing.

Lay off and Short-time Working

If an employee is 'laid off' or put on short time, he may be entitled to a redundancy payment.

Where there is a diminution of work of the kind the employee is required to perform under his contract, and because of this his pay for any week is less than half a week's pay, he is legally regarded as on 'short time'. Should he be on short time (or laid off altogether) for four or more consecutive weeks, or have been on short time or laid off for a series of six weeks or more in a period of 13 weeks, then the employee can claim redundancy pay if he gives the employer proper notice of his intention to do so. If there is a reasonable expectation that no later than 4 weeks from the termination date, the employee would enter a period of 13 weeks without short time or lay off, then the employer must notify the employee within 7 days that he contests the redundancy payment, as the employee would not under those circumstances be entitled.

Length of Service

The two-year minimum service must be continuous, and if any re-engagement has taken place, whether or not the service was broken will depend on the re-engagement, the length of the break being crucial (see paragraph above on re-engagement within a 4 week period).

The Amount of the Payment

The amount of the payment to which the employee has a legal entitlement is

Age 18–21 = ½ week's pay ⎫ for each year's
Age 22–40 = 1 week's pay   ⎬ service in these
Age 41–65 (60 for women) = 1½ weeks' pay ⎭ age brackets

This is subject to a maximum of 20 years' service, i.e. only the previous 20 years will count. The amount may also be reduced if the employee has a gratuity or pension from the time he leaves.

Carrying out Redundancies

Before making a redundancy payment, advance warning has to be given to the Department of Employment who will supply forms which set out details of the payment to be given to the employee.

Advanced Consultation with Trade Unions. Advance consultation with the representatives of a recognised union is necessary when a redundancy is proposed. The appropriate trade union is defined as the independent trade union which is recognised by the employer for bargaining or representation on behalf of that worker or group of workers.

Advance Notice

Table 12. Amount of advance notice to Secretary of State of Employment

Number of people to be made redundant at one establishment	Within following period of days	Minimum warning before first redundancy (days)
Less than 10	None	None
10–99	30 or less	30
100+	90 or less	90

Disclosure of Information to Union in Writing when Consultation Begins. The employer must disclose the following information:

(a) Reasons for redundancy.
(b) Numbers and descriptions of those to be made redundant.
(c) Total number employed at the establishment in question.
(d) Proposed method of selecting who is to be dismissed.
(e) Method and timing of dismissals.

Where an employer fails to comply with the consultation rules, a Tribunal may make a 'protective award', an order that the employer must continue to pay the employees according to the numbers of persons for the total number of days as set out in Table 12.

Time Off to Look for Another Job. An employee who is to be made redundant (provided he has at least 2 years' service) must be allowed up to 2 days' paid leave of absence to allow him the opportunity of searching for other employment. When the normal hours differ, week by week, the average weekly hours are taken over a 12-week period immediately preceding the day in which notice was given.

A Code of Practice on Handling Redundancies

A 1972 Code of Practice sets out a procedure which is still relevant as a model policy approach to redundancies, especially where there is no union with whom to consult.

Before contemplating redundancies, the Code suggests that management should stop recruitment, reduce overtime, consider retraining or transfer of the employees to other work, retire those over normal retirement age and introduce short-time working.

Where the redundancy is inevitable, employers should give as much warning as possible, use voluntary redundancy and early retirement, and offer help with the aid of the Training Commission in finding other work. Employers must also ensure that individuals are informed before any news leaks out, and should try to run down establishments slowly.

Where a transfer in the ownership of a business is contemplated then employers (either vendors or purchasers) must follow a similar consultative procedure as specified in the earlier section on carrying out redundancies. Section 10 of the Transfer of Undertakings Regulation 1981, states that representatives of recognised trade unions must be informed:

1. When the transfer will take place, and the reasons for the transfer.
2. Any legal, economic or social implications for the employees.
3. Whether or not any actions are intended with regard to the employees.
4. Where the employer is making the transfer, the expected actions of the buyer in respect of the affected employees.

Employers are required to consult with any recognised trade unions and to consider their representations. Where a reply is required, they must give reasons if they reject the Union's representations.

The union can complain to a tribunal about failure to comply with these regulations. If a tribunal upholds the complaint, the maximum compensation is two weeks pay per employee.

PAY

Methods of Payment
Following the repeal of the Truck Acts, manual workers do not have to be paid in coin of the realm, and payment is increasingly made by electronic funds transfer, direct into a bank account, such as the service offered by Bankers Automated Clearing Services Limited.

Itemised Pay Statements
An employee has a right to receive an itemised statement of his pay which shows:

1. Gross amount of pay.
2. Variable deductions (such as income tax).
3. Fixed deductions (such as pension contributions). If the

employer prefers he can issue a statement annually showing the aggregate of fixed deductions.

4. Net amount of pay.

Guarantee Payments

Employees have a right to a limited amount of pay if laid off or put on short time. The conditions under which this is granted to an employee are:

1. He must not unreasonably refuse suitable alternative work.

2. He must make himself available for work, and it must be a day on which he would normally be working.

3. The lay off or short time must not be a consequence of a trade dispute involving his own employer. Thus, if there is a strike in the company which is not associated with his employer, then guaranteed pay would apply if the employee was laid off.

The amount of guarantee pay is limited to a maximum of £10.90 per day (as at 1.3.88) and to a maximum of 5 days within any 3 months rolling period.

The formula for calculating a day's pay is:

Number of normal working hours × the guaranteed hourly rate

$$\text{The guaranteed hourly rate} = \frac{1 \text{ week's pay}}{\text{normal working hours per week}}$$

If the hours per week vary, the average over the last 12 weeks is taken as representative. Where the employee has less than 12 weeks' service, then the average for similar workers of his employer is taken.

Collective Agreements on Guarantee Pay

Where a collective agreement exists, which would result in the employee receiving more than the minimum guarantee pay under the Employment Protection (Consolidation) Act, then the employee receives the larger amount. Whether or not the legal minimum gives more than the collective agreement depends on how many days are involved, and on whether or not the collective agreement guaranteed a proportion of a week's pay instead of a day's pay as a basis for calculation.

The parties to an agreement on guarantee pay may apply to the Secretary of State for exemption from legal obligations, provided their scheme is as beneficial to employees as the State scheme.

Suspension on Medical Grounds

There are situations where the employee may be suspended on medical grounds because of a health hazard at his place of work, or because of a recommendation contained in a code of practice. Employees with a minimum period of 4 weeks' service, who are not absent for a personal health reason, are entitled to payment for up to 26 weeks of suspension. Employees must not unreasonably refuse offers of alternative work during this time.

A number of State payments are now made through the payroll. These are presently statutory sick pay and maternity allowance.

Statutory Sick Pay

This scheme involves employers being responsible for paying the first 28 weeks of sick pay through the payroll. This means employers must keep detailed records. The rules are:

1. Employees must notify their employers of their absence.
2. The period of incapacity for work (PIW) must be for at least four completed days for the employee to be eligible. This PIW may include Saturdays and Sundays. Two or more PIW may be linked if there is a gap of no more than 56 days between them.
3. The PIW begins with the first complete day of incapacity and ends, usually either when the employee returns or runs out of entitlement, or leaves.
4. SSP is paid for qualifying days only. The first 3 days are waiting days.
5. The employer must give the necessary information to the employee concerning exclusion etc. where required.
6. Employers must keep records showing dates of incapacity and details of sick pay paid to each employee, weekly, monthly and yearly as well as dates when SSP was not paid.
7. Employers must also keep evidence of the employee's incapacity.

Employees should be advised that failure to produce accurate information may be treated as misconduct and lead to disciplinary action.

MATERNITY PROVISIONS

A woman who is dismissed because she is pregnant will be regarded as unfairly dismissed unless by continuing to work she was in contravention of a statute, or her work was inadequately performed. In either case, the employer has a duty to offer suitable alternative work if there is a vacancy.

Statutory Maternity Pay

Statutory Maternity Pay (SMP) is now paid by the employer through the payroll and reclaimed in full from the State. SMP is payable to women who qualify for up to 18 weeks while the woman is on maternity leave.

Absence due to Pregnancy

A woman with two years' or more continuous service is entitled to return to work after her pregnancy, except in small firms where less than five people are employed. The employer is not required to offer exactly the same job back, however, if it is not reasonably practical to do so, provided he offers the returning woman work 'of a kind which is both suitable in relation to the employee and appropriate for her to do in the circumstances'. The absence entitlement is as follows:

Before the birth:	11 weeks
After the birth:	29 weeks
If unfit then:	4 weeks
	44 weeks

In order to qualify for a right to return, a woman must inform her employer in writing 21 days before the absence is due, or as soon as practical, that she intends to return.

The employer may request confirmation of her intention in writing 49 days or more after her confinement, and she must reply to this within 14 days. At least 3 weeks before returning to work, she must notify the employer in writing that she intends to return. Employers should use a system of forms so that the employee is aware of her obligations and the time scale.

An employer is required to give paid time off for antenatal care as instructed by the doctor.

DISCRIMINATION IN EMPLOYMENT

Equal Pay

The Equal Pay Act 1970 was designed to stop discrimination in the contractual area of terms and conditions between men and women. It applies to both sexes, and to employees of any age. There must be no difference in the pay and conditions of service for women or men on 'like work', or work which is rated as equivalent. The comparisons made are between people working for the same employer, and at the same establishment (where there are differences based on location).

Exceptions are in maternity provisions, life insurance benefits, and when there is a statutory reason as, for example, where women are forbidden to carry out certain work in factories. An employer must be able to prove that any difference between the contracts of men and women is due to a material difference in the work. Work which is 'broadly similar' is regarded as the same for the purposes of the Act. Job evaluation schemes which use non-discriminatory factors show the value of different jobs in relation to each other, indicating that no discrimination has occurred.

Equal Value

Following a case brought by the European Community against the UK Government, which succeeded in showing that the Equal Pay Act did not fully conform to the Treaty of Rome, and the EC's 1975 Equal Pay Directive, the Equal Pay Act was amended to ensure that the principle of equal pay for work of equal value, compared between men and women, was included in the Equal Pay legislation.

There are three ways in which a claim (by a man or a woman) may be made in respect of pay, terms and conditions of service:

1. Where she (in the case of a woman making the claim) is employed on 'like work' to that of a man.
2. Where she can show that she is employed on work rated as equivalent to a man under a job evaluation study.
3. Where she can show that the work she does is of equal value to a man's work, in terms of the demands made upon her, in such areas as effort, or skill etc.

A claim under the Act is made to an industrial tribunal. If no conciliation is possible, the tribunal will examine any job evaluation scheme, to see if it is valid. Where no job evaluation scheme is operating, the tribunal may still reject the claim if it thinks there are no reasonable grounds. Where there is a job evaluation scheme, and the employer can show that there are no grounds for the scheme to be regarded as sex discriminatory, the claim will not succeed. However, unless the employer is able to show that there are no reasonable grounds for saying the work is of equal value (for example, by showing that there is a genuine material factor which proves that the difference in pay or conditions is due to other reasons than sex differences), the tribunal must commission a report from an independent expert. This report will be considered when it is completed (usually within 42 days) and the tribunal, at its resumed hearing, will make a decision. Tribunals can require information to be given to the independent expert, and there are safeguards if the report is inadequate.

Sex Discrimination

The Sex Discrimination Act 1975 aimed at removing discrimination in the non-contractual areas of employment, and set up the Equal Opportunities Commission to oversee the working of the Act and the Equal Pay Act.

A distinction is made between direct and indirect discrimination, both of which are illegal. Direct discrimination is where a person is treated less favourably that the opposite sex because of their sex (for example, the recruitment of all males in managerial jobs). Indirect discrimination occurs when, although the conditions are applied equally to men and women, the effect of the condition is to preclude one sex. (For example, stipulating that all managers must be over 6'3" in height, this being less likely as a female characteristic.) Therefore, where the condition is irrelevant, and when the number of women who can comply is much smaller than men, then there is indirect discrimination.

Similarly, discrimination against people on the grounds of their marital status is regarded as illegal.

The only exception is where there is a genuine occupational qualification for:

1. Physiological reasons (e.g. a male actor).
2. For decency or privacy (e.g. a lavatory attendant).
3. Where the employee is required to sleep on the premises.
4. Where special care is provided (e.g. in prison).
5. Personal services for education or welfare.
6. Legal restrictions (e.g. The Factories Act forbids night shift work for women).
7. Where there are overseas restrictions and it is necessary for the person to work overseas (e.g. in some Muslim countries women might be restricted).
8. Where the job is for a married couple.

The Act does not apply when there are less than 6 people employed, nor to domestic workers in private households.

The main areas where personnel managers must watch for discrimination are in:

1. *Advertisements.* These should not have any particular reference to sex. Job titles which have a gender included should be avoided (e.g. 'salesgirl', 'office boy').
2. *Recruitment Procedures.* These must avoid discrimination, notably the person specification must not show signs of indirect discrimination.
3. *Promotion, Training, Transfer Policies.* These should be sufficiently well known and obviously non-discriminatory so that accusations of unfairness can be avoided.

Complaints may be made (within 3 months of the discrimination) to a tribunal which can award damages. The Equal Opportunities Commission can require an employer to stop discriminating, and to advise the Commission of action taken to remove discrimination.

Race Discrimination

The Race Relations Act 1976 follows the same broad principles, in seeking to remove discrimination, as the Sex Discrimination Act, and makes the same distinction between direct and indirect discrimination. The Commission for Racial Equality's role in promoting harmony between ethnic groups extends beyond employment.

Racial groups are defined as groups of people of particular origins, of specific race or nationality, or colour. Religious affiliations are not part of the definition (although there is legislation in Northern Ireland aimed against religious discrimination).

The segregation of racial groups is illegal. The victimisation of anyone who brings a complaint under the Act is also illegal (as is the case with the Sex Discrimination Act).

Employers must pay particular attention to their recruitment procedures to ensure that no discriminatory practices enter into their decisions (for example, in advertising, screening applicants, etc.), and should ensure that their employees are treated fairly so that promotion, training and development opportunities are not foregone because of discrimination. Terms and conditions of employment must apply equally to all racial groups, there must be no discrimination during disciplinary action, and unless membership of a particular race is a genuine occupational qualification (e.g. for a film or play), then there are no exceptions. The Race Relations Act applies to organisations of all sizes. The complaints procedure is similar to that of the Sex Discrimination Act.

The Rehabilitation of Offenders Act 1974

This Act (which does not apply in Northern Ireland) means that ex-offenders who have completed their sentences, whether imprisonment or fine, have a period of rehabilitation after which the conviction should be regarded as 'spent'. The period of time before the conviction becomes spent is dependent on the sentence. Thus, for example, for sentences of 6 to 30 months' imprisonment the period is 10 years before the conviction is spent, and at the other extreme an 'absolute discharge' is spent after 6 months. Further convictions during the rehabilitation period extend the time before the earlier conviction is spent so that both convictions are spent at the same time.

As far as personnel managers are concerned, when interviewing applicants for employment, they may ask about any previous convictions, but must not question the person about any spent convictions. If an applicant does not reveal a spent conviction, no action should be taken against him and he must be treated as though the offence had not been committed.

A spent conviction is not grounds for dismissal, or for not recruiting, promoting or in any way treating the employee differently from others.

Certain professions, such as barristers, accountants, medical practitioners, etc. are excluded from this generalisation, and spent convictions may be taken into account in their case.

When giving references no information should be disclosed about spent convictions. Such a reference would be slander or libel, and would also risk criminal prosecution.

DATA PROTECTION ACT

Personnel records are increasingly held on computer, and the provisions of the Data Protection Act 1984 should therefore be observed by those who use the data. The scope of the Act covers 'automatically processed information relating to individuals and the provision of services in respect of such information'. Individuals have the right to seek compensation through the Courts for damage or distress caused by loss, destruction or unauthorised disclosure of data, to apply to the Courts for the rectification or erasure of inaccurate data, and to obtain access, provided the individual is the subject of the data.

Data users are required to register with the Data Protection Registrar the personal data they hold, and the purposes for which the data are held, the sources from which they may receive them, and those to whom the data may be disclosed, as well as the countries outside the UK if the data is to be transmitted overseas.

Data users must abide by a number of principles in relation to personal data, which:

1. Shall be collected and processed fairly and lawfully.
2. Shall only be held for specified, lawful purposes.
3. Shall only be used for registered purposes or disclosed to registered recipients.
4. Shall be adequate, relevant to the registered purpose, and not excessive in relation to that purpose.
5. Shall be accurate.
6. Shall be only held as long as is necessary for the stated purpose.
7. Shall be protected by appropriate security.
8. Shall be open to an entitled individual, who is entitled to know whether any data relating to the individual is held, and who will have access to that data, and who may have it corrected or erased.

Personal data is defined as 'consisting of information which relates to a living individual who can be identified from that information (or from that and other information in the possession of the data user) including any expression of opinion about the individual but not any indication of the intentions of the data user in respect of that individual'. This latter point does not include the intention of third parties. Disclosure includes oral, handwritten, printed data and data displayed on a screen.

There are several exemptions. Amongst the conditional exemptions from the Act as a whole is personal data held for payroll purposes. It should be noted, however, that the exemption applies only for the purposes of calculating pay, pensions, making payments and calculating deductions from pay, keeping accounts and making forecasts. Unless registered for the purpose, the personnel department should not seek to use payroll data for other reasons. Exemption from subject access is also given for specific categories, such as data held solely for statistical or research purposes. There are also exemptions from the non-disclosure provisions in cases where the disclosure is made for law enforcement, for national security, where required by the Courts and where the disclosure is to the data subject or someone acting on his/her behalf.

Note: Quotations in this section are taken from *Guideline Number 1*, produced by the Data Protection Registrar 1985.

COLLECTIVE BARGAINING

Definition of Trade Unions and Role of Certification Officer

The Trade Union and Labour Relations Act 1974 defined independent trade unions as those which are free from control or interference by the employer. The 'Certification Officer' is responsible for certifying the independence of trade unions and for keeping a list of trade unions and employers' associations. The Certification Officer supervises the scheme for refunding costs incurred by Trade Unions in holding secret ballots. Under the 1984 Trade Union Act, the Certification Officer hears complaints concerning the ballots for the election of the principal executive committee of a trade union.

Trade Union Recognition

Employers are not obliged to grant any trade union recognition but the decision has considerable implications for the organisation's industrial relations policy. Recognition means recognition for collective bargaining purposes. It is possible to offer representational rights, this being a kind of half-way house, which allows the union representative to appear on behalf of a member in discipline or grievance hearings. Recognition can be withdrawn by a Company, and recognition agreements may contain clauses stipulating the period of notice to be given for the withdrawal of recognition.

Trade Union Immunities

The 1980, 1982 and 1984 Acts severely limit the immunities previously enjoyed by trade unions from tort liabilities—such as breach of contract, intimidation by threatening a breach of contract, interference with a contract, or inducement to break a contract.

Immunity is now restricted to actions which are 'in contemplation or furtherance of a trade dispute'. The disputes to which this applies are limited to disputes between workers and their employer which relate wholly or mainly to one or more of the following:

1. Terms and conditions of employment, or physical conditions of work.
2. Engagement or non-engagement, termination or suspension of employment or duties of employment of one or more workers.
3. Allocation of work or duties of employment between workers.
4. Discipline.
5. Membership or non-membership of a trade union.
6. Facilities for officials of trade unions.
7. Negotiation machinery, consultation procedures, including recognition issues.

Effectively this prevents official secondary action and political disputes, stops sympathetic strikes, and restricts disputes of an official nature to those involving the workers of the same employer. Official disputes purely about recognition are also banned. The Trade Union Act 1984 removes immunities from trade unions which take industrial action without the support of a ballot. This does not prevent unions from threatening action without a ballot, but they cannot carry out the threat without a ballot.

Under the 1982 Act, vicarious liability is defined. A union is only liable for acts 'authorised or endorsed by a responsible person'. Examples are members of the union's executive committee and those empowered by the rules to act. Damages are limited according to the size of union membership. For trade unions over 100,000 members the maximum is £250,000.

Union Membership

Every employee has the right not to have action taken against him which seeks to prevent him from joining an independent trade union, or from taking part in its activities (that is, if the union is a party to an agreement with his employer). Under the 1982 Act employees who work under a closed shop agreement which has not been approved in a ballot will have the right not to be dismissed or to have action short of dismissal taken, for not joining a trade union. A closed shop agreement is 'approved' at any given date only if it has been supported by a secret ballot. The required level of support is (for Agreements which took effect after 14 August 1980), over 80% of those entitled to vote or over 85% of those voting. A periodic ballot is required every five years. The statutory rules are supplemented by a Code of Practice on 'Closed Shop Agreements' produced by the Secretary of State, which is admissable in evidence in legal proceedings. Ballots may be at the work place, or by post. The code is critical of 'pre-entry' closed shops, advising that 'no new agreements of this type should be contemplated'. (Paragraph 45.)

Rights to Time Off

Trade Union officials (shop stewards, trade union safety representatives, etc.) in recognised trade unions have a right to time off during working hours, with pay, to carry out trade union duties, including training in industrial relations. Members of trade unions have the right to time off to take part in union activities other than strike activities. This includes meetings of the membership but there is no obligation to pay for this latter time off.

A similar right exists for time off without payment for public duties such as attendance as a JP or in local authorities.

Disclosure of Information to Trade Unions

Employers are required to disclose certain information to the representatives of an independent trade union they recognise for collective bargaining. This does not apply to employers' associations. The union representative (who could be a shop steward and/or a full-time official) can be required by the employer to put his request for information in writing.

The employer has an obligation to produce information only if:

1. It is in his possession.
2. It relates to his undertaking or that of an associated employer.
3. It is in accordance with good industrial relations practice (as per the ACAS code of practice).
4. The absence of the information would impede the trade union representative to a material extent in conducting collective bargaining.

There is no obligation to produce information relating to particular individuals, information given in confidence, or information which could cause substantial injury to the employer's undertaking, other than its effect on collective bargaining. There are similar exclusions regarding national security, information used in legal proceedings or if giving the information could break the law. The employer does not have to produce any original document or compile data where this would cost more than its value for collective bargaining purposes.

Trade unions may complain to the CAC when an employer fails to comply. In such circumstances ACAS would normally try to conciliate, but if this fails the CAC may make an award. To date, most references have been made by white collar unions and a large proportion have been settled without a full hearing.

Election of Union Officers

Part I of the Trade Union Act 1984 requires a trade union to hold a secret ballot of its members to elect candidates to a union's principal executive committee, a procedure which must be followed at least every five years. All members of the union must have an equal opportunity to vote without any constraint.

Political Objectives of Trade Unions

Section 12 of the 1984 Trade Union Act requires a union to ballot their members at least once every ten years if it is to retain the authority to devote union funds to political objectives. This legislation was retrospective as far as the ten-year period was concerned. The rules for the ballot are similar to those for electing union officials, except a wider constituency, embracing unemployed members, those in arrears etc. is given.

Secret Ballots

The 1980 Act provides for regulations to be made enabling the Certification Officer to contribute towards the costs of secret ballots held by Trade Unions for decisions on industrial action, the election of committees and officials, amendments to union rules and decisions on amalgamation or transfer. Management would be required to provide ballot boxes and facilities.

Picketing

Picketing is only permitted legally where pickets seek, by peaceful means, to communicate with and to persuade workers to work or not to work in support of a trade dispute.

Preventing people from crossing the picket lines by physical means, and picketing outside a private home are both unlawful. Picketing is permitted only where it is outside or near the employee's own place of work, and is conducted by the employees in dispute or with their union representative. The Secretary of State has produced a Code of Practice on Picketing which has to be taken into account by the criminal courts in any litigation. The code suggests that in general the number of pickets should not exceed six at any entrance to a work place, and recommends liaison between the picket organiser and the police.

HEALTH AND SAFETY AT WORK

The Health and Safety at Work Act 1974 places a general duty on all employers to maintain standards in health, safety and welfare of people at work, to protect the general public and visitors against risks to safety and to prevent pollution of the environment. A Health and Safety Commission was established with an Executive to enforce the law.

Scope

The Act requires the employer to provide for his employees, so far as it is reasonably practical, plant, machinery, systems of work, handling, storage and transport that are safe and without risks to health. The employer also has an obligation, so far as is reasonably practical, to provide information, instruction, training and supervision on safety, to maintain any places of work in a safe condition, to ensure a working environment which is without risk to health, with adequate facilities and a written safety policy. The policy must state how it is to be carried out, and who is to be responsible. Employers must not charge employees for the cost of safety equipment, or special protective clothing, such as goggles.

Sanctions for breaches of the Act are imposed in the criminal courts. The penalties are a fine of up to £1000 and up to 2 years' imprisonment for every person guilty of infringement.

Employees also have duties—notably to co-operate with management on safety matters.

Safety Representatives

Safety representatives, appointed by recognised trade unions where one or more employees belong to the union must notify management of their names and of any changes. Safety representatives who have no legal responsibility in this respect have the right to make representations to an employer on behalf of all or some of the people they represent, to inspect premises, be supplied with information about accidents, and to be consulted by the employer on safety matters. Employers must allow representatives time off with pay to perform these duties. When two or more representatives request it, the employer must set up a safety committee within 3 months, and he is obliged to consult the representatives on the composition of the committee. These safety committees review the provision of health and safety measures at the work place.

Inspectors, reporting to the Health and Safety Executive, have wide powers. They can enter premises at any time, make examinations, order a production process to stop, and can enquire into any practice which seems unsafe. The Inspector can issue 'improvement notices' requiring remedial action within a specified time or 'prohibition notices' which stop any work until remedial action is taken. Safety representatives can represent their members in consultation with the Inspector. Penalties under the Act can be imposed by Magistrates or Crown Courts, in the form of fines or imprisonment.

The Factory Acts

The 1961 Factories Act, which has over 200 consequential regulations and orders, details particular duties on employers, such as the fencing of machinery, and rules concerning the employment of women and young persons in factories.

For example, women and young persons must not work on 'bank holidays', and there is a maximum for them of 48 hours excluding meal breaks in any week (a maximum of 10 hours in any one day of a 5-day week or 8 hours in any one day of a 6-day week). First aid boxes and, where 50 or more persons work, a trained first aider are required.

A minimum temperature of 60°F (15°C) after the first hour of work is laid down, and there must be adequate ventilation etc.

The most important provisions perhaps are those covering the fencing of machinery, guards being obligatory on all moving parts. The periodic inspection of hoists, cranes, boilers, etc. is expected. Accidents causing absence of more than 3 days must be reported to the factory inspector, as must any accident which causes an interruption of work for 24 hours or more, or causes a death.

It should be noted that, in addition to any penalty for failing to comply with the regulations, there is the possibility of further civil actions for compensation for a breach of statutory duty.

The Offices, Shops and Railway Premises Act 1963

This covers the same sort of issues as the Factory Acts but for the premises named in its title. It deals with such matters as sanitary facilities, cleanliness, overcrowding, ventilation, lighting, etc., and lays down minimum standards in these areas.

QUESTIONS

1. Describe the main functions of ACAS.

2. Under what circumstances is a contract of employment formed? What written particulars of the contract must be given?

3. What is meant by 'unfair dismissal'?

4. What is constructive dismissal?

5. If you were advised by your Chief Executive that 12 factory workers (members of the Transport and General Workers Union) would have to

be made redundant because of a reduction in sales orders, what actions would you take and why?

6. Under what circumstances must a Trade Union ballot its members?

7. When is it possible for a trade union to organise a strike without losing immunity from legal action?

8. What is the difference between 'direct' and 'indirect' discrimination?

9. What rights to information for collective bargaining purposes do trade union representatives have?

10. When is picketing lawful?

11. What is the main objective of the Health and Safety at Work Act?

12. What is the difference between a 'prohibition' notice, and an 'improvement' notice?

FURTHER READING: PART 6

ACAS, *Codes of Practice on Discipline, Information to Trade Unions, and on Time off for Trade Union Duties*, HMSO, London.

Atkinson, G. G., *The Effective Negotiator*, Quest, London, 1977.

Bain, G. S., *The Growth of White Collar Unionism*, Oxford University Press, London, 1972.

Batstone, E., et al., *Shop Stewards in Action*, Basil Blackwell, Oxford, 1979.

Brewster, C. and Connock S., *Industrial Relations: Cost Effective Strategies*, Hutchinson, London, 1985.

Croner's Personnel Law and Practice, Croner Publications, 1987.

Dunlop, J. T., *Industrial Relations Systems*, Southern Illinois University Press, 1970.

Elliott, J., *Conflict or Co-operation? The Growth of Industrial Democracy*, Kogan Page, London, 1978.

Flanders, A. (ed.), *Collective Bargaining*, Penguin, Harmondsworth, 1971.

Fox, A., *Industrial Sociology and Industrial Relations*, Research Paper No. 3, HMSO, London, 1966.

Goldthorpe, J.H., et al., *The Affluent Worker*, Cambridge University Press, Cambridge 1970.

ILO, *Conciliation in Industrial Disputes*, ILO, Geneva, 1973.

Lupton, T., *On the Shop Floor*, Pergamon, Oxford, 1963.

Marsh, A. I. and Evans, E. O., *The Dictionary of Industrial Relations*, Hutchinson, London, 1973.

Marsh A. I. and McCarthy, W. E. J., *Disputes Procedures in British Industry (Parts I and II)*, Research Paper No. 2, HMSO, London, 1966.

PART 7

The Future of
Personnel Management

24

Personnel Management in a Changing Environment

Managers need to be aware of the forces shaping society and to plan strategies to meet the challenges to come. Predictions of the future are becoming more difficult as the pace of change accelerates. The slogan 'the future is now' could well be adopted for the last decades of the twentieth century. Technological change has become so commonplace that no one shows surprise at space exploration, the wonders of micro-electronics, telecommunications, robots and test-tube babies.

Changes in Western society are also taking place, in the movements for sexual equality, improved education standards, better health, more leisure, the greater degree of home ownership, more mobility and increased foreign travel. From these changes have sprung the rejection of traditional attitudes to authority and higher expectations about future life styles.

In this valedictory section we wish to outline the likely impact of these changes on personnel management. Personnel managers will inevitably face the brunt of social changes, in their consultancy, problem-solving and resourcing roles.

THE CHANGING ENVIRONMENT OF WORK

Technological Change
The application of micro-electronic technology has been to the manufacture of capital and consumer goods, and there are robot factories making motor cars, computer-aided production systems in batch production, and in mass production industries. Mechanised 'paperless' offices are now possible, with word processors and data retrieval systems linking in to 'intelligent' reprographic equipment.

The 'Information Revolution'
Visual display units connected to computerised information stores make enormous quantities of data available at a touch of a switch, on stock control, storage, distribution, personnel records, individual

performance data and financial information for control and for planning.

The 'Advanced Developing Countries'

These ADCs are now major trade competitors. Countries such as South Korea, Singapore, Taiwan and Brazil have developed an industrial base very quickly and their products are often cheaper, of better quality and more available than those of the old industrialised West.

The Decline in Manufacturing Industry in the West

This decline, notably in steel, cars and ship-building, has resulted in the need to restructure British industry. There is also a trade recession, which together with the deflationary economic policies and the four factors above has resulted in high unemployment (approximately 2½ million in the UK).

CHANGING EXPECTATIONS AND VALUES IN SOCIETY

1. There are now more women than ever before in the work force. The movement towards sexual equality and the effects of inflation make dual careers much more common.

2. The idea of a lifetime's employment in one occupation or company is neither attractive nor feasible to many people. Mid-career change is now often sought, and with rapidly changing technology, a new occupation is sometimes essential. There are anticipated to be 1½ million more people entering the labour force (including more women) in the period 1980–1990. Given the unemployment figures above, this means over 4 million more jobs will be needed.

3. Improved general living standards, represented by home ownership and labour-saving gadgets in the home, have tended to make the home and family the focus of friendship and leisure. The 'black economy' (spare time work often not declared in tax) is a sign of a desire for autonomy, for self-employed status and the freedom to choose when and how to work.

FUTURE ISSUES FOR PERSONNEL MANAGEMENT

The very pace of change itself is a central issue for personnel managers. Of necessity, they will need to be extremely flexible and imaginative in formulating solutions.

1. New technology places semi-skilled jobs in manufacturing and distribution at most risk. Unfortunately, the people displaced are

often the least able to find other work. There is an element of 'de-skilling' in the new technology. Workmen are to become subservient to machines, servicing their needs, watching, and easing the work of the machines. Potentially, many of these jobs could become tedious and very routine with little prospect of livening up the day. Service industry jobs are less likely to be affected by the 'mighty chip'. The productivity gained by using word processors, however, could be in excess of 100%, so one might expect the adoption of word processors, initially to overcome the shortage of typists, but ultimately to replace typing pools and routine secretarial tasks. Shortages of skilled electronic engineers will probably continue, and personnel managers will be expected either to convert existing staff into these occupations or to find a competitive advantage in recruitment.

2. It is now clear that the 1980s have been a time of major structural change for British industry. The growth of service industries and massive unemployment have had important effects on labour markets. The growth of secondary labour markets employing large numbers of women on a part-time basis, and increasing numbers of people working as sub-contract labour or on short-term contracts has influenced employee relations and personnel policy. Human resource managers are now able to propose non-employment options when assisting in planning future requirements. The spread of micro computers should assist managers to model labour supply and to plan future needs by examining alternative scenarios.

3. Structural changes have been but one factor in the new industrial relations scene. The changing occupational structure combined with massive unemployment, and the defensive stance forced upon trade unions has resulted in an approach to industrial relations reminiscent of the 'Junta' of the 1850s. Trade unions are now keen to put their own house in order. Unions such as the EETPU and the AUEW have sought to gain recognition agreements with employers, based on a single union, by offering no-strike deals. There is thus a danger that trade unions will destroy their brotherhood within a battle for new members.

4. Human resource managers are now able to exploit the opportunities available with the new atmosphere in industrial relations, by adopting broad employee relations policies. The elements of these policies are an emphasis on communications, on improved flexibility (of task, time and contract), employee involvement, a drive for better quality in services and products, and a more strategic approach to managing change. As current government policy forces more responsibility back on to the individual, there may be corresponding moves by employers; for example company health policies are likely to enjoy an enhanced status to cope with the problems of stress and of AIDS.

5. New approaches to management development will be necessary. Careers are increasingly built between companies as individuals move around to gain relevant experience, and for domestic reasons. The transferability of pensions, and better information on job markets will encourage this movement. Managers will therefore need to make more entry and exit points to management jobs, and to accommodate dual career needs.

The Handy and Constable reports on management development have reinforced moves towards improved management training. The MBA degree is increasingly seen as a necessary passport to managerial status. New techniques in education technology, computer-based training, distance learning and the movement to professionalise management are set to revolutionise the development of managers and supervisors. Shortages of skilled workpeople, school leavers and graduate entrants are likely to be solved by broadening the search into the labour markets of the European Community. By 1992, all barriers to competition within the Community should have been removed. For multinationals, and for small companies employing expatriates, the mobility of labour is tied up with children's schooling, housing, dual careers and similar issues. A personnel policy response is required which recognises and offers solutions to such difficulties.

6. Organisation change and development. We outlined at an early stage the ideas behind 'organisation development' (OD)—this being a term used to describe behavioural science applications to the process of managing change.

There is pressure to devolve power downwards as decision making becomes more complex, and there are initiatives for worker participation originating with the EEC. This may result in experiments with formal reporting relationships allowing for more participation. Functional specialism may be reduced, and a tendency towards smaller organisations with more autonomous work groups is one possible answer to some of the problems outlined.

Greater attention to task-oriented structures (i.e. matrix-type) organisations which are more adaptive and make good use of expertise will bring the need for team building to the fore. Management style is important here, and this in turn brings in the whole question of how work is organised, and jobs are designed. We mentioned job design in one response to conflict (see p. 294). Most design schemes are concerned with:

(i) Increasing autonomy, responsibility and control. The responsibility is for choice of methods, target setting, programming, etc., and gives autonomous groups power over work allocation.
(ii) Increasing task identity. The job needs to be broken down into meaningful units, and is dependent on the length of the work cycle.

(*iii*) Learning will take place if there is feedback on the quality and quantity of performance. Feedback also provides a feeling of achievement.

(*iv*) The work itself should be meaningful and should have some obvious relationship to the organisation's end product.

These notes on job design exemplify the practical side to OD, but the larger scale work of OD consultants takes them into the industrial relations area, when a fundamental change is planned. Here, we might anticipate attempts to harness the change in technical processes to the sociological requirements of the organisation—to the way people interact, and to the groupings they form. Above all, new investment or reorganisation can be seen as an opportunity to change attitudes, to gain a greater commitment from all levels of the organisation. This can only be achieved if a climate of honesty and trust is established, and we might therefore expect to see management setting out their attitudes towards their workforce, and their adherence to goals which include the provision for fair rewards, dignity and respect to their workforce in addition to the economic goals of the organisation.

The future is thus seen not as a threat, but as an opportunity for growth and human development.

Index